HOME SECURITY

THE HOMEOWNER'S LIBRARY

HOME SECURITY

**Sydney C. Cooper, Anne Scott,
and the Editors
of Consumer Reports Books**

**Consumers Union
Mount Vernon, New York**

Library of Congress Cataloging-in-Publication Data
Cooper, Sydney C.
Home security.
Bibliography: p.
Includes index.
1. Dwellings—Security measures. 2. Burglary
protection. I. Scott, Anne.   II. Consumer Reports
Books. III. Title.
TH9705.C66   1988   643'.16   88-71054

Design by Jeff Ward
Illustrations by E. William Ward
First printing, December 1988
Manufactured in the United States of America

Home Security is a Consumer Reports Book published by Consumers Union, the nonprofit organization that publishes *Consumer Reports,* the monthly magazine of test reports, product Ratings, and buying guidance. Established in 1936, Consumers Union is chartered under the Not-For-Profit Corporation Law of the State of New York.

The purposes of Consumers Union, as stated in its charter, are to provide consumers with information and counsel on consumer goods and services, to give information on all matters relating to the expenditure of the family income, and to initiate and to cooperate with individual and group efforts seeking to create and maintain decent living standards.

Consumers Union derives its income solely from the sale of *Consumer Reports* and other publications. In addition, expenses of occasional public service efforts may be met, in part, by nonrestrictive, noncommercial contributions, grants, and fees. Consumers Union accepts no advertising or product samples and is not beholden in any way to any commercial interest. Its Ratings and reports are solely for the use of the readers of its publications. Neither the Ratings nor the reports nor any Consumers Union publications, including this book, may be used in advertising or for any commercial purpose. Consumers Union will take all steps open to it to prevent such uses of its materials, its name, or the name of *Consumer Reports.*

Contents

Acknowledgments

Many individuals in a number of different agencies and organizations have shared their time and expertise with us in the course of preparing this book. The authors are grateful for the generous assistance and information received from New York City Police Commissioner Benjamin Ward as well as the following active and retired members of the department: Deputy Inspector Frank Biehler, commanding officer of the 24th Precinct; Assistant Chief John P. Moran, commanding officer of the Internal Affairs Division; Lieutenant John Kidd of the Internal Affairs Division; Director Philip McGuire of the Criminal Analysis Section; Lieutenant John J. O'Connor and Sergeant Robert N. Tellone of the Crime Prevention Division; Deputy Inspector Raymond M. Hanratty, Jr., and Detective John Eaniello of the Auto Crimes Division; Deputy Inspector Arthur Katz of the Safe, Loft and Truck Squad; as well as Retired Chief Inspector Sanford Garelik; Retired Chief of Detectives Albert Seedman; Retired Inspector Benjamin Hellman; and Retired Deputy Inspector Robert Krell. In addition, New York City Transit Police Chief Vincent Del Castillo and Detective Bernard M. Jacobs, crime prevention specialist, have made themselves unsparingly accessible for advice and information.

Other law enforcement officials and specialists to whom the authors are indebted include Lieutenant Robert R. Reed and Detective Richard Alfiano of the Nassau County (N.Y.) Police Department's Community Projects Bureau; Commissioner Anthony Schembri of the City of Rye (N.Y.) Police Department, as well as Sergeant Gene Rosenberg and Detective Gene Berry, crime prevention specialists with that agency. In addition, thanks are owing to Susan Jacobson, director of the New York State Office of Crime Prevention; Arthur Randall, executive director of the Nassau County Criminal Justice Coordinating Committee;

Thomas Reppetto, president of the New York City Citizens' Crime Commission; John A. Neeb, assistant manager of the National Auto Theft Bureau; and Eugene Pasternak, president of Special Security, Inc., Long Island City, N. Y.

Special thanks are also owing to faculty and staff members of the John Jay College of Criminal Justice, including Dean James T. Curran, as well as Debra Hairston and Gregg Ward, executive assistants, for invaluable technical support. Professor Anthony T. Simpson, director of the John Jay College Library, gave unstinting bibliographic assistance, as did Dorothy Moore, Ellen Coschliano, Caryl Montheard, and Evelyn McNamara of the Oyster Bay (N.Y.) Public Library; Mary Johnston, director of the Locust Valley (N.Y.) Public Library; and Maryam Puller and Karen Jackson, chief librarian and assistant librarian, respectively, of the Ardmore (Pa.) Free Library.

The editors of Consumer Reports Books wish to give special thanks to S. J. Sussina, Robert McGuire, David Tallman, and A. Larry Seligson.

HOME SECURITY

Introduction

To say that a man's home is his castle is to make a statement about security, not lifestyle. The point of a castle is its ability to keep outsiders out and insiders in—safe from intruders, wild animals, and other kinds of harm. To satisfy these requirements, the classic medieval castle came with a drawbridge, a moat, and fortified artillery posts. But these traditional defense items are not available to the average apartment dweller or suburban homeowner.

What is available is an array of high-tech electronic, wrought-iron, and tempered-glass security hardware, at various levels of expense, as well as a variety of low-cost or free psychological and "aesthetic" deterrents to intrusion that can protect and reduce the anxiety of even the most security-conscious homeowner.

Home security is among the leading growth industries of the American economy today, with an annual growth rate of 12 to 15 percent. In 1987, Americans spent $8.2 billion on equipment and labor to make their homes more secure from intrusion. In addition, driven by local ordinances and a rising level of consumer consciousness about fire and other hazards, smoke detectors for the home have also begun to command a growing market.

To serve an expanding and increasingly sophisticated consumer lobby for public and private safety, American consumer publications have run many articles on security devices in recent years. Some of these devices (e.g., pickproof door locks and heavy-gauge lock guards) came under the heading of better or more innovative mousetraps. Others (e.g., system multiplexing alarms) are direct spinoffs of electronic and computer technology undreamed of as little as ten years ago.

But in the fast-growing area of home security, someone is always developing a better mousetrap, and last year's electronic miracle is as hard to keep up with as last year's mousetrap. *Home Security* examines and analyzes these innovations to help you decide which ones are likely to make a good fit with your security needs, budget, and lifestyle.

This book is not a "how-to" but a "what-to" manual. Although it contains helpful advice for the average do-it-yourselfer, proficient home handypersons will have to go elsewhere for detailed drawings, blueprints, and specs. For readers with little or no home repair or installation skills, however, this book will provide all the background they need to make informed decisions and hold intelligent discussions with carpenters, locksmiths, and security alarm installers. You may not want to, have time for, or even be capable of doing the job yourself—but you should still be knowledgeable enough about the existing problems and desirable solutions to discuss them with the people you ultimately choose to do the job for you.

The emphasis throughout this book is on the doable, the affordable, and the realistic. In making your house as impregnable as possible to outsiders, there will always be certain factors to consider. Cost is one; convenience is another. Some state-of-the-art security systems are so challenging to install, test, arm, and maintain that all but the most compulsive and gadget-happy homeowner will be reluctant to turn them on and use them. Current choices range from fully automated electronic field volumetric motion sensors with vibration detector transducers, down to the humblest arrangement of bolts and window latches. In a house with many children, pets, and assorted visitors, the latter may add up to as much security as any family needs or wants to live with on a steady basis. At the other end of the scale, in a house full of priceless objects and irreplaceable collections, no cost may be too great and no system too sensitive or complex.

Aesthetics present another, different kind of challenge. The proverbial chain-link or barbed-wire fence that protects many industrial and warehouse installations would be an eyesore in the average tree-lined suburb. Window bars turn houses into figurative prisons. Additionally, what is gained in security by barring the windows can be lost in fast and easy exit in case of fire.

Only individual homeowners can decide what combination of convenience, aesthetics, and physical fortification adds up to overall peace of mind. As with audio and other electronic equipment, security equipment comes in an almost infinite range of choices and costs. You will have to decide for yourself what kind of installation you need and how much you can afford to spend.

It is beyond the scope of this book to suggest long-range strategies for minimizing the risk of break-ins and burglary on a communitywide basis. The incidence of such crimes is so high, and our ability as a society to deal with their root causes so elusive, that the likelihood of any dramatic change in the next few decades is minimal.

Nor can any book take the place of an individualized, on-the-spot security check of your home. The best source for this kind of advice remains the crime-prevention unit of your local police department, the office of your own grassroots community crime-prevention organization, or a reputable private security company. These groups are still the only locally authoritative source for neighborhood crime patterns, statistical trends, and other local risk factors, and can be counted on for the most up-to-date information about deterring crime in your home or neighborhood.

This book should therefore be used as an adjunct to local security checks and advisories. It does not offer a blanket prescription for ways and means of burglar-proofing and/or fireproofing any one particular house. What it does offer is an overview of the problem, a description of existing equipment, and a compendium of new ideas and security strategies. This book differs from other current books on the subject in four major ways:

1. It goes straight to the criminological research, crime statistics, and consumer literature for a close look at the most recent findings on burglary, burglars, burglary prevention programs, and anti-burglary devices. Based on this review, it brings you a reasoned evaluation of what measures you can take to prevent break-ins.

2. It deals realistically with the dollars and cents of safety and security. Equipment prices change from year to year, but it's a safe bet that the most complex systems will always command top dollar. However, you may or may not need the best that money can buy. If you do, this book will help you shop for the best values in security equipment. If you do not, it will steer you to commonsense low-cost or no-cost approaches that may turn out to be all the security you need.

3. The authors are concerned not only with home safety and home security hardware, but also with such intangibles as research findings on the geography, architecture, landscaping, and other risk factors of safe homes. Where a house is located in relation to other houses, neighboring streets, and surrounding neighborhoods may have as much to do with its security as its own locks, bolts, door chains, and alarms. This book will help you to offset or minimize the local risk factors that you are not immediately able to change.

4. Last but not least, this book brings the weight of recent research by Consumers Union to bear on a subject that few laypersons are equipped to judge for themselves. By expanding on articles published in *Consumer Reports* over the past five years, and scanning a wide range of new products, new research, and various government publications on the subject, this book provides a guide to the best, the latest, and the most commonsense ways of making your home as safe as possible.

PART I
PERSPECTIVES ON HOME SECURITY

1

BURGLARY: AN OVERVIEW

Definitions of burglary are not uniform. Some jurisdictions define burglary as any unlawful entry by a person having no legal right to be in your home, whether or not he has to break down the door or smash a window to get in. Others define the act only as forced entry to locked and secured space. During a ten-year period from 1973 to 1982, the Justice Department's National Crime Survey reported 73 million incidents of "forcible entry," "attempted entry," and "unlawful entry." These distinctions reflect differences in the wording of individual states' laws, but for purposes of this book they can all be termed burglary.

In 1986, 5.3 percent of American households were touched by burglary—marking a decline from a high of 7.7 percent in 1975. In these burglaries, the average value of the items and/or cash taken was $991. However, these numbers reflect only reported crimes; police officials estimate that the number of unreported crimes is at least equal to that of reported crimes. In addition, any realistic discussion of burglary must look beyond the numbers; whether it is on the rise or on the wane, whether it happens when we are at home or off the premises, burglary is an act of physical invasion and takes its toll as much or more in psychological terms than in financial terms.

DAMAGE

To gain access to your house the burglar may pry out your lock, kick in your door, splinter your door frame, smash your windows, or cut through your walls. Once inside he may rip up your upholstery and bedding, break into locked desk drawers, pull pictures out of their frames, and rip cabinet doors from their hinges looking for cash, jewelry, and other salable items. The costs of the break-in may therefore greatly exceed the value of the items taken in terms of repairs, replacements, and shattered nerves.

VIOLENCE

Burglary's potential for violence skews the burglary figures themselves toward the low side through an unfortunate quirk of national crime-reporting practices. Three-fifths of all rapes in the home, three-fifths of all home robberies (against the person), and about a third of aggravated and simple assaults are committed by burglars. If you confront a burglar in your home, there is a better than fifty-fifty chance that the encounter will end in physical violence of some kind. Paradoxically, though, whenever the break-in leads to violence, it automatically deflates the national FBI crime statistics on burglary itself, because the resulting incident is no longer classified and listed as a burglary but gets recorded in the FBI crime index as rape, robbery, or assault.

UNLAWFUL ENTRY

An "unlawful entry" is where the burglar had merely to walk through an unlocked door or window to gain access to the premises. Clearly, the first line of defense against such residential break-ins is securely closed windows and tightly locked doors. "No-force burglary ranks as one of the most prevalent crimes measured by the crime survey," writes Harold Lenzner of the U.S. Census Bureau's Crime Statistics Analysis staff. "In 1975 it accounted for 44 percent of the total number of residential burglaries, compared with 34 percent for completed forcible entry. Judged as a component of all measured household crimes, no-force burglary, with 17 percent of the total, was second only to household larceny of less than fifty dollars. And for every hundred no-force burglaries committed in 1975 there were five rapes, thirty-eight robberies, and fifty-five aggravated assaults."

STRANGER-TO-STRANGER BURGLARIES

Burglary is not overwhelmingly a stranger-to-stranger crime. In the 1985 National Crime Survey (which questions victims, rather than police jurisdictions, about the incidence of household crime), just under 48 percent of all burglaries in which offender characteristics were obtained were committed by people completely unknown to the homeowner or tenant. By contrast, 25 percent were committed by acquaintances. Divorced or separated spouses and other relatives accounted for over 10 percent, and neighborhood familiars known to the victims only by sight accounted for another 6 percent. Another 10 percent were committed by offenders whose identity was uncertain. So, although your overall chances of being burglarized are small, if and when it happens, the possibility that the crime will be committed by someone you would at least recognize is over 40 percent.

SEASON

Burglary has traditionally been a warm-weather crime. Burglars, like homeowners, are more apt to spend the cold winter days and the even colder nights in the warmth of their own homes. Seasoned police administrators have long maintained that bad weather is the law's most reliable long-term ally—although the increasing use of drugs, and the year-round habits they engender, are starting to tip the scale back toward year-round burglaries.

Cold weather tends to make householders more aware of possible openings in their home. Windows left open in warmer months for ventilation and cooling are likely to be tightly closed during the heating season, especially at night. Still another factor may be that Americans are more apt to take their vacations in the summertime, or head for the beaches and mountains on warm-weather weekends. Nationwide crime statistics indicate that burglars favor the long summer weekends from Memorial Day to Labor Day for the vast majority of their crimes. Empty suburban houses and streets, where better than half the residents may be away during the warm summer weekends, mean reduced chances for burglars of being seen. Not surprisingly, therefore, burglaries, forcible entries, and attempted forcible entries all peak in August.

TIME OF DAY

Time of day seems to make less difference to burglars than is commonly supposed. Most of us picture burglary as taking place furtively under cover of darkness on a moonless night. But in fact, in those incidents where police and residents were able to say with any degree of precision when the break-in occurred, the crimes were distributed pretty evenly between daylight and nighttime hours.

In roughly 30 percent of cases, the time of day that a break-in occurred is simply impossible to pinpoint. There is no reason to suppose, though, that the round-the-clock distribution is any different in these cases than it is in those in which it is known exactly when the break-in occurred. If anything, a slight trend toward increased frequency of daytime burglaries can be expected to grow as the number of two-income families grows and more and more homes stand empty during the daylight hours.

WHAT GETS STOLEN

To determine the kinds of property favored by burglars, U.S. Law Enforcement Assistance Administration (LEAA) researchers analyzed a sample of 255 cases of unlawful no-force entries in which there was some kind of property stolen. At the head of the list, with 22 percent of recorded losses, cash was the target of choice; tools and building materials held second place; and entertainment equipment such as televisions, stereo components, and cameras or recorders tied for third place, along with bicycles, bicycle parts, and home furnishings.

TYPES OF ITEMS STOLEN
(from *The Cost of Negligence*, LEAA 1979)

Types of Item	% of Incidents
Cash	22
Tools and building supplies	15
Home furnishings	11
Television, stereo equipment, cameras	11
Bicycles/parts	11
Jewelry, furs, silver	8
Food and drink	8
Clothing	6
Sporting goods	6
Motor vehicles/parts and equipment	5
Gasoline	4
Guns and ammunition	2

Some of the items on this list may represent targets of opportunity rather than any active preference on the burglar's part. Such items as furs, valuable jewelry, and silver are not generally found in the average city or suburban home. But more houses, in a wide range of neighborhoods, do contain cash and/or electronic gadgets of various kinds.

"If thieves were rated solely on the basis of the value of their heist, how would we rate our [no-force] burglars?" ask the authors of the LEAA survey summarized above. "Considering all of the sampled offenses, both successful and unsuccessful, and the sum total of all kinds of items lost in each successful incident, we would have to conclude that these offenders were not very skillful. To begin with, a sizable number of incidents failed, that is, no cash or property was taken, even though an entry was made. Many more offenses produced some stolen property, but the purloined items were of types not likely to provide profitable return on the illegal market."

Other Department of Justice studies show that the monetary value of property stolen in the course of a real break-in (as opposed to a no-force) corresponds to the degree of force used to get into a home. Where a burglary netted items or cash worth over $1,000, it was almost always as the result of a real break-in, not a walk-in, and it presumably required some degree of planning and effort to gain access to the place where the goods were housed.

PLANNED VS. UNPLANNED BURGLARY

The degree to which burglary is or is not planned remains open to debate. "Few offenders said that their decision to commit a crime resulted from the chance discovery of a crime opportunity," according to U.S. Department of Justice analysts. Instead, "the majority said that the decision was precipitated by a specific factor, usually the need for money or the influence of others." A 1984 study that included in-depth interviews with convicted burglars in the south of England found that the most important factor in the decision to commit a given break-in was the surveyability of the target, and whether or not there appeared to be anyone at home at the time. One convicted burglar, interviewed by Vera Institute of Justice researchers in 1983, said, "If you're working and you see something you want, you wonder how you're going to save money to buy it. If you're not working and you see something you want, you wonder how you're going to take it."

BURGLARY AND ECONOMIC CONDITIONS

The relationship between burglary and the economic scene is not as simple as it might appear. It is a paradox of American criminological theory that crime went down during the Depression, when vast numbers of people were economically disenfranchised, and up in the 1960s, when the national economy was on the rise.

But the figures supporting this paradox are subject to dispute. Elliott Currie, whose recent book, *Confronting Crime,* presents a reasoned reassessment of the available literature on economic factors and crime, cites a number of studies to support his argument that economic factors are paramount in economic crimes like burglary. Writing in 1931, Emily Winslow tracked crime against the business cycle and found that burglary and other property crimes, including robbery and housebreaking, peaked in bad years and receded in good. And researchers Sampson and Castellano, writing in 1981, found an 80 percent increase of theft in urban neighborhoods with high unemployment rates as opposed to other neighborhoods with lower rates.

Another factor that seems to have some bearing on the burglary statistics is the availability of welfare programs. In 1956 James Short studied the business cycle in relation to crime and found that "although the murder and aggravated-assault rates were not much affected by the availability of public welfare, rates of robbery and burglary were strongly influenced by it." Thus, when other funds are legitimately available, burglary is not the preferred method of earning an income.

The evidence adduced by these researchers supports the assumption that burglary is indeed, first and foremost, an economic crime. Evidence of the connection between burglary and poverty is pervasive both nationally and internationally. It is a crime committed by reasonably rational human beings operating in their own economic interests to the detriment of others; and it is a crime committed by people with a relatively realistic assessment of the economic—and social—odds.

2

THE GEOGRAPHY
OF SAFE COMMUNITIES

SAFE NEIGHBORHOODS

Statistics demonstrate that approximately every ten seconds a burglary is committed somewhere in America. But national data may not reflect local facts. Burglary rates in neighboring
geographical areas vary according to the residents' age and lifestyles, proximity to high-
crime areas, zoning regulations, and land use. The geography of safe communities is an
issue that has received increasing attention over the last twenty years. The proximate causes
of burglary and other property crime were formerly considered to be a combination of
population density, opportunity, and local economic conditions. Books like Jane Jacobs's
The Death and Life of Great American Cities (1961) and Oscar Newman's *Defensible Space*
(1973) looked below the surface and considered the importance of such variables as building
size, land use, and neighborliness in promoting the safety of any given street.

Public/Private Space

Jane Jacobs staked out new sociological territory by suggesting that street layout and land
use played a critical role in public safety. Jacobs stressed the need for "mixed street use,"
streets with a blend of shops, churches, homes, and commercial offices. "A well-used city
street is apt to be a safe street," Jacobs wrote. "A deserted city street is apt to be unsafe."
The same principle can reasonably be extended to suburban roads and cul-de-sacs, housing
projects, and rural villages.

In Jacobs's view, the difference between safe and unsafe streets hinges on the dividing line between public and private space. Jacobs defines private space inside the householder's fence, garden patch, building lobby, or locked doorway, with public space being everything outside those lines. She called for a blending of the two that would utilize "mixed street use," where shopkeepers and residents rub elbows in the same street and keep up an informal, round-the-clock surveillance of each other's children, customers, and visitors, providing a friendly background bustle in which a potential criminal could be more easily detected.

Oscar Newman, an architect with a strong commitment to the social issues involved in urban planning, made it his goal to put Jacobs's principles into practice. He studied a cross-section of public-housing projects in inner-city neighborhoods to see what they could teach him about the relationship between space design and public safety, and came up with a few insights and prescriptions of his own. Newman and his colleagues coined the phrase "defensible space" to describe the area that one inhabits directly and/or feels responsible for, socially and legally.

Defensible Space

Newman contended that in poorly designed blocks and streets, defensible space stops at the homeowner's or the tenant's front door. He theorized that many tenants in traditional high-rise buildings do not feel responsible in any systematic fashion for the area outside their own front doors—including the long "double-loaded" corridor that their quarters open onto, or the stairs, elevators, and lobbies that they routinely use. But when this corridor is redesigned so that it is accessible only to a handful of neighbors, the corridor will suddenly become "privatized." Families whose front doors open onto that particular section of corridor will tend to treat it as a continuation of the private space behind their own front doors, provided it is physically blocked off from other sections. In theory, therefore, they will keep it under daylong surveillance, ensure that it is swept, lighted, and scrubbed, and police it for vandalism and unwanted intruders.

To support his theory, Newman invoked the well-known territorial instinct that makes most animals guard their lairs against trespassers. Humans are not the only mammals concerned about the inviolability of their homes; dogs, cats, foxes, and rodents are also highly territorial, and even birds and some species of insects take elaborate precautions to ensure the security of their nests. In fact, some animals are as sensitive to intrusion as the most advanced electronic geophones or building-penetration sensors are—a fact well-known to dog and cat owners.

Even more than Jacobs, Newman contended that a predator's selection of his target is not a random choice. On the contrary, he assumed that burglaries and other break-ins are usually crimes of opportunity, and that predators go where the access is easy and the visibility low. It is the task of urban planners, architects, and remodeling homeowners, in Newman's view, to reverse the odds by tightening the approaches and generally making access more difficult for predators.

Surveyability and Curious Neighbors

Jacobs and Newman established the terms for a whole generation of urban planners and for public policy research on safe streets. Central to their work was the idea of what we might call "surveyability."

Newman and Jacobs both asserted that public space, if it is to be kept safe, must be visible to the people on whose private space it borders. To maintain security, streets, corridors, and building entrances must be "surveyable" from the resident homeowner's windows, doorways, and outdoor sight lines. Most criminals like their privacy; they need unsurveyable spaces to go about their "business." Half the battle of preventing crime is therefore maintaining clear sight lines on the space outside the homeowner's doors and windows, and locking up or otherwise restricting access to the areas that cannot be easily surveyed.

Research Findings

How well have Jacobs's and Newman's theories stood up to the test of time and real-life crime statistics? The message on this is mixed. Certainly, the safe-streets theorists made a valuable contribution by raising national consciousness about the role of architectural and planning factors in security. But on an individual basis, their specific hypotheses have not always proven valid.

Since the early 1970s, a number of researchers have set out to test Jacobs's and Newman's theories. Among the most systematic approaches is a carefully controlled study done by Stephanie Greenberg, William Rohe, and Jay Williams at North Carolina's Research Triangle Institute in 1981. Greenberg and her colleagues selected three pairs of high- and low-crime neighborhoods in Atlanta and tried to determine what factors contributed to their vulnerability or strength, including architecture, land use, and local geographic and social factors.

The neighborhoods that Greenberg studied were closely matched for such factors as ethnicity, income, and social class, so that any differences in their crime patterns could not be explained away by race, social class, or standard of living. Of the three pairs of neighborhoods, two were essentially black and one was essentially white. All were middle- to lower-middle-income, and several had quasi-suburban two- and three-story row houses, with driveways between them, small gardens in front, and larger yards in back.

The study involved twenty-one interviewers working in teams of two. Researchers contacted a total of 801 neighborhood residents, and in-depth interviews were conducted with 523. Newman's areas of "defensible space" and Jacobs's notion of "mixed street use" were found to have little pertinence. The researchers concluded that how close one lives to potential predators, where the neighborhood is situated in relation to railroad tracks and major traffic arteries, how built-up it is, and the average age of the neighbors affect local crime rates more than the residents' incomes, their community-mindedness, and the "busyness" of their streets.

Land Use With regard to land use, Greenberg, Rohe, and Williams had several major findings. First, they found that low-crime neighborhoods tend to be predominantly residential—not the mixed residential and commercial groupings that Jacobs had postulated for safe streets. However, the housing stock in the low-crime neighborhoods tended to consist of single-family dwellings as opposed to high-rises or apartment clusters—thereby supporting Newman's hypothesis that building population density does indeed tend to foster higher crime rates and that high-rises, with their minimally surveyable "public" spaces, indoors and out, provided good opportunities for intrusion, burglary, and other crime.

Low-crime neighborhoods also had certain key physical characteristics in common. They had less vacant land than high-crime neighborhoods did, for example, and they were less likely to have major traffic arteries running through them. On the other hand, they were also more likely to be transected or bounded by a railroad line, "usually surrounded by a small industrial concentration." The authors speculate that railroad tracks, expressways, and large industrial concentrations may limit access and act as buffer zones between residents and those outside the community who are intent on committing criminal acts. As Greenberg and her colleagues point out, "Objective physical, social, and boundary characteristics presumably have both a direct effect on crime and an indirect effect, by promoting or inhibiting informal territorial control."

Access Even so, boundaries themselves—in the sense of access barriers like railroad tracks, viaducts, roadcuts, and waterways—may turn out to be less important in keeping criminals *out* of low-crime areas than well-traveled thoroughfares are in letting them *into* high-crime areas. Living on or close to a main traffic artery was a significant risk factor in neighborhood crime rates. Residences that fronted on a major throughway lined with commercial (or commercial/residential) buildings were much more likely to be the sites of crime than streets lined with residential properties alone. And Greenberg's findings on this issue reflect similar findings in Hartford's Asylum Hill area, where crime went down by 50 percent after local traffic patterns were redesigned to minimize through traffic.

Demographics The sex, income, and education level of a neighborhood's inhabitants had no effect on the difference in crime rates between low- and high-crime neighborhoods. Surprisingly, though, there was a significant difference in the age of residents in safe neighborhoods as opposed to less safe ones, with low-crime areas having older residents than high-crime areas.

This finding came as a major surprise, since the elderly were commonly assumed to be victimized much more often than other age groups in the community. In fact, crime statistics from London and other English cities covered by the British Crime Survey in 1982 found similarly lower victimization rates among the elderly, even when differences in exposure and activity patterns were taken into account.

Street Design   Certain physical differences can be identified between safe streets and less safe ones. Greenberg and her colleagues made it clear that you are less likely to be victimized on a street that is either totally or predominantly residential than you are on a street with a mixture of residential and commercial buildings. In addition, the physical configuration of the street itself may make it more or less conducive to crime.

The message of Greenberg's and other studies is that safe streets are short streets. The anonymity imposed by long streets seems to make them inviting to criminals; short streets, cul-de-sacs, circles, and dead ends seem to make intruders think twice about their chances of making a quick getaway. By inference, winding roads and natural dead ends or round-abouts seem to be security pluses for homeowners and other residents.

Acting on this inference, a number of communities in St. Louis and elsewhere have taken steps to make their city streets private by installing gates at either end and restricting access to all but residents and authorized visitors. But such initiatives raise a myriad of administrative, legal, financial, and traffic issues, and may be more trouble than they are worth.

Lighting   Street lighting did not turn out to be a critical variable in Greenberg's study, but in this instance the Atlanta research is at odds with a whole body of accepted opinion on the part of police and other crime-prevention organizations. A well-lighted street or property decreases the chances of a burglary. Common sense suggests that neighbors and passersby are more apt to see and remember suspicious cars, people, and behavior if the street is well-lit. Furthermore, good street lighting usually makes residents feel safer, and should be maintained for that reason alone, since persistent fear of crime can be almost as unsettling as crime itself.

"Safe" Neighbors   All in all, Greenberg and her colleagues found that differences in the physical characteristics of a neighborhood were more important factors than differences in the behavior or mindset of neighborhood residents—including the more informal features of so-called territorial control. For example, residents of both high- and low-crime neighborhoods were about equally likely to be on the lookout for strangers, to belong to neighborhood organizations, to have strong local ties to the community they lived in (in terms of friends and relatives who lived nearby), or to get involved in neighborhood problems when they arose.

Nor were there any significant differences between the two kinds of neighborhoods in terms of fear of crime and precautions taken to prevent it. If anything, residents of high-crime neighborhoods tended to be more watchful than residents of low-crime ones, suggesting that watchfulness itself may be a reactive strategy and not necessarily an active means of forestalling or curtailing crime.

The one way in which residents of low-crime neighborhoods distinguished themselves psychologically from those in high-crime areas was the degree to which they felt attached to the neighborhood itself. This factor was judged in terms of how long residents had lived there and how long they intended to stay. Not surprisingly, low-crime neighborhood residents expressed more affection for their neighborhoods than high-crime residents did. But here again, it may be that their affection for the neighborhood was in part a reaction to the crime rate itself, and not the other way around.

High-Crime Neighborhoods Factors that distinguish high-crime neighborhoods provide a mirror image of those that prevail in low-crime areas. High-crime neighborhoods tend to have a lower number of residential properties and more vacant land than low-crime neighborhoods do. They also have a lower proportion of single-family houses and a much higher proportion of multiple-family dwellings, commercial properties, and "mixed" land use. High-crime neighborhoods in Greenberg's study were also marked by a higher percentage of blocks with major thoroughfares and a correspondingly lower percentage of blocks with small, short, winding neighborhood streets. In addition, they had more parking lots and less private, off-street parking than low-crime neighborhoods did.

In demographic terms, there were only two variables that distinguished high- and low-crime neighborhoods. People who lived in low-crime neighborhoods were more residentially stable than people who lived in high-crime areas, and the average age of residents was also higher in low-crime neighborhoods. This was true even though there was no difference in the two kinds of neighborhoods in terms of family composition, percentage of households with children, or mean number of adults per family. And, of course, differences in basic socioeconomic factors had been ruled out by the original design of the survey itself.

Based on their study, the authors suggest such crime prevention strategies as "limiting the amount of commercial development at neighborhood boundaries, discouraging the city from widening streets in predominantly residential areas, and minimizing the amount of nonresidential land use in residential blocks." If these suggestions sound familiar, it may not be coincidental. The researchers' prescriptions bear a more than passing resemblance to the average suburban zoning board's most closely defended and long-cherished planning agendas. The zoners intuitively understood that low-density single dwellings and residential streets are safer than their high-density, multiple-dwelling, mixed commercial and residential counterparts in other parts of the same city, township, or community.

But knowing the risk factors implicit in this difference—and acting on them—is no guarantee that you, as an individual homeowner, may not be the victim of a burglary. You will need to know more than relative local risk factors to make your home secure from crime.

3

BURGLARS
AND THEIR HABITS

Who are the burglars, and what do they usually look for in the pursuit of profit? In the past decade, some serious efforts have been made to find out, and at least one practitioner of the trade (Jack MacLean, whose 1983 book, *Secrets of a Superthief,* in many respects closely parallels the more formal findings of credentialed researchers) has gone public on the subject. Systematic research on the self-reported crimes of drug addicts and repeat offenders has also contributed to an increasingly comprehensive profile of the American burglar at the end of the twentieth century, and there is common agreement on several issues.

AGE

Criminologist Thomas Reppetto studied residential crime in and around Boston in the 1970s, and his research included detailed interviews with ninety-seven convicted burglars. Reppetto concluded that in terms of age and "modus operandi," there were two major categories of burglars operating in the Boston area at the time of his study.

The first (and larger) group was made up of young, unskilled burglars who operated close to home, were more apt to choose a target for its proximity and easy access than for the value of the goods within it, and were easily deterred from breaking into a given site by evidence that there was someone at home. A second, smaller group of burglars was older, more mobile, more skilled, and more concerned with the value of the property. These men were more likely to plan their jobs ahead, act on detailed information about the occupants and their belongings, and operate within a larger geographic field.

But there are indications that burglary—like most crime—is increasingly a young man's game. In MacLean's informal interviews of more than 300 burglars, over two-thirds said that they had committed their first break-ins between the ages of eleven and twenty-five, and English researchers have had similar findings. Like other American offenders, burglars are overrepresented in the sixteen-to-twenty-five-year-old age groups, with the majority clustering at eighteen to twenty-one. This means that your chances of being burglarized by a seasoned pro with a sophisticated modus operandi and a high-tech tool kit are relatively low. The other side of this coin, however, is that with or without a personal confrontation, the possibility for vandalism, impulsivity, and overreaction is high.

The age of American burglars and other criminals is declining steeply. In 1985, youths fifteen years old and younger were responsible for 50,993 cases of burglary, in addition to 381 cases of murder and manslaughter, 18,021 aggravated assaults, 13,899 robberies, and 2,645 rapes. "Four or five years ago, even two or three years ago," says Daniel P. Dawson, an Orlando, Florida, district attorney, "it was very unusual to see a child younger than twelve or thirteen in the system, particularly with multiple charges. Now you see kids aged seven, eight, or nine come in with a whole string of burglaries."

In part, these figures reflect changes in juvenile justice policies and practices over the last ten years. With fewer federally funded programs to divert young offenders from the criminal justice system, more and more young criminals are ending up in police custody, juvenile court, and detention. But the rise in referrals also reflects long-term upswings in index crimes for all age groups, and with the projected jump in the youth population predicted for the 1990s, as the children of baby-boomers mature into the high-risk years, the figures can be expected to go higher still.

EMPLOYMENT STATUS

Burglary is not so much a way of living for many burglars as it is a job supplement or moonlighting scheme: something they do when they are laid off or can't make ends meet on what they earn. MacLean's burglars bore this assumption out. Only 35 percent of them said that they committed property crimes "for a living." Most had other jobs, or at least sidelines—including unskilled service jobs and selling drugs.

The crucial element here seems not to be just the lack of income alone, but, even more important, the lack of normal social rewards from the kind of jobs that are available to men who have not finished high school and who have no career training or goals. "One of the most consistent findings in recent research," says criminologist Elliott Currie, "is that unemployment is less strongly associated with serious crime than underemployment—the prospect of working, perhaps forever, in jobs that cannot provide a decent or stable livelihood, a sense of social purpose, or a modicum of self-esteem."

FAMILY

Most burglars are unmarried, and many of them come from homes without adequate social or financial resources. But poverty may not be the crucial variable here. Daniel West's recent research among working-class delinquents in London concluded that family discord and violence were more accurate predictors of delinquency in children than was poverty alone.

The same factors that steer younger children toward delinquency may also propel them, as they grow older, away from marriage and family life. The street life that forms the social matrix in which most criminals operate is a poor social substitute for the more communal avenues of family and work, and breeds what one journalist has called "the loneliness of a life in which one's friends are just as dangerous as one's enemies." All indications are that burglars, like other criminals, lead what most of us would judge to be a lonely life, and that their attachments to family members and other people are as tenuous as their attachments to the job marketplace.

GEOGRAPHY

Burglars do not tend to cross state lines to commit their crimes, and may not even leave their own neighborhoods to do so. Most criminals inhabit the same neighborhoods as their victims, and there is evidence that most break-ins occur within a five- to ten-mile radius of the burglar's own home.

In New York an informal analysis of burglary patterns by the New York City Police Department's Safe, Loft, and Truck Squad showed that there was a close correlation between the site of a burglary and its proximity to a local subway station. The commanding officer of that squad reasons that burglars are as concerned with "convenience shopping" as other consumers are. "In a big city with strictly enforced parking regulations and heavy mid-city traffic congestion, public transportation is just as convenient for burglars as it is for their victims," says the officer.

For this and other reasons, from a statistical viewpoint, burglary also tends to be a big-city crime. A recent study of Dutch burglary statistics shows a direct correlation between the size of the city and the rate of burglaries it reported per 10,000 inhabitants. This is because, as city size increases, so does the size of that city's various subcultures—including the criminal subculture. As the size of the criminal subculture increases, so does the likelihood that other city dwellers will have dealings—planned or unplanned, wanted or unwanted—with any of its members.

SKILL LEVELS

In his Boston study, Thomas Reppetto classified the burglars he interviewed into three different subgroups with respect to their skill at breaking and entering. From picking locks at one end of the skills scale, to smashing windows or kicking in doors at the other, the preponderance of burglars in this study preferred prying, disabling, or removing a lock, "loiding" it (sliding a thin piece of plastic along the door edge to open a spring lock), or using a passkey to get into the house. By this measure, the vast majority (84 percent) were what Reppetto classified as "semi-skilled," and the "most consistently carried tool for all categories of burglars was the simple screwdriver, or the crowbar."

However, this self-reported preference is somewhat at odds with the FBI's national Uniform Crime Reports figures, as well as police statistics from Reppetto's own target areas, all of which indicate that kicking in a door or smashing a lock is by far the preferred way of gaining access to a house targeted for burglary—and perhaps the easiest. It also requires the least skill. Either way, though, the burglars interviewed by Reppetto estimated that it took them five minutes to get a door opened and three minutes for a window. Most agreed that they would spend no more than ten minutes trying to open any given door, or five minutes for a window.

DRUGS: CAUSE OR EFFECT?

The myth of the addict who has no other recourse to support his habit than to turn to a life of crime is contradicted by a number of studies on this subject. A number of researchers in the 1970s found that most offenders had significant histories of delinquency before they turned to drugs; addiction may have merely increased the urgency of the user's economic "need." Some analysts even argue that, at least in the case of heroin, addiction can sap the drug user's energy and thereby diminish his ability to plan or carry out a break-in.

But this argument clearly does not apply in the case of drugs like cocaine and its derivative "crack," angel dust, and amphetamines, all of which have exactly the opposite effect on the user's energy level to that of heroin and other "downers." In keeping with this and other commonsense expectations about the effects of drugs on crime, Reppetto concluded that of all the factors analyzed in his study, drug use correlated most strongly with local increases in residential crime. His conclusions were confirmed in January 1988, when *The New York Times* published the first findings of the Drug Use Forecasting System, a program founded by the National Institute of Justice. The program tested for illegal drug use in the preceding twenty-four to forty-eight hours those arrested for such serious street crimes as burglary, grand larceny, and assault. Based on urine tests of more than 2,000 men arrested in twelve major U.S. cities, the findings showed positive results for drugs from 53 percent in Phoenix to 79 percent in New York, with a national average of 70 percent. "It was much higher than anyone had anticipated," said James K. Stewart, the director of the National

Institute of Justice. "If we are going to do something about crime, we are going to have to confront the drug problem."

ACCOMPLICES

In Reppetto's research, the youngest and least skilled burglars were the ones most likely to work with accomplices, and burglary was often a kind of group activity. ("I'm just walking down the street and a couple of friends say, 'Hey, do you want to break into a house with us?' I say, 'Okay, if it's a good hit.' ") Otherwise, burglars tended to prefer either one accomplice, who usually acted as a lookout, or none. Security experts characterize the professional burglar as a compulsive loner who makes it a cardinal rule to operate solo and keep his exploits to himself.

ETHNICITY

Reppetto found a distinct preference among both white and nonwhite burglars (especially the younger ones) to operate among their own kind—in part because they thought they would attract less attention, and in part because they feared racial violence if they crossed the ethnic line.

RECIDIVISM

Burglary is a crime with a very high probability of recidivism. British researchers Trevor Bennett and Ted Wright at the Cambridge Institute of Criminology interviewed 128 incarcerated burglars ranging from sixteen to sixty years old in 1983. The majority admitted to more than fifty burglaries in their lifetime. Almost all had committed at least one other property offense, but most of them regarded burglary as their chosen "specialty." In talking to the burglars, the authors of this study were searching for the deterrent effects—if any—of the criminal justice system alone (police, jail terms, etc.) as opposed to the deterrent effects of the targets themselves (locks, alarms, dogs, etc.).

Most offenders had approached their targets without any anxiety about getting caught by the police. In explaining why they had considered themselves so safe, some said that they had taken care to minimize any risks, and others said they simply refused to think about the possibility of being caught. One said: "I thought about it I suppose. I knew there's a chance of getting caught, but you don't think you're gonna when you do it. You just think, 'I won't get caught for this one.' " Another said, "Well, I don't think about it, that's just it. I push it to the back of my mind."

To the burglars who did admit the possibility of getting caught, the prospect did not seem to trouble them unduly. "I expected six months," said one. "What's six months? By the time you go in one door, you're outside again." The idea of prison itself, except for first timers, was not a serious deterrent. Some interviewees even professed to welcome the respite from family problems and other less pleasurable aspects of daily life. "Once you've been in prison, it's easy. Prison is only a deterrent if you've never been to it. Once you've been to it, it's a laugh."

These are English burglars speaking, and they are talking about English jails, but the American experience is not too different. The attitude on both sides of the Atlantic seems to reflect the American recidivist's street wisdom that "if you can't do the time, don't do the crime." MacLean's colleagues in the Florida prison where he was incarcerated were equally philosophical about their time behind bars. Sixty-four percent of them had been jailed for burglary before, and of the remaining 36 percent who were behind bars for the first time, many had already been on probation. Most professed to see prison as—among other things—an eye-opening educational experience. "Prisons are places where inmates can get together and tell stories of all kinds," writes MacLean. "They explain how they got caught, and the next guy learns from the other's mistakes, so he won't make the same one when he gets out."

There is conflicting evidence on the subject of repeated break-ins at the same site. The burglars interviewed by Reppetto said that they would fear being recognized if they showed up at the scene of the crime too often and tried to minimize the risk by maximizing their territory. But recognition may be a less significant factor for burglars who operate at night, and other issues may outweigh any initial anxiety about being seen. Like Reppetto, MacLean also asked his interviewees whether they ever burglarized the same address twice. One said that he had hit the same house nine times in a four-month period. This was a record, but 60 percent said they had hit the same house or business more than once. "If you burglarize a place one time and there's money lying all over the place and you score well, what do you have to lose in trying again?" writes MacLean.

SUMMARY

The composite picture of burglars that emerges from such studies as Reppetto's, Bennett and Wright's, and MacLean's is of a social and economic outsider who has fallen through the cracks in the educational system at an early age and into a sociopathic way of life.

Most burglars are not ambitious men, even inside the limits of their own small worlds. Far from conceiving a grandiose strategy for instant and/or long-term wealth, burglars view their break-ins as a way of making ends meet and staking themselves to such luxuries as drugs. In England, researchers Bennett and Wright asked convicted burglars what kind of money it would take to make them give up burglary, and they were surprised at the seemingly modest sums the burglars named.

But if burglary is not a get-rich-quick scheme, neither does jail hold any terror for them.

If anything, prison institutionalizes the street culture that burglars were born into or fell into when they dropped out of school and/or the working community, and may come as close as anything in their adult lives to the communality of family and community life.

Burglars as a group are apt to be young and unskilled, and their preferred method of entry is to kick in a door or climb in through an open window. But if there is no handy window open, they are not as afraid of breaking glass to get inside as householders have been told by the standard authorities on this subject. And the younger and less sophisticated they are, the greater the likelihood that they will choose to work in, or relatively close to, their own neighborhoods.

Young or old, they are apt to be either unemployed or underemployed, and marginal to the local economy. Many of them are addicted to drugs and high on them at the time of the break-in, and most are either "earning" money for drugs by burglary, or are looking for drugs themselves as a primary target of the break-in.

Basically, there are two ways to minimize your risk of being burglarized. One is to "harden the target" as police say—that is, to make your house or apartment as difficult as possible for any unwanted outsider to get in. This means installing locks, window guards, jimmy-proofing devices, alarms, and/or fences that will make it so difficult and time-consuming for the burglar to get in that he will give up in disgust and go elsewhere in search of an easier target.

The other—and almost equally effective—way of protecting yourself and your house is to exploit what facts we currently know from studies like those mentioned in this chapter, and to make your home look and sound impregnable, even if it is not.

4

DETERRENCE

Burglars respond to economic and social cues, and they are easily disheartened, persuaded, or misled. "Burglary is a mind game," says Jack MacLean, "played by people who are using their heads to decide whether or not to hit your house. Hundreds of considerations run through a burglar's mind, and he either says to himself . . . , 'Let's go for it,' or 'Pass.' "

The purpose of burglary deterrence strategies is, in a nutshell, to make the burglar say "Pass." There is wide agreement among crime analysts and criminologists that some targets are simply more attractive than others to burglars. The attractive qualities can be deduced from the kind of residences that end up being burglarized, and the deductions corroborated by interviews with burglars themselves. The object of a well-thought-out deterrence strategy is to make your home as unattractive to burglars as possible, based on an analysis of such studies as those reviewed here.

OCCUPANCY

It is the unanimous finding of research both here and abroad that burglars are unlikely to attack an occupied building. In 1972 Reppetto showed sentenced burglars pictures of potential targets and asked them which ones they would have been most likely to hit. The answers varied widely. Some preferred corner houses as targets, others liked houses in the middle of the block; some liked houses on a busy street, others preferred seclusion. But there was one thing they all agreed on: the house should be empty at the time of the hit.

Almost ten years later, Bennett and Wright showed convicted English burglars videotapes and color photographs of selected "targets," and the results were strikingly similar.

The first line of anti-burglary defense is thus the ability to project the appearance that there is somebody at home. Burglary, like most other crimes, is a very private affair. It is meant to take place behind closed doors without anybody watching—particularly the victims. The burglar's fear of discovery is probably a very strong and primitive impulse; anyone who has ever purloined typing paper from the office can understand this sentiment. An empty house provides the ideal environment for burglary because it guarantees invisibility.

The impression of round-the-clock occupancy is best projected from the outside—if possible, from the sidewalk or the street. This means even the perimeter of your property should suggest that there is someone inside the house day and night, summer and winter, spring and fall. The usual prescriptions stressed by police community protection officers and responsible manuals on this subject (e.g., don't leave on vacation without making provisions for someone to mow the grass, shovel the snow, or pick up the newspapers and mail) are the cornerstone of any sensible burglary-prevention strategy. But they are only the beginning. In a high-crime neighborhood—or in households with special reasons to fear burglary and break-ins—these basics don't go far enough. There are a number of other subtle and not so subtle ways to project an impression of occupancy that can prejudice a potential burglar's original reading of the site and induce him to go elsewhere, or, better still, give up the whole idea.

How to Make Your House Look Occupied

Burglars and sociologists are probably alike in their understanding that there are three basic kinds of householders who stay home all day: mothers with small children, people who work at home, and retirees. How to project the appearance of any of these categories of house residents—even if you happen to have a full-time job, spend many of your weekends at the shore, or travel extensively for business or pleasure—is one of the major challenges you face in working out a comprehensive deterrence strategy. In the discussion that follows, we have tried to come up with a mix of imaginative low-cost or no-cost strategies to make a house look lived in. This includes some down-to-earth projections of what does and doesn't make a site attractive to would-be burglars, and various ways to manipulate these factors in the homeowner's favor.

House Sitters   The easiest way to make your house look occupied is to arrange for it to *be* occupied. This suggestion is not as frivolous as it sounds. If you are seldom or never at home, you may want to consider sharing your house with somebody else who is. House sitters—especially students and retirees, who are on flexible daytime schedules and come and go unpredictably around the clock—are probably the invitees of choice. For suburban and rural residents, cars at the curb or in the driveway, curtains drawn and shades raised or lowered at appropriate hours of the day or night, garbage in the garbage pails, and lights going on and off are all legible signals to burglars that there is someone up and around and, by implication, standing guard.

Introducing another person into the privacy of your home can mean a change of status and/or lifestyle that only the most burglar-shy resident may be willing to incur. Short of taking on a spouse, a roommate, or boarders, then, what can you do to give your house a look of round-the-clock occupancy? Here you have your choice of human agency, mechanical contrivances, and, for want of a better term, front-yard camouflage.

In the first category, for example, a trusted neighbor who spends more time at home than you may be happy to park in your driveway, pull your curtains closed at the end of the day, or make the motions of going in and out several times a day. A part-time gardener, dog-walker, or cleaning person is another suggestion. The caution here is that you must pay very strict attention to workers' credentials before you hire them. Check references and hand out as few keys as necessary to get the job done. If and when you fire a worker, change the lock or locks. It is only wise to assume that an unknown percentage of burglaries are the result of inside information collected by people with legitimate and easy access to your home.

Lights   There are a number of electric and electronic devices that can do some of the work of human hands in your absence. An electric timer can be programmed to turn lights on in the late afternoon and off in the late morning inside your home. Outside, photosensitive floodlights and door lights can take the place of a human lamplighter. These devices, which consist of a light-sensitive cell screwed into the existing light sockets, respond to levels of daylight in the immediate environment and turn themselves on at dusk and off at dawn, regardless of who is or is not at home. They have the added advantage that you need never come home to a dark house, and don't have to worry about leaving the front- or back-door lights on all day either.

An important product in this area is the automatic outdoor floodlight that uses infrared sensors to detect people, cars, and other heat-disseminating objects in their path. These have a range of up to fifty feet and an adjustable delay that you can time to go on for three to twenty minutes. These gadgets sell for anywhere from $65 to $120, and are designed to simulate the reactions of a wary homeowner who hears unexpected footsteps outside the house and runs to turn on the lights.

Several caveats are in order here. First, police advise homeowners to cover any kind of outdoor light with wire mesh, so that the bulb can't be smashed—and inactivated—by would-be burglars or vandals. Second, timers may be a better choice than photocells where outdoor lights have to be located close to trees or tall shrubs, since such obstacles may create their own artificial dusk, or delay the onset of daylight in the immediate vicinity of their shade. In this case, you will paradoxically get a more natural effect by setting the timer to the hours of dusk and daylight yourself. Finally, any timer, whether it is manually set, photosensitive, or infrared-activated, is vulnerable to blackouts if it is wired into the house's central electric power supply, so look for those with battery backup.

Camouflage   Other variations on this theme are less technical and come under the heading of front-yard stage management and set design. The purpose of such camouflage is the same as in the theater: to suggest a setting and create an expectation about it in the audience's mind. Snow shovels in winter, unplanted seedling trays in spring, a child's tricycle in the summertime are all possible props, but the possibilities are as various as the homeowner's imagination. Anything that makes the house look occupied—at that very moment—qualifies. Obviously, the decoy object should not be attractive or valuable enough to invite being stolen itself, and with some imagination its eyesore quotient can be minimized—or even contravened. Your stage-managed "disarray" can consist of decorative objects like flower baskets, clay pots, an antique garden rake. In fact, anything goes, so long as the burglar is in some doubt as to what it is doing there and whether you will poke your head out the door at any moment to retrieve it.

Such "arrangements" may go against the grain of proud homeowners trained from childhood to keep the front porch tidy, but it should be noted that minor infringements of standard neighborhood aesthetics may be a small price to pay for the illusion of round-the-clock occupancy. If your neighbors object to the resulting disorder, explain the reasoning behind it. A minimal degree of carefully considered disorder may work in the homeowner's favor without necessarily compromising suburban property values and neighborhood goodwill.

Apartment dwellers have less leeway than homeowners because their discretionary area does not extend to the common corridor outside their front doors. But even here, there are some stage effects that can deter burglars or at least give them pause. For example, in an apartment building where most tenants have only one lock, you can install another. Where two locks are the norm, install a third. You don't have to use them all; all you really want is to give the impression that trying to break into your particular apartment will be a tedious, time-consuming chore and not worth the effort it takes the intruder to get out his tools. (See chapter 11, "Apartments.")

First Impressions   A corollary of the "unattractive nuisance" strategy is the impression of affluence reflected in the general state of repair of your house and grounds. Some of Reppetto's burglars walked around the neighborhood looking for "the house that stands out, in really good condition, the lawn really cared for; paint; TV antenna." The implication was that the same kind of affluence and pride of property inferable from the condition of the outside of the house and the tidiness of the grounds will be reflected in the value of the target's contents, once the burglar gets inside. People with perfectly manicured shrubs and well-maintained driveways, roofs, and shutters are more likely to own large color-television sets, expensive jewelry, and other high-priced household effects.

A certain degree of calculated shabbiness relative to other homes on the block may lower the odds that your house will be singled out for a burglary. There are no conclusive research findings on this issue, but common sense suggests that there is probably something to be said for keeping down a notch or two from the Joneses—at least from a burglary-deterrence point of view. On the other hand, a yard that appears too unkempt or slovenly, with derelict lawns and unswept walkways or porch steps, may in fact invite burglars by implying that you are far from home and may not be back for months.

So if you have it, don't flaunt it. Expensive cars are best kept behind closed garage doors. Picture windows that display a high-priced entertainment center or family silver are best kept discreetly curtained at all hours of the day and night.

Curious Neighbors   Curious neighbors may be a source of irritation, but they are also a dependable burglary-deterrence device. Research supports the assumption that burglars are as uneasy about your neighbors' curiosity as you are. In addition to an obviously occupied house, for example, the burglars in Bennett and Wright's study said they were most likely to be deterred from picking a given target by the visibility from nearby vantage points. Houses that fronted on streets with other visibly occupied houses were a turnoff, even if the immediate target appeared to be unoccupied at the time.

An important consideration here was whether other nearby buildings were themselves visible from the burglar's chosen entry points. "A frequently repeated fear among the burglars was that neighbors knew better than passersby who was a stranger to the area, or to the occupants of the target dwelling, and also would be more likely than passersby to do something about it." The message here is that you, the concerned homeowner, should keep the sight lines as open as possible between your house and the houses on either side— as well as those to the rear and facing you across the street. Tall fences and hedges, trellises, or privacy walls may work against you.

Informal neighborhood "crime-control" programs are apt to work better in some places than others, and they are probably most effective in small towns and rural neighborhoods where residents know each other well and are less inured to the presence of strangers than city dwellers are. Instances of the indifference of city dwellers abound. "In Hartford," notes urbanologist Fred Du Bow, summarizing the preliminary findings of a well-known communitywide crime-prevention program launched in the 1970s, "the most common response to seeing suspicious strangers was to ignore them."

When neighbors do notice someone or something amiss, they may be less than prompt to take any helpful action about it. Research indicates that block watchers are most useful when they know that they are supposed to be watching the block. In 1975, psychologist Thomas Moriarty mounted a field experiment in which bystanders were tested to see how they would respond to a "theft" staged by the experimenters. Altogether, only half of the respondents intervened. However, fully 90 percent of those who had made a previous commitment to keep an eye on the "stolen" object did so, as opposed to only a quarter of those who had made no such promises.

Such commitments are, or should be, part of any well-planned burglary-deterrence strategy, and if you don't know your neighbors well enough to do so, we suggest that you start laying the groundwork. Research indicates that such ad hoc neighborliness pays off in terms of reduced burglary risks. In the Asylum Hill area of Hartford, over half of the community worked out regular cooperative surveyance or house-watching arrangements with their neighbors; similar strategies have been implemented effectively in Seattle, St. Louis, and in the Midwood section of Brooklyn in New York City.

The next time you come home and unlock your door, make a quick assessment of your probable visibility to neighbors. If you are easily spotted from one or more of your respective neighbors' windows, you score high for surveyability—and correspondingly low for the attractiveness of your house as a prime target for burglary.

Hedges   In a recent University of Utah study, short hedges were found to be significant deterrents to burglary in communities where the houses were evenly matched for everything except the presence or absence of hedges. Social psychologist Barbara Brown hypothesizes that hedges suggest territoriality and therefore have some potent psychological effect on would-be intruders. But there is another, simpler explanation, too: thick hedges, with or without a closed gate between them, are highly uncomfortable and relatively impenetrable barriers to most humans, large dogs, and other kinds of intruders, and are therefore effective barriers in the average suburban setting.

Marking Your Belongings   Another increasingly popular deterrence strategy is the use of engraving devices to mark common household items, which makes them more difficult for a burglar to cash in. "Operation ID" is frequently promoted by local police jurisdictions, which often lend electric engraving tools to homeowners without cost. Household effects such as television sets, cameras, electronic equipment, and jewelry, if the piece is big enough to accommodate it, are marked with the owner's Social Security number or some other easily remembered code. The police then issue the owner a sticker or sign with an Operation ID logo, to be posted on or close to the front door. This is done to warn the would-be burglar that even if he does burglarize your home, chances are he will later have more difficulty selling the stolen articles. Whereupon he will theoretically give up on the idea of breaking in, at least for the time being.

Is Operation ID an effective deterrent? Skeptics have their doubts. It would seem, especially in America's big cities, that a few numbers scratched on the back of a piece of equipment would be highly unlikely to affect its "resale" value on the street. Even law-abiding bargain hunters are notorious for not questioning the origin of goods they can purchase at a significant discount.

So on the one hand, engraved items are apparently just as easily disposed of as nonengraved items; fences have no problem accepting them, and burglars have no problem fencing them. Nor are engraved items more likely to be retrieved than nonengraved items after a successful burglary.

At the same time, however, houses that display Operation ID stickers do seem to have lower victimization rates than nonposted houses; and there is evidence from Portland, Oregon, that homeowners whose houses had previously been the victims of repeated break-ins could break the cycle by posting Operation ID decals. This suggests that houses displaying the decals are not as attractive to burglars as houses without them. Everything else being equal, burglars would evidently prefer not to burglarize a house where the property is engraved—either because they accept the police logic that the goods would be more difficult to sell, or because they assume that a house where the owner has gone to all the trouble of engraving his belongings is also probably too well defended in other ways to make it worth their while.

Alarm Decals   The effectiveness of burglar alarms as deterrence devices is still an open question. (See chapter 9, "Burglar Alarms.") Although there is some evidence, especially in commercial premises, that functioning alarms result in a higher percentage of burglars being caught in the act, that message does not seem to have reached the burglars themselves. Only 36 percent of the burglars interviewed by Reppetto said that they were deterred by the presence of a burglar-alarm system; when asked what measures homeowners could take to protect themselves from break-ins, only 20 percent recommended buying a burglar alarm.

Pat Mayhew of the British Home Office Research and Planning Unit brings up another issue: the way in which an alarm affects the burglar once he is actually inside the house. "Research says . . . that houses with alarms might experience relatively small losses in a burglary," asserts Mayhew, "possibly because the offender has to make a hasty retreat" once the alarm goes off. This inference makes sense; unless a burglar knows exactly what he is looking for and where to find it, the sound of the alarm bell means that police will soon be on the scene, thereby greatly cutting down on the time he can safely spend searching for lucrative items and cash. Burglars are probably highly sensitive to the time factor involved in breaking into any given home; if so, an alarm sign in the front yard or a decal on the door may be all that is needed to make a burglar decide to "pass."

Sound Effects   The example of alarms proves that setting the stage need not be limited to visual cues alone. Human beings make a certain amount of noise as they go about their daily business, and one way for burglars—especially those who work at night—to find out if someone is home is to put their ear to the door and listen for sounds of life. Daytime burglars often go to the front door, ring the bell, and wait for someone to respond. If there is no action on the other side of the door after a reasonable amount of time has elapsed, they go into action of their own.

A radio or a TV left on all day was once considered a clever burglary deterrent device. But burglars are on to this trick and, although it may give them pause, in the absence of other signs of occupancy it may not slow them down as long as it did in the days when such ruses were still fresh. However, there *are* variations on the all-day radio theme which may still pay off. One such possibility is a long-playing tape programmed with random radio voices, ringing phones, bits and pieces of real conversation, and the clanking of various kinds of household machinery (the noisier the better). A current item in many mail-order catalogues is an alarm that can be connected to doors and windows; it is programmed to play a tape of a barking dog when the alarm is activated. This device is battery-operated and costs between twenty-five and thirty dollars, a reasonable enough price unless there are an excessive number of doors and windows to protect.

Dogs   If your tape includes stretches of dogs barking, so much the better. Circumstances permitting, the bark should be as deep and thunderous as possible. Although dogs are in general strong dissuaders to many burglars, it stands to reason that the worse the bark, the more threatening the implied bite attached to it will seem.

Why a recording of a snarling guard dog and not the real thing? Guard dogs come in all shapes, breeds, and sizes, but to perform their duties they must also submit to their fair share of training, and once trained they may be embarrassingly difficult to untrain—or to control. A dog trained to bark at footsteps outside the house will bark at all footsteps, friendly or unfriendly, and in doing so may incur the anger of your neighbors. A dog trained to keep an intruder at bay will keep anyone else at bay whose smell he doesn't recognize immediately—including the mailman, the delivery boy, and visiting relatives.

Dogs trained to attack intruders will do just that. Nobody has yet come up with a way of training a dog to make the distinctions between strangers, semi-strangers, and long-lost friends. To be able to control the dog's responses, you have got to be on the spot physically, calling the shots.

The characteristics of dogs that make them such good choices for guarding their masters' homes may have their drawbacks in the chaos of a burglary in progress. To the dogs, helpful neighbors and/or police arriving at the crime scene may seem to be intruders, too, and dealt with accordingly.

For this and other reasons, if you feel you must have a trained guard dog, professional trainers strongly advise giving all members of the family a hand in the training process, as opposed to bringing home a dog already trained by professional handlers.

PART II

HARDENING
THE TARGET

5

DOORS

"Hardening the target" refers to physical procedures, gadgets, and equipment that will make a property less vulnerable to burglary. Appropriate hardware, thoughtfully planned and carefully installed, can prevent some burglaries and slow down others so drastically that either the intruder has a good chance of being caught in the act, or is in such a hurry that he leaves the house before perusing its contents thoroughly.

Target-hardening should ideally start at the outer perimeter of the property with gates, walls, and fences. A second line of defense begins at the outside of the house itself, with locks, chains, grates, bars, and assorted hardware to reinforce entry points like doors and windows. Inside the house a third line of defense includes alarms, timers, and an array of electronic sensors that can be programmed to detect intrusion and send out an alarm.

INTRODUCTION

"Most doors are a joke," wrote Jack MacLean in his book *Secrets of a Superthief*. "They can be kicked in easily, or at least have a foot poked through them to make a hole that can be enlarged quickly. Forget about hollow doors. Forget about most wooden doors, unless they are solid and thick enough to resist an axe."

MacLean's disdain echoes the caveats of most professional security experts. "An issue that crops up regularly on council estates [public housing projects] with high rates of break-ins is the weakness of outside doors and their frames," says British environmentalist Michael Burbidge. Since practically two-thirds of all illegal entries are made through doors, with the remainder made by climbing through windows, these access points deserve the home-owner's first and most systematic security review.

Door as Point of Entry

Even burglars who eventually get into a house through a window will generally have tried a door first, since they are less likely to draw the suspicion of neighbors and passersby that way. Doors are designed to offer quick and convenient entry. For security purposes, however, the trick is to build, equip, and reinforce them so that they offer this convenience only to the people who are actually authorized to go in and out of the house.

Primary vs. Secondary Doors

Doors come in many shapes, sizes, and functional categories, including front, side, and back doors, service doors, garage doors, cellar doors, porch doors, and—in apartments and other multi-family dwellings—corridor, lobby, and vestibule doors. But beyond these primary exterior doors there are also interior "secondary" doors, like the ones between the garage and the house, the porch and the house, or the cellar and the house. From a burglar's point of view, such secondary doors are choice targets since they are usually not visible from the street. Once inside the secondary area between the exterior door and the house, the burglar has additional time and privacy to work on the secondary door that leads directly into the house itself.

Secondary doors are usually less sturdy and have more vulnerable locks than those found in primary doors. But even if they are as strong as primary doors, their seclusion still means that whatever sounds the intruder makes are muffled from neighbors and passersby. Locks can be drilled, glass broken, and doors pried or wrenched from their frames—either with tools the intruder brought with him, or those that he may have found in the homeowner's cellar, porch, or garage—affording opportunities that would not be available in the open.

Doors that are meant to serve as barriers to unwanted intruders, whether they are inside the actual perimeter of the house or not, should require a great deal of effort and noise for an intruder to enter. This is particularly true for doors that are located in the least visible areas of the house.

Door Assemblies as Systems

To test the security of a working door you should think of it as one element in an integrated system. Typical door assemblies include a variety of components: some of them are visible, while others are known only to the carpenter and/or locksmith who installed them. Their working elements include the supporting walls; the invisible part of the rough structural door frame concealed by the exposed outer frame or jamb; the door itself; its hinges; the lockset, including the strike and protective plates; and the screws, bolts, and nails that hold the whole assembly together. A weakness in any one of these elements can defeat the purpose of the entire assembly.

DOOR FRAMES

To visualize the structural parts of the door assembly, it may be helpful to think of them as three interlocking frames or pieces, each one cut marginally smaller than the next. All three structural elements must work tightly together for the doorway to be effectively secure.

The door frame is often the weakest point in a typical door assembly, and is thus frequently the first point of attack for burglars. Research shows that most burglars do not pick locks; they either kick through a door or pry it away from its door frame. Prying the door away from the frame allows the lock's bolt or latch to pop out of the strike, and represents the easiest way for an intruder to get past a locked door. No matter how strong the lock or kickproof the door, both are all but useless in a weak frame.

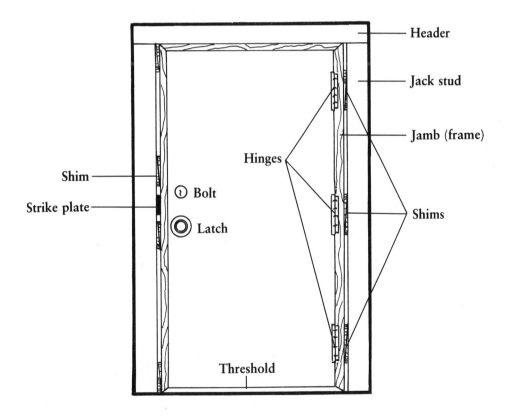

Figure 1 Typical door assembly

Door-Frame Construction

In the vast majority of new housing construction since World War II, cheap materials and standard labor shortcuts have meant serious deficiencies in doors and door assemblies from a security point of view. The rough outer door frame is a rectangle constructed of two-by-four-inch stock lumber, usually at least three feet wide by eighty-six to ninety inches tall. The sides of this rectangle are called the *jack studs*. The top is called the *header*, and the bottom is the *threshold*. Together, these four pieces of lumber define the structural opening that holds the inner frame or *jamb*, which in turn holds the door and its hardware. Outer frames are cut slightly larger than the inner frame or jamb, to permit easier insertion and adjustment for plumbness, and easy opening or closing of the door while it is being installed.

The door jamb is the vertical inner frame that encloses the door itself. In most instances the jamb and door are preassembled and fitted in place in a single unit. After insertion, any space that is left between the jack studs and the jamb is taken up by driving in thin wedges or shims. It is this space between the jamb and the jack studs, especially in the immediate area of the locks, strike, and hinges, that is most vulnerable to prying and jimmying with crowbars and other tools.

Metal Door Frames   Door frames can be made of metal as well as wood. A wood door can be hung in a steel frame, but most one-piece steel frames come as part of a metal door-and-frame assembly. A cautionary note: rolled steel door frames may leave a space between the jack studs and the hollow jamb. To make the door secure if it is being refitted into a new steel frame, this space should be backed up with a crush-resistant filling such as cement grout, especially in the area of the strike, so that it won't give way to the bending action of a pry-bar inserted between the door and the frame. Another consideration if you are installing a steel door frame is to be sure to use steel that is at least twelve-gauge or thicker. This means using steel with a gauge of twelve or *lower*, because the thicker the steel plate the lower the gauge number. (See section on steel doors, below.)

Door-Frame Weaknesses   Like any other opening cut into the continuous façade of the house (windows, electrical service line openings, water mains, gas lines), door frames represent interruptions in the house's solid exterior casing and have inherent structural weaknesses intensified by constant use. As a newly constructed house settles, shims may loosen and frames may separate and shrink away from the door as well as the enclosing jack studs.

In older houses, time and the weather also take their toll on the wooden elements of the door assembly. The wood in the door, jamb, and frame is subject to drying, cracking, termites, and rot. Screws and nails rust and loosen, contributing to the wear and tear. As time passes, doors contract with dryness and swell with moisture or caked paint. To compensate, you may be tempted to plane them down to prevent sticking, but this contributes further to the widening space between the door and the jamb.

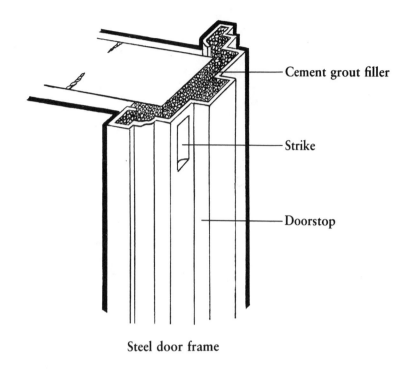

Cement grout filler

Strike

Doorstop

Steel door frame

Figure 2   Stiffening a steel door frame

Doorstops   One part of the jamb that receives a great deal of wear and tear is the doorstop. The jamb itself, the vertical frame component that encloses the door, includes a protruding wooden lip or doorstop that prevents the door from swinging all the way in either direction. The doorstop is often simply a piece of wood nailed to the center of the jamb, which can be pried off with a screwdriver or some other jimmying device. Instead, if at all practical, the doorstop should be rabbetted, or cut into the wood of the door jamb itself, forming a protruding stop or offset that can't be pried loose from the underlying jamb.

Strengthening the Frame

In strengthening the structure of the door assembly, certain guidelines should be kept in mind. The door must fit closely into the jamb, with no more than $1/32$ inch of space. If it doesn't, you should either shop for a new door or build up the existing jamb to take up the excess space. Once you have a good fit, the rest of the framing can be examined for rigidity in either of two ways.

Testing the Door Frame   One simple test to find out if the door frame has too much play is by spreading it with two pieces of two-by-four lumber. (See figure 3a.) One short piece, tapered slightly to form a wedge, is held vertically against one side of the door frame in the area of the strike box. The second piece is cut to a length just shy of the distance between the narrow top of the vertical piece and the other side of the door. When you press the longer piece down against the thickening vertical wedge, the door frame begins to spread. If the door frame offers little resistance to the spreading action, it indicates weakness; you may want to replace or at least reinforce such a frame. *Note:* Do not press too hard on the horizontal piece, as too much pressure on the spreading frame may crack the plaster surrounding it.

Another way to test the tightness of the door frame is to remove the casing around it, unscrew the door strikes, and make an actual physical inspection of the area around the

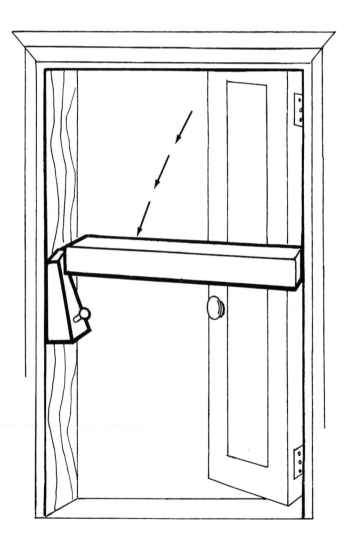

Figure 3A   Testing the door frame

strikes and hinges. You should pay close attention to the shims, which fit in the gap between the door frame and the jack studs and header that make up the outer frame. You may find that the play in the frame is due to loose or splitting shims, or in some instances to no shims being present at all.

Reinforcing the Door Frame with Shims   If the frame itself is sturdy, but the play in the frame is due to loose-fitting shims, you should replace them with strips of plywood. (While some home builders initially use a pair of shingles for this purpose, shingles usually consist of softer wood that can split easily, so plywood is preferable.) Split or weakened shims are most common behind the hinges and in the areas immediately above and below the strike box or strike plate, since these are the areas that receive the greatest wear and tear over the years.

When reinforcing an existing frame with new shims, the shims should make a tight fit, tight enough to require a mallet to drive them in. To ensure a tight-enough fit, use two thinner shims instead of one thicker one (e.g., two 1/4-inch pieces of plywood rather than one 1/2-inch piece). The shims should be tapered (planed, sanded, or chiseled down at one edge) in matching pairs, and inserted with the thick end of one against the thin end of the other. (See figure 3b.) This procedure will result in a tight-fitting shim with little risk of splitting the jamb.

As far as the outer door frame and jamb are concerned, if you have any doubt about their strength, replace them. This job may best be accomplished by a hired professional, but if you feel sufficiently confident with your own skills to take on the task yourself, remember to use screws of sufficient length to go all the way through the finished frame and the shims and into the jack stud. Countersink the screw and fill in the depressions with a plug or wood filler shaved flush; then stain the screw heads or paint them to match the door jamb.

DOOR CONSTRUCTION

There are two reliable security tests of the material components of a door. One is the material's relative ability to resist drilling, sawing, cutting, and brute force. The second is its ability to anchor the lock assemblies attached to it so that they resist being pried, jimmied, or twisted off. If the door opens outward, with its hinges on the outside, then a third concern is the hinges' ability to resist tampering or removal.

Doors in most single-family houses are generally made of wood. Other choices are combinations of wood, steel, glass, and aluminum. The strongest wood doors are constructed of a solid hardwood core, and consist of oak or other hardwood planks and/or blocks, laminated together and covered with a veneered facing on either side. Next best to solid-core hardwood doors are doors with interior cores of particle board or softwood. Prices

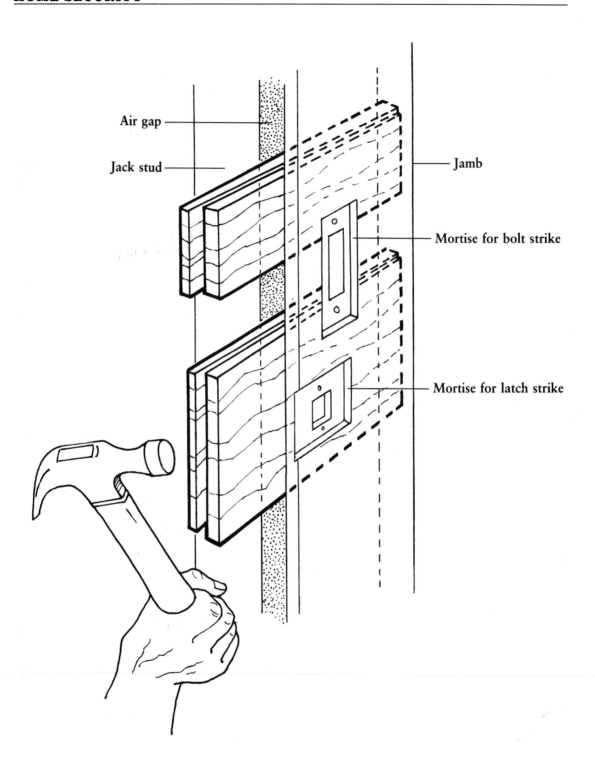

Figure 3B   Strengthening the door frame by driving tapered paired shims into the space between the jamb and the jack studs

for doors currently range from $400 for a hardwood-filled door down to $125 for one with softwood filler.

Other, less adequate construction includes the hollow-core door, which consists of two facing panels attached to a frame and filled in with such materials as pressed wood or various other insulating or stiffening materials. A single sheet of wood veneer is used as a facing on either side. Also popular are wood-panel doors.

To find out whether your door's core is hard, soft, or hollow, push a thumbtack into the flush panel about eight inches above the bottom of the panel, so as to avoid the frame of the door panel. If there is no resistance, the door is hollow. If there is some resistance, the door is probably softwood; and if the thumbtack will penetrate the wood only with great difficulty, if at all, your door is probably made of solid-core hardwood.

Solid-Core Hardwood Doors

The solid hardwood door, covered by laminated wooden panels, is recommended for all but high-crime areas, and it is an economical choice when fire regulations do not require metal doors with fire-resistant core materials. Solid-core wood doors should be no less than 1¾ inches thick, a dimension that offers sufficient resistance to hacking and brute force.

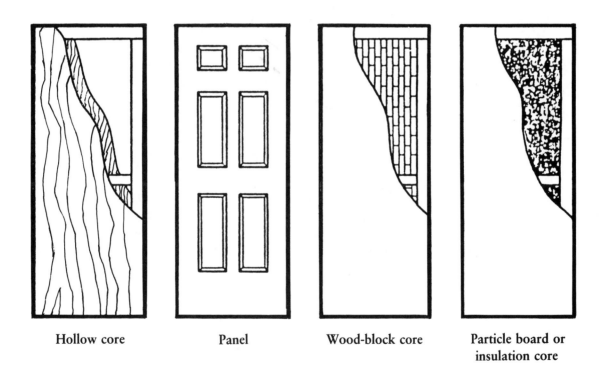

Hollow core   Panel   Wood-block core   Particle board or insulation core

Figure 4   A selection of wood doors

Some solid-core doors are built around softer materials like particle board or white pine wood interiors. Although less resistant than solid hardwood, these are still better than the typical hollow-core wood or hollow-core sheet-metal door.

A solid hardwood door can be cut or drilled, but not easily. Solid-core doors also offer the best support for the locking devices they carry, and when reinforced with inserted metal rods surrounding the lockset, the locking devices become almost totally resistant to attempts to cut the door from around the lock.

Reinforcing the Lock on a Wooden Door   Some solid-core wooden doors are vulnerable to attack by hacking or sawing around the lock, permitting the locking mechanism to be worked out of the strike plate, especially if the door's wood is soft or otherwise not very sturdy. This weakness can be compensated for by inserting steel rods around the lock area. To insert steel rods, open the door and, with its lock-side edge facing you, drill holes into the door about eight inches deep and at about two-inch intervals. You will need to use a drill guide and special long drill bits. The holes should be slightly larger in diameter than the rods you plan to insert in them, so that there will be some room for the rods to rotate, if and when an intruder tries to saw through them. This makes it difficult for the saw's teeth to catch and cut through the rod. Drill about six holes above and below the lock area, being careful that the nearest holes are no closer than one inch from the bolt or latch plate. The holes can be kept parallel at a ninety-degree angle to the door's edge by using a drill guide. Select solid steel unthreaded rods 7½ inches in length and drive them into the eight-inch holes. Fill the remaining space with wood filler or glued-in hardwood pegs, then paint or stain as appropriate.

Calamine Doors

This flush-type, solid-core metal-sheathed door provides excellent security. Most calamine doors consist of enclosed cores of pressed or soft wood with a metal sheathing of thin, twenty-four-gauge steel. But although such panel doors are more vulnerable than flush doors faced with heavier steel sheeting, they are almost equally fire retardant and represent a better security barrier than the more decorative thin-gauge metal doors whose cores consist of little more than fiberglass or other unresisting insulating material. Calamine doors are available pre-hung in their own pre-fitted metal door frames and are most often found as connecting doors between the garage and living portions of the house in recently constructed homes.

Steel Doors

Most municipal fire codes require metal doors in multiple dwellings, but there are mixed opinions about the use of steel doors in the average residential situation. Steel doors are generally of the hollow-core type, with a metal frame of heavier gauge than the thinner

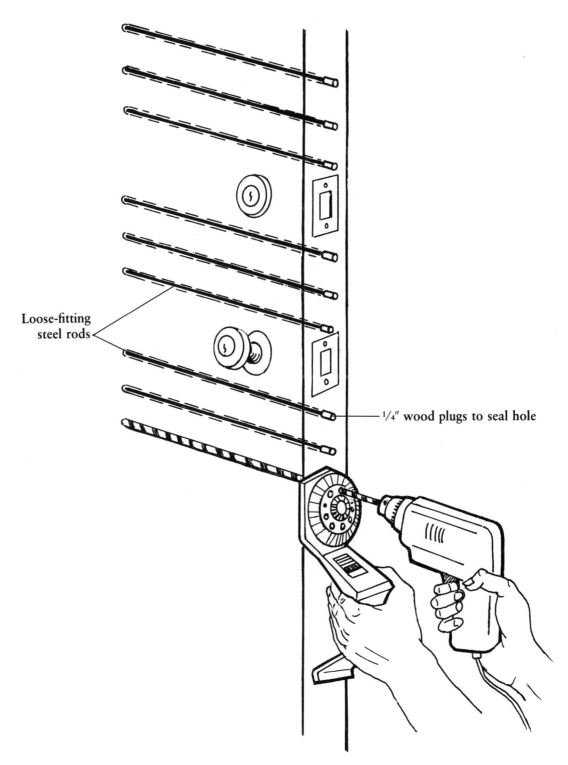

Loose-fitting
steel rods

¼″ wood plugs to seal hole

Figure 5   Sawproofing the lock area of a door

sheet metal of the facing panel that covers them. Since most panels are twenty-gauge or more (i.e., $1/_{32}$ inch or less in thickness), they can be punched through with a pair of common tin snips, and therefore do not represent a serious security barrier. Some are constructed of thin-gauge steel with so little internal bracing that they can easily buckle under the pressure of a strong kick or a sturdy pry-bar.

There are almost as many variations on the construction of steel doors as there are on wooden ones, but a steel door of sufficient gauge can offer the best level of protection available to the homeowner. If the gauge is thick enough (i.e., $1/_{16}$ inch or thicker), the panels are highly resistant to brute force, cutting, or punching in. When hung in a matching steel frame, and properly mounted and grouted, they can withstand the prying action of almost any kind of jimmying tool, from a strong screwdriver to a crowbar.

Steel doors offered at the average lumberyard or home-improvement center come in many shapes and sizes, stamped or pressed in varying designs. They are usually cut from twenty-four-gauge sheet steel. The best steel doors are those of the lowest (i.e., thickest) possible gauge, with an internal structure of metal bracing or hardwood core, and are usually designed for installation at commercial or industrial establishments where a high level of security is required.

Prices for good low-gauge steel doors in 1988 were one-fourth to two-thirds higher than those for comparable wooden doors. But in free-standing suburban houses or condominiums, the added security may be only marginally better than comparable solid-core wooden doors, and the cost may therefore only be worthwhile to the homeowner who lives in a very high crime area, whose house is not visible from other houses in the neighborhood, or who owns unusually valuable furnishings, belongings, or collections.

Steel Replacement Door Assemblies   A recent development in the door market is the steel-door replacement package, which may provide a good solution for householders faced with weak, old, or poorly fitting wood doors and frames. This package has the advantage that it requires relatively little skill to install. The door assembly consists of a steel door prehung on a metal frame, with such accessories as knobs and locks, and the entire assembly should fit snugly into the existing door's inner frame, jamb, and studs. As a general rule, only the existing threshold has to be removed when measuring for the correct height and width of the existing inner frame.

When it comes to choosing the steel-door replacement package, you should give the same care and attention to choosing the materials for the door and frame as you would if you were buying the pieces separately. Remember, too, that all the accessory hardware—including securing screws, bolts, and nails—should be long enough to penetrate all the way through the replacement frame and the old jamb, and into the old jack stud. Also, the knobs and locks that accompany such assemblies are frequently lightweight, so be sure that the preparation for the lock hardware will permit upgrading it with sturdier replacements.

DOOR DESIGN

The flush door is probably the most commonly used door design. It consists of flat wooden or metal facings, the same height and width as the door's frame, mounted either on a solid wood backing attached directly to the core, or on the interior framework of the hollow-core door itself.

After the flush door, the next most commonly used design is the panel door, chosen for its looks and fidelity to certain architectural styles. The standard Colonial-style door is probably the most familiar panel-door design. On a panel door, the framing members of the door enclose various indented or raised panels of varying thickness, and the aesthetic interest is achieved by beveling or inserting thinner wood panels at regular intervals along the face of the door. Both flush and paneled doors may be designed to include glass "lights" (windows) and/or louvers, both of which present serious security problems.

Hollow-Core Wood Doors

A hollow-core wood door used as the front-entrance door on many homes constructed since World War II is of little value for anything but preserving the occupant's visible privacy from curious passersby. In terms of security it is a point of great vulnerability.

Hollow-core doors are usually constructed of thin sheets or panels of wood veneer covering either side of an inner frame of slightly less than 1¾-inch wood stock. The center consists of empty space which may include some insulation but most often does not. At best its hollow center may enclose some thin egg-crate filler or corrugated material to help it maintain some semblance of stiffness. The vertical members of the inner frame are barely wide enough to provide support for the lock, knob, or hinge assemblies that are to be attached to it. This kind of door offers only token resistance to burglary. To get past it, a reasonably strong intruder can kick or shoulder his way through. It can be cut, drilled, or sawed through with relative ease, or the facing itself can be peeled off to give the burglar direct access to the lock.

To test whether your front door is hollow core, tap it in the center part of the door, away from the inner supporting frame, and listen for a hollow sound; or drill a small, inconspicuous hole. If your front or back door does turn out to be of hollow-core construction, the best treatment is to replace it with a solid-core wood, metal-clad, or metal door. If for some reason this is not practical, it may be necessary to reinforce it with sheet steel or plywood.

Reinforcing a Hollow-Core or Softwood-Core Door   Your own evaluation of the existing security risk in your community should determine whether or not to reinforce the door, and if so, what material and what thickness of reinforcement to use. Again, it is more strongly recommended that you replace a weak door than reinforce it, but if you opt for reinforcement, the two best choices are steel or plywood. For security purposes, steel of at least $1/16$-inch thickness is the best choice.

Steel reinforcements: Steel reinforcement panels vary by thickness, weight, and size. While you get maximum protection by covering both the entire exterior and interior surfaces of the door, you still receive extra protection by buttressing such obvious weak spots as the thin wood panels on a wood-panel door, or the glass window lights in a windowed door alone. The chart below gives some indication of thickness and weight of various gauges of steel.

Gauge	Thickness	Weight of Full-Size Door Panel (36″ × 80″)	Weight of Partial Panel (12″ × 20″)
12-gauge	$1/8$″	100 lbs.	10 lbs.
16-gauge	$1/16$	50 lbs.	5 lbs.
20-gauge	$1/32$″	25 lbs.	2½ lbs.
24-gauge	$3/128$″	15 lbs.	1½ lbs.

You get maximum protection by covering the entire surface of both sides of the door. However, if you decide to cover the surface of only one side of the door, it is best for security purposes to do it on the exterior side. On the other hand, if you reinforce only a part or parts of the door, such as window lights or panels in a panel door, the interior surfaces should be reinforced.

The choice of sheet steel presents special considerations—notably, weight and thickness. As you can see from the chart above, the weight of full door panels in twelve-gauge steel is about 100 pounds. While most hinges for residential exterior doors can carry such weight, some may not be able to. In addition, the thickness of the steel may interfere with opening and closing the door when the space between the exterior surface and the doorstop on the frame is not wide enough to accommodate it. This may call for remounting the entire door in its frame.

Templates: If you decide on a steel reinforcement, your next step is to make a full-size template for it. Don't trust the details to diagrams, because you will have to show the vendor the exact shape, dimensions, and locations of the cutouts needed to accommodate the lock cylinders, knobs, handles, and (if necessary) door viewers.

At this point you must decide whether or not to cover the entire lock cylinder—except for the keyway—with the steel cladding. One consideration here is what you will do if and when the cylinder has to be replaced at some later date, and can't be removed from the inside. Probably a better choice is a square or round cutout for the cylinder, with an additional guard plate affixed over it in the final assembly. (*Note:* When attaching a full or partial panel, such as a guard plate, to the door's exterior, use carriage bolts spaced no farther than twelve inches apart.)

Plywood reinforcements for hollow-core wood doors: Plywood, which is made of thin layers of wood glued together so that each layer's grain runs at right angles to the layer above and below it, is sturdier than solid wood of the same thickness. While not as sturdy as a thick steel panel, plywood is readily available, relatively inexpensive, and lends itself conveniently to the average handyperson's level of skills. Three-quarter-inch plywood is recommended if only one side is to be reinforced. A minimum of one-half-inch thickness for each side is advised when both sides of the door are going to be reinforced.

As with steel, weight varies according to thickness. A thirty-six-by-eighty-inch panel will weigh about forty pounds if it is ¾ inch thick, or twenty-five pounds in a ½-inch thickness. Double these weights—and thicknesses—if you are covering both sides of the door. Remember that a heavier door may require an additional hinge for support.

Material specifications: Exterior-grade plywood should be used for exterior surfaces, but interior panels can be chosen from a wide variety of decorative veneers and finishes. These panels should be glued to the door's surface, then screwed flush with carriage bolts or one-way screws. (A carriage bolt is a round-headed, mushroom-shaped bolt threaded along part of its shank. The round head has no slot for purchase that would allow it to be removed from the outside. A nut and sometimes an additional washer are screwed onto the threaded shank from the inside to secure it.)

Although plywood gives an added measure of strength, it also adds weight to the door, so you may need to replace the existing hinges with ones that can carry the added weight. Also, the added thickness may mean that the spindle of the existing doorknob is not long enough, and a new doorknob will be required. If the plywood is added to the outer surface of an inward-swinging door, you will probably also have to replace the strike plate and doorstops, too. An easier, though less secure and less attractive, alternative is to use plywood panels cut just wide enough and tall enough to cover the weak areas of the door, such as glass window lights, thin wood panels, and mail slots. In these cases, a hardwood molding can be used to frame the partial panel and improve its looks.

Wood-Panel Doors

Doors with raised or recessed panels, although attractive and architecturally accurate in the right context, offer little more resistance to burglars than the typical hollow-core door. Beveling the wood to produce an interesting design may also make the panels so thin at the edges that they can be shattered with a good kick. Where security is a factor, such doors should be replaced. If architectural fidelity and aesthetic considerations dictate retaining them—at least on the outside—the inside facing can still be reinforced, as on hollow-core doors, with sheet metal or plywood.

Doors with Glass "Lights"

Residential entrance doors that contain glass "lights" or windows present serious security problems. While such glass may afford you a view of the outside, so, too, does it afford anyone on the other side of the door a view of what's inside. When the pane is of ordinary window glass it can easily be broken, allowing an intruder to reach in and unlock the door from the inside—especially if the glass is less than forty inches from the interior lock.

To make such doors secure, you have several choices. Perhaps the most obvious (and probably the most expensive) is to replace the glass panes with special security see-through plastic made of 3/16-inch-thick transparent polycarbonate. (See section on patio doors, below.) Another choice is to reinforce the glass on one side with iron bars or iron filigree, patterned in a dense-enough design to prevent a human hand from getting between the openings and reaching the inside latch or doorknob. The panes can also be replaced by heavy glass embedded with wire mesh and backed by a metal grating or filigree on the inside. Or, as a makeshift in an emergency situation (glass panes broken, a rash of burglaries in the neighborhood, etc.), the glass can be backed with a temporary covering of plywood or steel plate.

Similar precautions should be taken with glass panels that are set into the outer walls close to or adjoining the doors. If the existing wall construction permits, the glass in these panels can be replaced with thick glass blocks, which permit light to enter but make it difficult for the intruder to get in, or to see through clearly.

Any exterior door containing glass or flanked by windows containing ordinary window glass should be equipped with a double-cylinder dead bolt which prevents the door from being unlocked from the inside by someone on the outside reaching in. (See chapter 7, "Locks.") Check your local building codes to determine if double cylinder locks are permitted in your area.

Louvered Glass Doors

Glass louvers consist of long, narrow glass panels set into a metal frame that permits the louvers to be adjusted from a vertical to a horizontal position, allowing for ventilation in warm weather. Of all doors containing window lights, these are the most vulnerable.

While louvers are acceptable on an auxiliary storm/screen door, louvers on primary exterior doors are a security hazard. Their long glass panels can be broken or worked out of their metal frames with minimal effort, so that intruders can either reach in and free the lock or remove the panes and climb through the opening. If your present exterior door has louvered glass panes, you should replace it, or if not, at least have the glass and its frame removed and replaced with 3/16-inch polycarbonate (see page 60). Or, as a final though probably less desirable alternative from a security point of view, the glass panels can be immobilized in their framed holders with epoxy glue and the glass portion backed up with metal grillwork. As with all doors that contain any kind of glass, this type of door should be equipped with a double-cylinder vertical lock (where permitted by local building codes) that can be opened only by key from the inside.

Dutch Doors

Dutch doors have separately cut and mounted top and bottom sections, either of which can be opened. If your house has a Dutch door as an exterior doorway, you should either replace it or else permanently fasten both halves together so that they act as one unit. However, even after you have reinforced a Dutch door in this way, it still will not have the stability or security of a door that was originally built as one unit, and the best advice is therefore to secure both halves with separate dead-bolt locks. Or, as an alternative, run a vertically mounted slide-bolt lock extending past the original division to connect both halves, and strengthen both of them in the process. Dutch doors sometimes have windowed upper portions with a paneled lower half. The precautions described earlier for windowed doors and paneled doors apply to these sections as well.

French Doors

A French door is basically a floor-to-ceiling window, hinged to open like a door. When used as primary exterior doors, French doors are usually designed to open onto patios, porches, or balconies, where light and view are a prime consideration. Where security is also a consideration, though, the glass in French doors should be replaced or reinforced with polycarbonate, grillwork, or iron shutters.

French doors come in pairs opening from the center, but usually only one-half of the door is opened for daily use, and unless the other side of the double door is made stationary it can easily be pried open. One of the two doors should therefore be permanently closed by fastening it to the frame's threshold and header. If this isn't feasible, one side of the door can at least be made relatively stationary by installing concealed, flush-mounted bolts or cane bolts that project by at least an inch into receptacles in the header and threshold. In this case the stationary side of the door acts as a jamb for the active part of the door, and encloses the strike plate for the locking mechanism on the active door.

Double Wood Doors

Double wood doors are rarely found as exterior doors in residential construction, but if you have one of these all the precautions for wood doors, especially panel doors, apply, in addition to the cautions outlined for French doors described above.

Storm and Screen Doors

Storm and screen doors should never act as security barriers. Their main purpose is to keep out insects and/or serve as an extra thermal barrier in cold weather. Whether they are made of wood or metal, they tend to be flimsy and lightweight, and can easily be forced or pried open. The locking devices designed for these doors are only adequate for keeping small children and animals in or out of the house.

Hatch Doors

Slanting hatch doors leading to the cellar are often found in houses built over twenty years ago. If these doors are constructed of wood planking and are original to the house, they may have deteriorated seriously with age. If so, they can easily be ripped apart, and their locks and hasps pried off.

The best recommendation is to replace them. Prefabricated steel doors sunk into concrete provide the best protection. A hasp and high-quality lock should be used to secure the door, preferably from the inside. (See chapter 8, "Padlocks . . .") If it is to be exposed on the outside, use a hinging hasp of hardened steel installed with carriage bolts in such a way that when it is closed all bolt heads are covered.

Detached Storage-Shed Doors

Target-hardening techniques used for the house are hard to apply to detached sheds and other outbuildings, since their construction is often lightweight and rudimentary. The best you can do is slow the burglar down with door and window security, good padlocks, and hasps; but you might want to think twice about using the shed to store various cutting, sawing, and prying tools that can be used to attack the house itself. If you must store such valuable items as bicycles, ladders, and lawnmowers in the shed, it would be best to chain and lock them to the frame.

Sliding-Glass Patio Doors

Sliding-glass patio doors are an immediate, visible target for burglars. More experienced burglars may attempt to get into the house by lifting them out of their tracks; others may prefer to smash, slide, or lift their way in.

In addition to their large areas of vulnerable glass, patio doors come with their own unique set of security problems:

- They are generally hung in malleable, lightweight aluminum frames and channels that can easily be bent with a crowbar.
- The individual panels are lifted into position when installed, and, unless secured in some manner, can just as easily be lifted out of their tracks and thrown aside.
- If the door panels consist of plate glass, they can be broken or cut with little effort; if they are made of tempered glass, the panels can be shattered with a little more effort.

- The locking mechanisms that come with patio doors are typically unsubstantial; some can even be forced by hand. Others secure only the sliding panel, providing no security for the stationary panel.
- The large glass areas that open up the patio door to its attractive suburban vista are just as handy in opening up a view of the house's contents to outsiders looking in.

Patio doors are at additional risk if they face a secluded terrace or garden, with no easy sight lines to other neighbors or the street. This gives the intruder a degree of privacy and cover beyond that at the front or side of the house.

Security for such doors is relative, but sliding-glass patio doors can be buttressed by addressing the door's weaknesses step by step.

Securing a Patio Door in Its Tracks   The growing use of patio doors for terraces and balconies in high-rise luxury apartments as well as suburban single-family houses has led to the development of a wide range of locking and other security mechanisms designed especially for them. Some of these are designed to keep a burglar from lifting the doors out of their tracks; others are designed to strengthen the sliding mechanism that moves them sideways in their frames.

Sliding-glass patio doors are usually constructed with a one-inch clearance in the upper track and about a half-inch lip defining the lower track. The doors are installed so that their tops slip into the upper trough, giving it enough clearance to slip over the shorter floor-level lip, with the sliding panel fitting into the inner track. The resulting half-inch play in the upper track can be reduced by installing 1¾-inch number-twelve sheet-metal, pan-headed screws vertically into the top of the upper track of the sliding part of the door, spaced so that there is only marginal clearance between the heads of the screws and the top of the sliding door. If the top edge of the track is hollow, though, the inserted screws will not have enough purchase to resist the door's being lifted from its tracks. In this case, the screws should be inserted horizontally, rather than vertically, into the frame along the top edge of the sliding door.

The stationary door panel is often easy to pry open or lift out of its track because the barriers of the troughs which hold the door in the track can be bent, allowing the door to be slipped out. Installing a bracket made of a 1¼-inch angle iron as a barrier outside the stationary panel makes it virtually impossible to pry the panel up high enough to clear the barrier.

Preventing Opening or Sliding   Inexpensive devices are available that can increase the difficulty of sliding open the movable panel of a sliding patio-door assembly. Most of these devices secure both the sliding and the stationary panels of the door by pinning them together at a point where their two frames overlap, thus resisting efforts to force either panel sideways. This two-panel protection consists of devices that may be as simple as push-in pins. Others use keys or have some other provision for locking the pinning device in place.

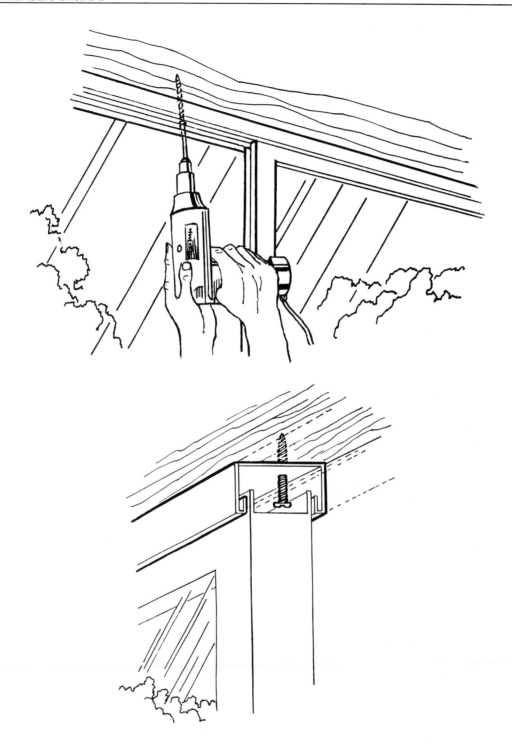

Figure 6A   Securing a patio door using sheet-metal screws in the upper track to reduce the clearance between the upper channel and the top of the door. This prevents the door from being lifted out.

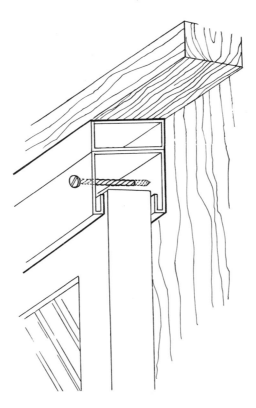

Figure 6B   Securing a patio door with a horizontally driven screw

Another, less secure group of devices provides protection only to the sliding panel. These include a variety of latches, bolts, and pins that fasten the sliding door to the track, to the framing channel, to the header, or to the sill. Included in this group are an assortment of hinged metal bars that swing down from the door frame and block the sliding door in its track.

You can get the same blocking action by wedging a thick dowel, rod, or broomstick into the exposed lower track of the sliding door. Another suggestion that prevents sliding as well as lifting the panels out of their tracks is to fasten both panels to the upper track with a bolt or pin. This can be done by drilling a hole through the inside face of the upper track at the point where both panel frames overlap. The hole should be angled downward and should penetrate through the frame of the inner sliding door, and into but not through the frame of the outer stationary panel. The hole should be of sufficient diameter to accommodate a ¼-inch nail or eye bolt that will serve to secure both panels to the upper track. The downward angle helps to prevent the bolt from slipping out of the hole. An additional method of permanently securing the stationary door panel is to drill a hole and insert a number-ten or larger sheet-metal screw through the upper channel and into the panel's upper frame.

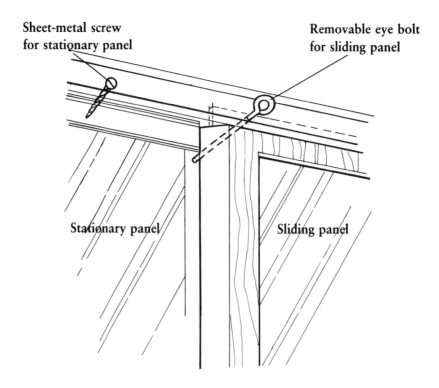

Figure 7   Pinning a patio door with a sheet-metal screw and an eye bolt through the upper channel

Using Angle Irons to Secure the Stationary Panel of a Patio Door   There are two ways to use steel angle-iron brackets to keep the stationary panel of a patio door from being pried out of its sill. The first is to install a bracket of about 1¼-inch steel angle iron a little shorter than the width of the panel. After marking the bracket's position on the sill, remove the door's retaining hardware and slide it out of the way. Attach the bracket to the sill where the stationary panel had been, using three-inch-long flathead screws in the drilled-out countersunk holes. Then slide the door back in place.

While this will prevent the stationary part of the door from being lifted out, it may not prevent it from being worked away from the protection of the bracket itself. To provide sliding protection for the stationary part where there is only one panel for the sliding door, drill a hole for a carriage bolt ⅜ inch in diameter through the vertical leg of the angle iron and the door; the nut holding it in place should be thin enough not to interfere with the free movement of the sliding panel.

The second way to secure the stationary panel with an angle iron is to replace the thin angle-iron block that may already be installed with a more substantial block made of a 1¼-inch angle iron cut to the depth of the door, and screw it into the sill and the vertical stile with three-inch tamperproof screws. If such screws are hard to find, use sheet-metal

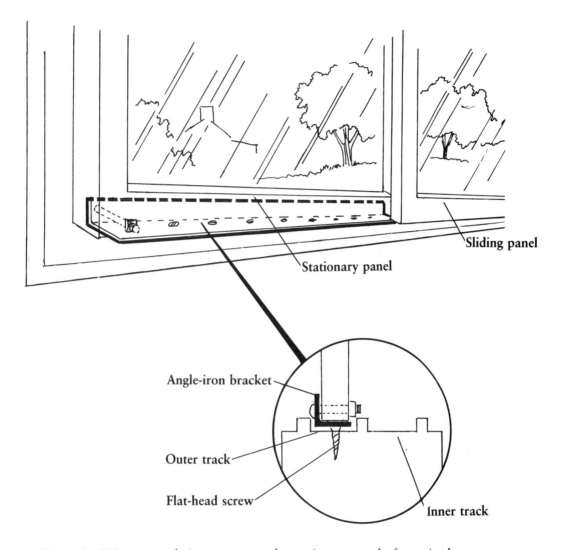

Figure 8   Using an angle iron to secure the stationary panel of a patio door

screws and file down the head so that the screws' slots are not usable. The horizontal screw is inserted into a hollow-core door stile, and may therefore call for reinforcement in the area of the stile.

Patio-Door Glazing Materials   Once the panels have been secured from lifting and sliding, the patio door is as secure as it will ever be, except for the integrity of the glass itself. While older patio doors contain plate or thermal glass that can be subject to dangerous splintering and fracturing when they break, most building codes now require that sliding-glass doors be glazed with tempered glass. This is a safety rather than a security measure.

Tempered glass: Tempered glass can be broken, but when it breaks it crumbles into tiny pieces. The crumbling process affects the entire surface of the glass, and automatically activates the metallic tape applied in many burglar alarm installations. (Burglars can circumvent the alarm-triggering tape by cutting a hole in a section of ordinary glass and reaching inside to bypass the alarm.)

Polycarbonate "glass": It is also now possible to replace the glass in patio doors with either a polycarbonated plastic or a laminated glass similar to auto safety glass, but far sturdier. Polycarbonate plastic is 300 times stronger than flat or plate glass, and at least thirty times stronger than most other acrylics. However, it can be burned through with a portable propane torch, and it can also be sawed through or drilled. Earlier fabrications also used to be susceptible to scratching, but most recent versions are said to be relatively mar-resistant.

Laminated glass: Another choice is laminated acrylic glass, which consists of two sheets of ⁵/₁₆-inch glass sandwiched over a thin plastic layer. This combination strongly resists assault, burning, or sawing. It also resists bending, unlike glazing material, which can easily be popped out of its frame. Thus, if the area to be covered is over forty-eight inches wide, the laminated products are a better choice than the single-layer polycarbonates. Both laminated and polycarbonate plastics are expensive; the cost of a single panel may be about $500 at 1988 prices, but these products offer invaluable solutions to some intractable security problems.

Sliding Grills and Gates

Some security experts suggest installing inside accordion gates that can be folded back and out of view during the daytime, and unfurled at night or whenever the homeowner is away. Similar installations include fixed grills attached to the inside of the door frames, as well as steel roll-up doors like the ones used on the outside of commercial establishments. (See chapter 11, "Apartments.")

HINGES, SCREWS, AND OTHER HARDWARE

Hinges

On ordinary wood and steel doors, hinges are another obvious place for target-hardening, especially if they are old, loose, or mounted on the outside of the door. Most exterior doors open inward and are hung with their hinge pins on the inside of the house. Where they open outward, the hinge pins are on the outside, and the burglars can simply knock out the pin and pull the door open from the hinge side.

Where the hinge pin is on the outside of the door and therefore easily subject to removal or damage, it is best to replace the existing hinge with a security hinge, which has a nonremovable pin. If that is not practical, you can ball-peen the exposed bottom of the hinge pin by flattening it with a hammer from the bottom, so that it can't be pushed up and out of the hinge.

Preventing the Removal of a Door with Outside Hinge Pins   The easiest way to keep the door from being lifted out—even with its hinge pins removed—is to take out one pair of screws (usually the middle ones) facing each other on their respective hinge leaves. Then drill a one-inch hole in the now empty screw hole in the door, and drive a twenty-penny nail into the empty screw hole in the jamb-side leaf of the hinge, directly opposite the screw hole in the door. The head of the nail should be sawed off so that only one inch of it protrudes. When the door is closed, the hole in the hinge leaf on the door will close over the protruding nail stud in the hinge leaf on the jamb, and act as a bolt on the lock. This treatment is appropriate for both the upper and lower hinges. As an alternative to the nail, use a two-inch wood screw with its screw head sawed off so it can act as the one-inch stud.

Screws

Examine the screws and screw holes holding the hinges and the strike or strike box that holds the lock. Screws may be loose or rusted, and the screw holes may be powdery—either

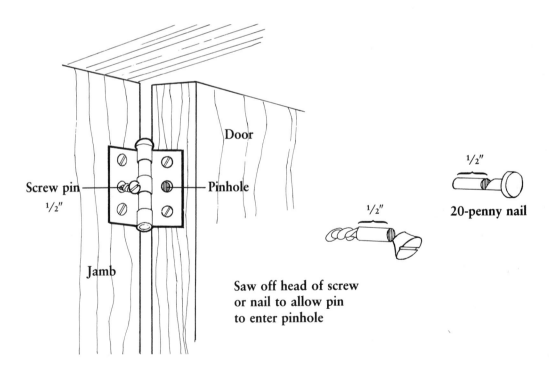

Figure 9   Pinning an outward-opening door with exposed hinge pins

because they have deteriorated with age or because the screws were improperly installed in the first place. Look at the screws and other hardware on both sides of the door. You may find the hinge side of the door more vulnerable than the lock side. Either way, the original screws may have been too short to take firm purchase through the jamb into the stud, or they may have rusted through. If so, they should be replaced with screws at least three inches long, assuming the wood in the frame and back stud is still sound.

Replacing Screws in Door Hinges   To grip the wood more firmly, some carpenters advise using self-tapping sheet-metal screws, which are threaded all the way to the head. In some cases, where the existing screw holes do not provide enough hold for the new screw, new hinges with newly drilled, repositioned screw holes may be required. In such a case, remember to plug up the old holes with glued-in hardwood pegs, and shave them flush with the surface. This will help retain the integrity of the frame.

Even the longest screw will not hold if it is not driven into a properly drilled screw hole. For an ordinary wood screw, electric drills can provide a drill hole with two widths or bores—a narrower bore for the pilot hole using a drill bit that is equal to the inner diameter of the thread portion of the screw, and a wider bit the diameter of the shank portion, with a countersink to accommodate the head of the screw. (On hinges the countersink is tooled into the leaves of the hinge.)

Tamperproof or Nonretractable Screws   Throughout this book, we will be making frequent references to tamperproof or nonretractable screws. Such screws have special heads that permit the screw to be tightened only while it is actually being driven into its wooden or metal frame. The slots on a nonretractable screw head are cut in such a way that a screwdriver has no purchase when you try to turn it in a counterclockwise direction, making it difficult to remove the screws unless they are gouged out of the wood itself. This leaves little room for error when you are inserting the screws, so before tightening such screws, it pays to make sure that they are positioned exactly right.

An alternative to nonretractable screws is to use a regular slotted screw and grind down the slot with a file or the tip of a conical grindstone in an electric drill, after tightening.

Twist-Off Bolts   Twist-off bolts are similar to carriage bolts, but with an additional feature that facilitates tightening: a twist-off hexagonal head affixed to the permanent head. Once the hardware or panel is secured, applying additional pressure to the hexagonal bolt head allows it to twist or shear off, leaving a rounded head which has no purchase and therefore cannot be removed from the outside.

Angle Irons

To make a door even more resistant to jimmying, protective L-shaped angle irons provide additional security for inward-swinging doors that either do not have rabbetted jambs or where for some other reason (i.e., the terms of a tenant's lease or other legal or economic considerations) the gap between the door and the frame cannot be properly fixed.

Angle irons are long strips of metal that are shaped like an L when you look down on them in cross section. To reinforce the door with an angle iron, one side of the L is attached to the door frame and positioned so that the other leg of the L butts up tightly against the door when it is in a closed position. The result is that a crowbar or other jimmying tool can't get between the angle iron and the door frame, or reach the strike plate to force the lock. Attaching an angle iron is a simple, low-cost way to protect the lock and the strike plate from jimmying, and may be all that is needed to shore up a door that no longer fits tightly in its frame.

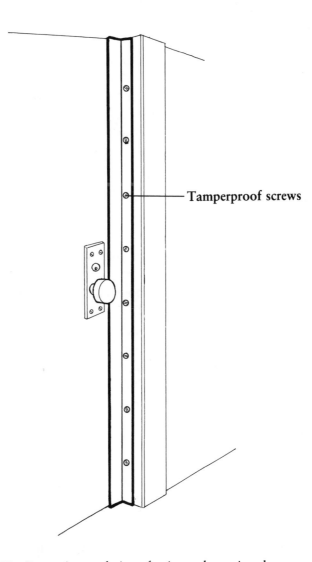

Figure 10   Protective angle iron for inward-opening door

The angle iron is a good solution for doors that open inward. It should be installed with tamper-resistant connectors such as one-way screws or, if practical, round-headed carriage bolts. For outward-swinging doors, where L-shaped angle irons would act as a door stop and therefore cannot be used, a flat metal iron strip can be mounted to the face of the door. This strip should extend beyond the edge of the door so that it fits flush against the jamb when the door is closed. As a precaution, one-way screws should be used in this attachment, too.

While some carpenters and security experts recommend that angle irons need only be mounted in the area of the strike plates themselves, for maximum safety it is recommended that these reinforcers should run the entire length of the door or frame.

Peepholes and Interviewers

Peepholes or door "interviewers" are more commonly seen on apartment doors than on those of free-standing homes. They are a substitute for windows or door "lights" in solid wood or metal doors that would otherwise have no view outside. Interviewers should have wide-angle fish-eye lenses capable of viewing from 160 to 200 degrees. (See chapter 11, "Apartments.")

Interviewing Chains

Interviewing door chains let you open the door a few inches so that you can see or talk to the person outside without actually permitting him entry to the house. Most of them use chain links of case-hardened steel with a catch on the free-swinging end that fits into a horizontally mounted slide track on the door jamb when the chain is in place.

Chain-door interviewers are notoriously easy to defeat. The two-to-three-inch play they allow between the door and the jamb makes them vulnerable to any strong force exerted from the outside, especially if the attachment hardware is flimsy. In its October 1984 issue, *Consumer Reports* suggested replacing the standard chain with a homemade interviewing chain made from a length of plastic-clad bicycle chain, cut to loop over the doorknob and fastened to the door frame with a 3¼-inch-long bolt installed two inches from the edge of the door frame. The bolt can be fitted with washers to allow the chain to swing freely. To use the chain, slip the loop around the doorknob and open the door.

SUMMARY AND SUGGESTIONS

The following suggestions are a recap of some of the factors to consider in tightening the security of your doors.

- *Protect secondary doors as well as primary doors.* Interviews with burglars indicate that secondary doors are the entries of choice for a break-in, planned or otherwise. Don't limit your target-hardening to the front or outer doors.
- *Door frames must be secure.* The door frame is probably the most overlooked and most vulnerable part of the door assembly. When a burglar tries to pry a lock's bolt free from the strike, it is the frame rather than the door that is the most likely to give. All door frames should be tested for excessive play. If there is more than a $1/32$-inch gap between the door and the jamb, examine the space between the jamb and the jack stud and replace soft, rotting, or split shims, especially in the vicinity of the hinges and strike. If the frame is of stamped metal, there is likely to be a hollow space between the jamb and the stud of the supporting wall. To prevent bending the frame with a pry-bar, fill in this hollow space with cement grout.
- *Install anti-pry plates.* To protect the bolt from being popped out of its strike, metal strips can be fastened to the door or jamb to cover the gap between them—especially in the vicinity of the lock assembly. For an inward-swinging door, an L-shaped angle iron should be fastened to the jamb with nonretractable screws. For outward-swinging doors, a flat metal plate fastened to the door and overlapping the jamb will block ordinary prying tools. For maximum protection, either angle irons or metal plates should run the full length of the door.
- *Install anti-saw rods.* Protect the lock assembly in the door by installing rotating metal rods above and below it. This will frustrate efforts to get at the lock by sawing or cutting through the door, by preventing a saw blade from getting sufficient purchase on the rotating rods to saw through the door.
- *Install steel doors.* A flush steel door made of sheet metal at least $1/64$-inch (sixteen-gauge) thick offers one of the best types of door barriers available. A door made of thinner steel is too flimsy to resist vigorous attack and can be cut, sawed through, or bent by a determined intruder. Decorative metal doors filled with insulating materials may be weatherproof but are not highly burglarproof. Doors made of steel thicker than sixteen-gauge are available from special security product outlets but cannot be bought at ordinary door stores or lumber supply houses.
- *Upgrade flimsy construction.* The post-war construction of many doors leaves much to be desired in terms of security. Hollow-core doors, doors with thin central panels, and doors with glass window lights, louvers, and the like offer privacy and some protection from the weather but are of little value in keeping intruders out. Such doors can be reinforced as described below; otherwise, you may want to replace them altogether. When you do replace them, the next best thing to a good steel door is a flush-panel wooden door with a solid core of laminated hardwood.

An otherwise sturdy door that is flanked by window lights can be fortified by backing up the window glass in the lights with transparent polycarbonate. This is expensive but effective, and has the advantage of preserving the light and visibility that were designed into the door in the first place. Without this protection, doors with glass window lights should have double-cylinder locks that lock with a key both from the inside and the outside. Auxiliary keys for such locks should be kept in a safe place, out of sight of burglars but close to the door for a quick emergency exit in case of fire. *Note:* Some local codes forbid use of double-cylinder locks.

- *Install steel panel replacements on wood doors.* If the door is sturdy enough to hold them, steel panels can be installed to tighten security. Use panels no thinner than sixteen-gauge, fastened to the door by nonretractable screws or through-the-door carriage bolts. Two sheets, one for the inside and one for the outside of the door, will weigh about one hundred pounds, which is roughly the limit the standard door hinge can bear. To be safe, install heavier-duty hinges and sturdier screws when you put in steel reinforcement panels.

- *Install plywood panels.* Plywood panels can also be used to reinforce otherwise lightweight doors and to back up paneled doors, hollow-core wooden doors, window glass in doors, and nearby windows set so close to the doors that a burglar can break the glass, reach in, and unlock the door itself. Plywood of ³/₄-inch thickness should be used on both sides. The exterior sheet should be fastened with through-the-door carriage bolts or nonretractable screws. If the existing hinges are weak, replace them.

- *Reinforce glass side windows.* Some houses have glass side panels on either side of the front door for aesthetic and/or lighting purposes. They may not be big enough to admit a burglar, but if they are set close enough to the door he can break the glass, reach in, and unlock the door from the inside. Treat these windows as if they were glass window lights set into the door itself, and back them up with plywood, see-through polycarbonate, or a metal grate or screen.

- *Don't depend on screen and storm doors.* These are good for letting air in and keeping flies and other bugs out, but are negligible in terms of security, and should never be used without a good primary door as well.

- *Protect sliding-glass patio doors.* The glass in patio doors is easily shattered, and their soft aluminum frames can be bent so that the doors can be lifted out of their tracks. Locking mechanisms on most patio doors are flimsy; to secure them, dowels can be dropped into the lower track and hinged bars can be used to keep the movable panel from being slid open. Pan-head screws inserted into the trough of the upper track will prevent both the sliding panel and the fixed-glass panel from being lifted out of the track. Or pin both panels together with a ³/₈-inch eyebolt where they overlap and where the lip of the upper track extends over the overlapping panel frames. Also, you may want to replace the glass with a see-through polycarbonate or laminated plastic. Otherwise, it may pay to protect your glass patio doors with tape and breakage sensors wired into a central burglar alarm system. (See chapter 9, "Burglar Alarms.")

- *Protect exposed hinge pins.* If the door opens outwards, the hinge pins are usually exposed and vulnerable to removal; replace the exposed hinges with ones that have nonremovable pins, or insert metal studs in a screw hole in each hinge.

- *Strengthen interviewer chains or install peepholes.* Don't rely on factory-made door chains. An intruder can force his way past them. If there are no windows in the door, you can see who's at the door without opening it by installing a peephole with one-way glass and at least a 160-degree viewing angle.

6

WINDOWS

Window security is a function of three components: locking mechanisms, frames and sashes, and glass. Window locks come in various forms. There are friction devices that inhibit sash movement up and down or sideways; wedge devices that are designed as jams between the sashes; various stops and bolts that act to block upwards or sideways movement; and key-locking devices that pin the sashes together where they overlap. Even the most sophisticated key-locking devices may not hold up to moderate effort, though, because window sashes are made of such light material that their locking devices can only be held in place with rather short screws. These do not hold both parts of the window securely in place, or support a locking pin long enough to provide much resistance against determined pressure.

Even when such locks do hold, moreover, there is still the glass to contend with. Noise is the intruder's enemy, and the sound of breaking glass can act as an audible alarm, calling attention to itself. Burglars are often aware of this, and may consider breaking windows a riskier way (more so than loiding locks or forcing doors) of getting into and out of the house. However, glass is notoriously easy to break, and there are several ways to break it soundlessly. Glass can be cut with an inexpensive glass cutter, and when it is held in place with adhesive or surgical tape, a section can be removed virtually without noise. In normal glazing installations, glass panes are held in place with clips, glazier's points, and putty. But old putty can dry and then be chipped out easily. Dried putty in a deteriorating window sash may signal a state of general disrepair, and to a potential burglar suggest vulnerability. The only definitive way to make a window unbreachable is to secure it with grills, gates, or shutters—and replace the standard plate glass (or back it up) with something sturdier than normal window glazing.

Despite these cautions, target-hardening can make a crucial difference when it comes to windows. Burglars are particularly exposed when they choose windows over doors as break-in points, and there is much that you can do to add to their visibility, audibility, and frustration.

WINDOW DESIGN

Double-Hung Windows

The double-hung window is standard in most modern residential construction. It consists of two glazed sashes, each one cut half the size of the window opening itself, and each sliding up and down in its channel built into the frame. The upper and lower sections overlap so that they make a watertight joint when the window is closed; and this overlap in turn makes a convenient support for any kind of fastening device used to hold both frames, or sashes, together.

Window Locks   In most houses and apartments the standard fastening device for the double-hung window consists of a crescent or butterfly closure which is erroneously referred to as a "lock." These serve only to latch the two sashes together to prevent them from rattling in their frames in a strong wind, and provide little resistance against entry from the outside. A window secured with this kind of lock can be opened easily by inserting a blade of some kind between the two sashes, and working them free of each other.

There are sturdier models of these devices on the market now, including many kinds of wedges, friction screws, and stops—some with and some without keys. Several of the newer devices can pull the two sashes so tightly together that a knife cannot be inserted between them. But here again, the narrowness of most wooden and metal window sashes means that they can only accommodate short screws, and these are easily pried out and offer only modest resistance to any kind of serious pry-bar attack.

Window "Pins"   A better security remedy than most of those currently on the market is the simple, do-it-yourself nail or bolt window stop. To install this stop, drill a hole at the far edges of the window sash where both sashes overlap, drilling all the way through the top of the lower sash, and about three-quarters through the bottom of the upper sash. When an eye bolt or a twelve-penny nail is inserted in the resulting hole from the inside, it pins the two sashes together. The hole should be drilled at a slightly downward angle to prevent the burglar from jiggling the pin out of the hole under pressure. One stop per window is probably all you need, but two pins, at opposite sides of the sash, add an additional measure of protection. When drilling the holes, remember that they should be wide enough to allow the pins to be inserted and removed easily by hand. Tests indicate that eye bolts $5/16$ inch

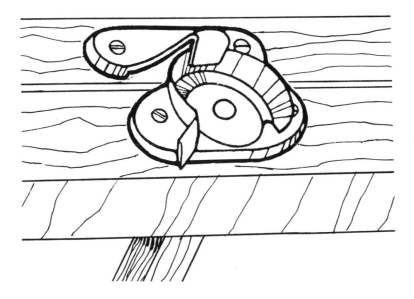

Figure 11   Crescent or butterfly closure provides little resistance to an inserted knife.

in diameter are stronger than nails and easier for you to grasp, and this kind of bolt has been found to resist considerable assault.

If you want to have the option of leaving the window open for ventilation while you are out of the house, drill a second hole an inch or so above the first one in the upper sash, and pin the sashes together in a slightly opened position. A one-inch opening will not be wide enough to permit a burglar to get his hand in and unpin the stop.

Semi-Permanent Sealing   Windows that are never used (unless they could conceivably be your only means of escape from a particular room in case of fire) should be fastened shut by screwing the overlapping sashes together. This prevents the burglar from breaking the glass and reaching inside to unlock the window itself. Some security experts suggest countersinking the screw so that the head is sunk below the level of the wood.

There are commercial products available that use the double-sash pinning method with the added advantage of a recessed screw. Each screw is screwed into a recessed cup to prevent an intruder who may have broken the glass pane from reaching in and turning the screw with pliers. The screw can be turned only with a special keylike wrench that fits into the recessed cup and engages the screw head. This kind of device can be used on windows that are seldom opened or as a vacation window lock.

Figure 12   These ready-made window locks offer modest resistance to attack.

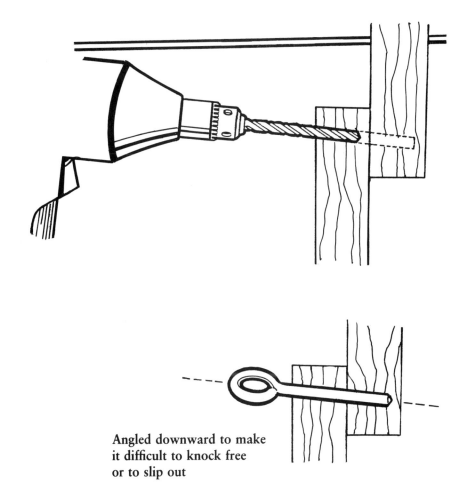

Angled downward to make it difficult to knock free or to slip out

Figure 13 Pinning a window—this do-it-yourself device offers more security than most ready-made, store-bought models.

Sliding Windows

Sliding windows operate on much the same principles as sliding-glass doors, with the difference that both panels are movable in the window version. Although sliding windows are available with wood frames and sashes, the most commonly installed are constructed with thin metal frames and channels. The same types of locks, stops, and pinning devices are available for sliding windows as for sliding doors, although those for windows are usually smaller and weaker. The storm pane or screen panels found with sliding-glass windows are often assembled in such a way that they are readily removable for cleaning and storage, and therefore offer little protection to the window itself. In addition, the lips of the sliding-window channels are usually rather short and thin. As a result, they can be bent easily, permitting a burglar to remove the whole glass panel itself; this creates enough space to climb through.

Sliding windows should be secured using the same methods described for securing sliding doors. One way to do this is to drill a hole through the upper and lower track where the frames overlap, and then insert a pin, bolt, or nail to prevent sliding and/or lifting out. If the channels do not extend up or down far enough to permit this, pan-head screws should be used in the upper channel to prevent lifting. Separately used pinning and bracing devices can be used to prevent sliding. As with sliding-glass doors, a wedging bar inserted in a channel or affixed to the frame will keep one panel stationary while a pinning device holds the other panel to the first.

Casement Windows

Casement windows are used to allow maximum ventilation, since they open like an outward swinging door. Hinges can be mounted on either side to allow the window to swing open from either the left or right. Casement windows are sometimes found on either side of a larger fixed picture window in a flat-wall or bay-window configuration, and another common spot for casements is in spaces too narrow for other window types. But even in this case, despite their smaller size, casements should get the same attention to security as other, seemingly more vulnerable windows do; the fact that they can be opened to 100 percent of the capacity of their frames makes them a convenient point of entry.

Closing Mechanisms   Like other kinds of windows, casement windows are constructed with either wood or metal sashes and frames, and are opened with either a crank or handle operating a gear—or by manually pushing them out. With windows that open with a gear and handle, the closed window acts as its own locking device—although a hard yank from the outside will often disconnect the window from the operating arm. Security is reinforced by removing the handle when it is not in use, and storing or hanging it nearby—more than an arm's length away, so that if someone breaks the glass there is no lever available for him to open it with.

A second, older, and less expensive kind of casement-window closure is a metal hook or receptacle mounted on the sash, which is designed to catch into a clasp mounted on the frame when the window is closed. But this kind of closure is almost as easy for a would-be intruder to defeat as the crescent closure on standard double-hung windows. It should therefore be replaced with a keyed locking handle designed for either the left-opening or right-opening window, as needed. Sizes of keyed handles are standard so there should normally be no difficulty in obtaining a replacement if one is lost, and if more than one window is involved you might want to consider having them all keyed alike so that one key would open all of the windows in the house.

Louvered or Jalousie Windows

These are constructed of narrow panels of overlapping glass panes set in a ladderlike horizontal series, and can be opened for ventilation by means of a crank. The narrow spaces between the slats are intended to keep an intruder from climbing through, but the thin metal lips that hold each panel in place can easily be bent back, permitting the glass to be pulled out of its holding channel with minimal effort, time, and strength.

Louvered or jalousie windows should be replaced by awning windows (see below), or by double-hung, sliding, or casement windows. If replacement is not an immediate possibility, you should consider covering the louvered glass with polycarbonate plastic panels of at least 3/16-inch thickness. Or, as an alternative, glue the individual panes into their holding channels with epoxy; ordinary or plastic glues will not hold.

Like casement windows, jalousies are opened and closed with a gear operated by a handle. The handle can and should be removed when the windows are closed. As a further safeguard, these windows can be backed up with a metal grill screwed into the frame from the inside.

Awning Windows

Awning windows are designed on the same principle as jalousies but present less of a security risk because of their heavier construction and the fact that each pane of glass is securely framed in its own metal or wood sash. Awning windows are mounted in a ladderlike series of two or more sashed panels that swing out from the bottom when opened with a crank handle. What makes them slightly more secure than louvered windows is that the sashes have to be of a fairly sturdy construction to support their own weight and that of the glass.

The number of sashes in the series of an awning window varies from two to as many as four. However, the smaller the sash, the more difficult it is to break a pane from the outside and climb in. These windows, like casement windows, can be equipped with a removable crank handle that is stored at just over an arm's length away from the window for extra security. Since the sashes open and close as a series, you might consider installing a key lock in one sash, which works to keep all of the panes from being moved.

Transoms

Transoms are narrow glass panels found over interior and exterior doors in some older houses, and over the corridor doors of apartments in older apartment houses. Transoms seldom serve any useful purpose and, if possible, should be screwed permanently shut. If the transom is large, the glass pane or panes should be replaced with, or backed up by, polycarbonate. If the transom is used for ventilation, it should be secured with mesh or grillwork mounted on the outside with round-headed bolts. A transom that is opened and closed frequently should have a good locking device or slide bolts affixed to the sash and the transom's frame.

Fixed Windows

Some windows are not meant to open. Sealed windows like these are found in fixed transoms, as side panels for entrance doors, basements, picture windows, and even glass "walls." Since they are sealed against movement, a locking device is not a security factor, but the glass itself is.

To prevent such panes from being lifted out, they should not be puttied or glazed from the outside, but should be installed from the inside into rabbetted jambs. The rabbetts, or stops, are screwed or nailed in place from the inside.

The choice of glazing materials in this kind of construction depends on the size of a single pane. In basement windows, transoms, and door side lights, impact-resistant polycarbonate should be used for glazing, or to back up the existing glass. For larger areas, like picture windows and glass walls, safety as well as security becomes a major consideration, and shatterproof or impact-resistant tempered glass laminates (or their plastic equivalents) are recommended. Where a single sheet is used to cover a large area, the panel should be sufficiently thick—and rigid—to prevent it from being popped out of the frame when it is bent.

Skylights

Skylights are found on the flat roofs of older houses and present a particularly vulnerable point of access, since the roof often cannot be seen from the street. As with ordinary windows, the glass in skylights can be shattered, frames pried open, and locks forced. And if the skylight is free from view, even grills and wire mesh may be dismantled.

Security should thus be considered at three levels: the glass, the sash, and the interior of the room itself. Your first step should be to strengthen the glazing with impact-resistant polycarbonate or a wired-glass laminate; then use a strong hasp and padlock on the inside to secure the sash to the frame. Finally, install bars, grills, or grates on the inside of the frame, in case the intruder gets past the glass and defeats the lock. This third line of security should be fastened securely to its supports with tamperproof screws or bolts.

If the skylight is not needed as an alternative escape route in case of fire, it should probably be sealed shut with a heavy piece of plywood or a sturdy sheet of steel panel. Sealing should be done from the interior, and screwed or bolted to the skylight frame.

Plastic Roof Domes

A popular modern version of the skylight is the plastic hatch cover or dome that brings additional natural light and/or ventilation to areas inside the house that otherwise would be difficult to light. These bubble-shaped domes are increasingly used as replacement hatches for decrepit basement windows as well. Most plastic roof domes are constructed of one piece or sheet of relatively thin acrylic or other lightweight plastic, set into equally thin and lightweight frames. Because of their vulnerable construction, neither the frame nor the locking or security device can withstand an attack with a pry-bar. Even the plastic itself can be cut through with a heavy knife or burned through with a portable propane torch.

To reinforce these installations, reasonable security can be attained by installing a sturdy metal grill to the inner frame below the dome. For greater security, the suggestions in the preceding section on skylights apply.

Window Air Conditioners

Unless a window-unit air conditioner is securely bolted or screwed to the sash, sill, or frame of the window, it can be pried loose and lifted out, creating a large opening. Lightweight metal mounting brackets do not present a serious obstacle to an intruder, since they can be worked free by cutting through the side panels—which are usually made of cardboard-thin plastic designed for insulating purposes only. To offset this weakness, use a sturdy L-shaped angle iron with holes drilled into it about every three inches, cut as long as the air conditioner is wide. One leg of the iron should be screwed into the cover of the air conditioner, with the other mounted snugly against the window sash with round-headed bolts that penetrate both the sash and the angle iron. The sides of the sashes should then be screwed together where they overlap, to resist sustained prying. For maximum security, the adjustable side panels for window-mounted air conditioners can be replaced with one-piece metal or heavy plywood panels screwed firmly to the sash and sill.

WINDOWS AS AN EMERGENCY EXIT

As noted earlier, one problem with fastening windows too securely is that you may be unable to open them in case of fire. A window which may have to be used as a means of escape from fire should never be sealed permanently by fasteners, screws, bolts, or nonremovable fixed gates and grills. According to the National Fire Prevention Association (1981 Life Safety Code Section 22–2.2, 1), windows must provide a means of unobstructed travel to the outside of the building at the street or setback. To be usable as an escape route, says the fire code, *"an outside window* [must be] operable from the inside without the use of tools, and provide a clear opening of not less than twenty inches (50.87 cm) in width, twenty-four inches (60.96 cm) in height, and 5.7 square feet (53 sq. cm) in area. The bottom of the opening shall not be more than forty-four inches (111.76 cm) above the floor."

Fire Escape Windows

Windows leading to fire escapes, and at least one window in each bedroom, should be looked at as possible escape routes. If nails, bolts, or other removable securing devices are installed in them, these devices must be capable of being removed easily in times of emergency

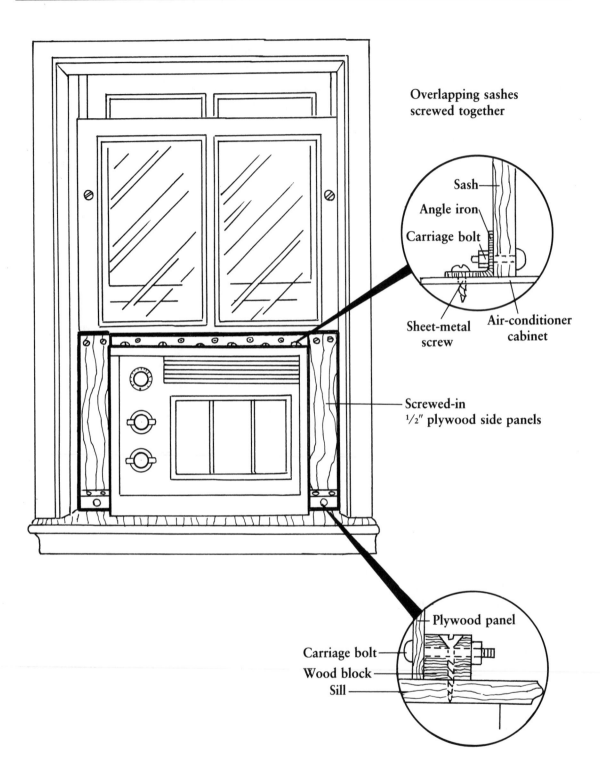

Overlapping sashes
screwed together

Sash

Angle iron

Carriage bolt

Sheet-metal
screw

Air-conditioner
cabinet

Screwed-in
¹/₂″ plywood side panels

Plywood panel

Carriage bolt

Wood block

Sill

Figure 14   Securing an air conditioner

and/or panic. Such windows should not be equipped with keyed locks, since keys are considered tools and are therefore prohibited by the fire code; but if they are already in place and you cannot change them, the keys must be located so that they are readily accessible to anyone in the room. As an additional precaution, a second key should also be hung at a place near the window in case the first key happens to get dropped and lost in the confusion and low visibility of a fire or other emergency.

Window Height

Windows found in bedrooms in some modern ranch houses can be much higher than forty-four inches from the floor. They are designed that way to allow more wall space for furniture placement and provide privacy from neighboring first-floor picture windows. If this kind of window is the only alternative to the door as an escape route in a child's bedroom, remember to provide something for a smaller occupant to climb on so that he or she can reach the windowsill in an emergency.

WINDOW-GLAZING MATERIALS

Standard Window Glass (Sheet or Float Glass)

Residential glazing often utilizes this lightweight silicon amalgam with a brilliant finish, little distortion, and great resistance to sun, sea, air, and most airborne chemicals, as well as various kinds of normal abrasive action. Standard window glass cuts easily and shatters into dangerous jagged shards when it breaks, making it a poor choice for use in large pieces indoors, or anywhere else where it may be subject to unusual stress.

Plate Glass

This glass, which comes in thicknesses of from ⅛ inch to one inch, is a form of ground and polished rolled glass. In lesser thicknesses it provides little security advantage over ordinary sheet or float glass. In greater thicknesses it is less breakable than these and is often used in residential picture windows and some of the older models of glass patio doors. Like standard glass, it shatters into jagged shards when it breaks. Where plate glass is found in an exterior door, it should be replaced with tempered glass.

Tempered Glass

This glass is from five to seven times as break-resistant as standard or plate glass. It acquires its additional strength through a process of heating followed by rapid cooling. Once cut or pierced at any point, the entire surface shatters completely into small and comparatively harmless shards and fragments. Because of this it cannot be cut to size but must be manufactured to the exact size required. The crumbling it undergoes under impact provides additional security advantage. An intruder may be able to cut through standard glass or various plastics without disturbing the metal foil of a glass-protecting burglar-alarm tape. He can then reach in and bypass the alarm. This is not possible with tempered glass, since the crumbling itself breaks the foil and sounds the alarm. Where safety and security are a consideration, tempered glass should be at least the minimum quality of glass considered for use. However, it costs about twice as much as plate glass of the same thickness, and it does present some marginal visual distortion.

Glass Security Film

Security film is a commercially available transparent adhesive overlay that can be applied over existing glass to limit smashing and slow down entering. It has been used extensively in Europe as a safety device against vandalism, bomb blasts, riots, and natural disasters. It is sticky on one side and smooth on the other, and can be applied to the outer surface of the existing glass like a kind of transparent contact paper. Security film is about three or four times as thick as ordinary Scotch tape, and if attacked, it keeps the glass underneath from fragmenting.

Wired Glass

This glass is made by embedding a continuous sheet of wire mesh between two layers of ordinary glass. While it is possible to break through this kind of glass, if the wire is heavy enough it will provide some useful resistance and slow the intruder down. The mesh serves the purpose of preventing the glass from shattering, since the shards tend to cling to the wire mesh as they shatter. In residences wire-mesh glass is most commonly used in skylights and in fire doors for some shatter resistance to heat.

Laminated Glass

Laminated glass is made by bonding a plastic inner layer between two outer layers of glass under high pressure and heat. When the layer of glass is broken it does not separate significantly from the bonding layer and therefore tends to remain intact. Its resistance to impact can be strengthened by increasing the number of layers. It is classified as "safety glass" when it consists of two layers and a relatively thin plastic interlayer. As the number of layers increases, its classification moves up to "burglar resistant." When the multilayers increase up to $3/4$ inch to four inches, this kind of glass is able to resist bullets from small- and medium-power firearms.

Laminated glass is sold in varying thicknesses and under a wide range of brand names by glass manufacturers. Costs range from six to ten times that of plate glass of the same thickness. Like tempered glass, it cannot be cut to fit a frame and must therefore be ordered to measure directly from the manufacturer.

Plastic Glazing Materials

See-through plastics offer another alternative to conventional standard glazing. They can be produced in strengths and thicknesses that are impervious to shattering or piercing by bullets. Plastics, however, are expensive, and in addition to their high cost they have certain other drawbacks as well.

1. *Flexibility:* Unless they are thick and heavy, plastics will bend under pressure and can be popped out of their frames when used on large picture windows and sliding-glass doors.
2. *Discoloration:* In industrial areas, airborne chemicals and acids may act together with sun or sea air to cause the glass to turn color and start to disintegrate.
3. *Flammability and toxic fumes:* While some plastics are supposed to be fire-resistant and self-extinguishing, most standard acrylics and polycarbonates support flames and produce toxic fumes as they burn, presenting a hazard to residents in the event of fire. Burglars familiar with the flame-supporting property of plastics have been able to burn through them noiselessly with a small portable propane torch, and without any serious danger of fire spreading.
4. *Noiselessness:* Some acrylics can be drilled, sawed, cut, and burned through completely noiselessly, without the natural alarm potential of breaking glass.
5. *Scratch resistance:* Although sometimes listed as abrasion-resistant, acrylic surfaces do have a tendency to scratch.

Listed below are some of the more common glazing plastics.

Standard Acrylics   You may know these materials under such common names as Plexiglas, Lucite, and others, but they are all basically the same product. These plastic "glasses," even though they are clearer than standard glass and have no visibility distortions, are seventeen times stronger than single-strength standard glass of the same thickness. The advantage of this kind of glass is its strength per unit of thickness. Its disadvantages are that it can be drilled, cut, or sawed through, and that it supports flames and produces toxic fumes when burned. In addition, it scratches easily.

Polycarbonates   These materials are probably less widely known by their trade names than the standard acrylics listed above, but builders and other specialists will recognize them under such names as Lexan, Lexiguard, and Tuffak. This lightweight see-through tempered plastic is 300 times stronger than standard window glass and up to twenty times stronger than acrylics of the same thickness; but even in lesser degrees of thickness it offers excellent resistance to impact and shattering.

Because of its flexibility, however, polycarbonate should be used in thicknesses of at least 3/16 inch when used as a backup to regular glass, and even greater thicknesses to provide sufficient rigidity when cut in large panes or in sliding-glass doors. In addition, it scratches easily, although it is also available with abrasion-resistant coatings.

Laminated Polycarbons   Where high risk and greater impact resistance are considerations, laminated polycarbons may be the answer. These have the visibility of glass but are impenetrable to ballistic or other attack, and there are a wide range available in degrees of thickness and numbers of plies. Some laminates consist of sheets of polycarbonates bonded together with special film interlayers which, in thicknesses of 3/4 inch or more, can resist many rounds from firearms. In addition, there are glass-clad polycarbonates which use elastic interlayers, allowing for expansion of both materials. Such laminates provide the surface resistance of glass to chemicals, abrasion, and fire, with polycarbonate's resistance to impact and breakage.

Extensive testing of such high-security glazing as polycarbonates has demonstrated that, given enough time and with appropriate tools and skills, even these can be penetrated. However, the same thing can be said of almost any kind of building material, including brick walls, stone foundation walls, and steel vaults. In terms of the time it would take a frustrated intruder to get past them, these laminates are probably a good buy even at the high prices they currently command.

Leaded Glass   This type of glazing can be found in the windows of some older public buildings and a few homes built in the late nineteenth and early twentieth century, especially in the eastern United States. Leaded glass gets its name from the distinguishing lead muntins that bind the small panes together into the window frame. This kind of glazing is also found in churches and in more modest residences in the form of door panels, fan windows, and other decorative touches.

Decorative leaded glass warrants protection. A clear, shatterproof, see-through plastic barrier is a good means of reinforcement. A strong impact-resistant 3/16-inch polycarbonate panel should cover the entire glazed surface. As with other backings, it should be bolted into place with round-head bolts or tamperproof screws which are then carefully painted or stained to blend in with the frame. Whether the windows themselves are casement, bow, fan, or even double-hung, the appropriate locking and frame precautions should be taken to secure them from intrusion.

BARS, GATES, AND GRILLS

Given the fragility of glass and the light construction of many window locks and of most window sashes, ground-floor windows should probably be backed up with something more substantial than window pins or other locking devices, particularly in easily reached places. One solution is to install bars, grills, gates, or shutters on the most vulnerable windows.

Metal Grills

Installation If the house is constructed of brickwork, stone, or masonry, permanent bars and grillwork can be anchored through the window frames into concrete plugs in the surrounding walls. Iron bars should extend at least three inches into the top and bottom of the masonry, and should be placed no more than five inches apart. To offer a realistic degree of resistance they should be at least 3/4 inch in diameter.

Wire-mesh grills are another possibility. If you choose wire-mesh grillwork, make sure that the wire is no less than 1/8 inch in diameter and the openings no more than two inches wide. The flat iron grill frame that holds the mesh should be at least 3/8 inch thick and positioned so that its screw fastenings penetrate through the window frame and into the underlying studs or masonry. For masonry walls, it is wise to use machine or round-head bolts, welded into the grill frame after installation. If the grill is set in wood, sturdy nonretractable screws should be used to attach it to the frame.

One problem with permanently mounted grillwork is that the grills cannot be removed for any purpose, including window cleaning, unless they are installed with hingelike supports. In this case, the frames must be secured with a padlock, and the grillwork itself is then only as strong as its weakest link, which may be the padlock that secures it.

Protecting Basement Windows Basement windows, especially those that are concealed behind shrubbery, should have a heavy grill covering either on the inside or outside. Most basement windows are seldom or never used, except to admit light, and the most accessible ones can probably be sealed safely, leaving one or two relatively inaccessible ones free for ventilation. If you need to use the window as an exit or entry point, you should install a folding gate or removable grill padlocked to the window frame.

Folding Gates

If you object to living behind iron bars, a reasonable compromise might be to install folding gates that can be locked in place at night or when you leave, but can be folded back out of the way when you are at home. Most important, they can still be opened quickly to let people out in case of a fire or other emergency. Accordion or scissor gates are popular for this purpose because they come in a wide range of heights and widths to fit ceiling-high windows, patio doors, or odd-shaped and smaller windows.

A good accordion gate should run at both top and bottom in steel U-shaped channels, which hold the gate in place against any attack. The lattice-grid pattern of the gate should be dense enough to prevent a potential intruder from getting anything more than a finger or two through it. The gate should also come with a hasplike locking mechanism at both the top and the bottom. The hasp fits over a sturdy eyelike staple firmly attached to the window frame on the side opposite the gate's mounting. A good commercial padlock with a 3/8-inch case-hardened steel shackle should be used as a lock on this kind of gate.

Figure 15   Accordion or scissor gates—the metal box with the hinged cover houses a lever that when pulled permits the gate to be opened quickly in case of fire.

If you use a padlock to secure a folding gate, be sure to have more than one key easily available inside the house. One key should be hung near the window, out of arm's reach from the outside, and the other kept in reserve nearby. This can save precious seconds when you are groping for an exit through thick smoke or fire.

Note: In some metropolitan areas, fire codes forbid the use of locks on gates installed on fire escape windows. One solution to this problem is a patented accordion gate that can be opened by turning a small lever enclosed in a metal box built into the gate's framing. (See chapter 11, "Apartments.")

Ready-made Window-Bar Assemblies

There are many ready-made window-bar assemblies on the market that come with adjustable widths so that they telescope sideways for quick removal and easy escape. These assemblies are offered in various degrees of sturdiness, and although some offer reasonable protection, others do not. If they are used, they should be mounted onto the interior frame of the window. Some can only be screwed permanently into the window, while others have special slip-out screw slots that permit quick removal in case of emergency. However, the same quick-removal feature is also available to the burglar, who can break the glass from the outside and reach in to disarm the window.

Even when they are mounted permanently to the window frame with nonretractable screws or bolts, some of these assemblies have bars made with hollow tubes so thin and stamped metal frames of such lightweight construction that they offer only token resistance to a determined attack with a pry-bar. Whatever deterrent effect they carry is therefore more a function of appearance than reality.

Shutters

The ultimate in security may be metal shutters and roll-down metal shades. These have long been used to protect storefronts and other entries, and are beginning to appear on residences. Such barriers can be installed on either the inside or the outside, with the locking mechanism inside. They are expensive and usually have to be custom-made and installed. As with other types of exterior barriers, the increased security that roll-down shutters offer must be weighed against their inconvenience in case of fire and smoke inside the shuttered area.

SUMMARY AND SUGGESTIONS

- Probably the best protection against window break-ins is an automatic alarm (either local or centrally monitored) that is triggered by the sound of breaking glass, the body heat of someone gaining entry, or the breaking of metal foil.
- Street-level or basement windows that are out of public view should have clear sight lines to the street or the neighbors, and should not be obstructed by shrubs.
- Since almost all windows represent access points, they should always be closed and locked except when needed for ventilation. Use existing locks, no matter how lightweight, since they represent several seconds' worth of delay that a prowler may not want to risk.
- If a window is rarely or never needed for ventilation, you may want to take some measures to keep it closed permanently so that a thief pushing his hand through a

broken glass pane cannot unlock it. To do this, screw overlapping sashes together in double-hung or sliding windows, and remove the crank handle or knob from the inside of unused casement, awning, or louvered windows.

- With very few exceptions, store-bought locking devices for standard double-hung or sliding windows offer little or no resistance to a screwdriver or pry-bar. The weakness of various other devices—such as wedges that jam between sashes, friction locks, and various keyed and unkeyed window stops—is that the sashes are so thin and narrow that they can't support the heavy-duty brackets that are needed to support them and are therefore held in place with short screws or weak pins. Better than any of these solutions is the use of homemade window "pins," which consist of drilling holes in the sashes of double-hung or sliding windows where they overlap, and "pinning" the sashes together with a removable eyebolt or twelve-penny nail.

- Casement, awning, and louvered windows are usually opened by turning a crank handle or a knob, but they can be pried open from the outside. Where these knobs do not have a key-activated lock, removable handles are available on the market and can be used to replace the existing handles. To lock such a window, you simply remove the handle. The handle should be hung close to the window but out of arm's reach of a would-be intruder, and you should have some spares on hand.

- Louvered windows offer little security, and instead of reinforcing them most experts suggest replacing them with more secure windows. If this is not feasible and if you need to use such windows for ventilation, they should be backed up with wire-mesh grates installed on the inside. The same applies to easily accessible transoms and skylights.

- Large picture windows or other fixed expanses of glass should be installed in rabbetted jambs with the solid wood or metal of the frame facing outward so that the glazing compound on the inside cannot be tampered with from outside the house.

- To replace ordinary window glass with something stronger, see-through plastic polycarbonate is recommended. Its impact resistance is roughly 300 times that of standard window glass. Polycarbonates should be at least $3/16$ inch thick; anything thinner than that is flexible enough to be bent and removed from the sash, unless it is one of the more rigid laminated polycarbonates. Although it is extremely break-resistant, polycarbonates can be sawn, cut, and drilled through noiselessly without setting off noise-sensitive alarms like those found on most perimeter alarm-system tapes and sensors. They can also be burned through with a hand-held propane torch, but except in high-security targets like banks and military installations this requires more work than most burglars are willing or ready to perform.

- Metal window bars or grills are a strong security deterrent for vulnerable ground-level windows. The best are folding awning or scissor gates, installed inside the house and made of steel heavy enough to resist bending. Openings should be close enough together to prevent an intruder's hand from getting through, and the gate should slide along U-shaped channels at both top and bottom to prevent the gate from being pushed out of its frame and allowing an intruder to wriggle through.

• Ornamental ironwork to protect windows and doors is custom-made, expensive, and comes in varying degrees of sturdiness. The same caution you would use to select a locksmith, a burglar-alarm installer, or anyone else dealing with security arrangements for your house should be exercised in choosing an installer for security grillwork. In all these instances it is wise to deal only with well-established, reputable companies, and check the materials when they are delivered to make sure that you are getting exactly what you ordered.

7

LOCKS

Despite their state-of-the-art hardware and sophisticated operation, a large number of the locks currently on the market are extremely ineffective for security purposes. Others may have a less sophisticated appearance and yet provide much better security than their more sleek and streamlined counterparts.

VULNERABILITY

To make an informed decision about what kind of lockset to buy, it may pay to visualize the kind of attacks that locks and their components are generally vulnerable to. In 1984, Consumers Union's technical department tested over fifty door locks and discovered a number of significant deficiencies. They found that locks are vulnerable to attack in a number of ways, which are briefly summarized below.

Picking

This term covers any surreptitious technique used to open a lock other than with the correct key. No one knows how many burglars can and do pick locks as part of their practice, though many experts estimate that it's 10 percent or less. However, for those who do practice the skill, there is really no such thing as a totally pickproof lock cylinder.

Traditional lockpicker's tools come in various shapes. The *hand pick* is a short length of strong spring steel, with a slight curve at its tip that allows it to feel out the lower pins along the keyway and lift them one at a time, thereby compressing the small springs that hold each set of pins in place. Another variation is the *rake,* which is similar to the hand pick except that the upper blade is shaped into a series of small ripples or waves. The rake is inserted into the entire depth of the keyway and drawn forward along the row of pins to raise them into the open position at the shear line. The *tension bar* follows the pick or rake and holds the pins up once they are released. It is then used as a lever to rotate the key plug and open the lock. Other lockpicker's tools include vibrating devices like the professional locksmith's pistollike "lock aid" gun, or the burglar's "snapper," which looks like a safety pin and is held in the hand and jiggled with the thumb as it passes along the keyway to feel out the upper pins and raise them.

Brute Force

In most cases, one or two well-placed kicks can usually open a seemingly secure door—often without making enough noise to alert neighbors or passersby. Lightweight door assemblies, poorly installed and equipped with weak locksets, are at greatest risk from this form of attack.

Prying

The most common tools used by burglars are a jimmy, pry-bar, or even a large screwdriver. Prying is popular because of its relatively quiet action and powerful effect. Prying can force a door and its jamb either far enough apart to cause the bolt to come out of the strike, or at least far enough to allow clearance for a saw blade or a chisel to get at the exposed bolt. Prying can also be used to tear a lock cylinder from the door.

Hammering

Because of the noise and the attention it draws, burglars generally avoid attacking a door or lock with a hammer, unless they are sure there is nobody within hearing distance. But hammering can be effective: Consumers Union testers used a hammer and punching tools directly on a door lock and were able to force some cylinders out of the lockset or even knock a rimlock off the door.

Cutting

A properly installed lockset will allow little or no access to the bolt. However, when the doors and/or jambs are weak or loose enough to be pried apart, an exposed bolt can be sawed through with a metal-cutting hacksaw.

Forced Separation

All the reinforcement and sophistication a lock may possess in other respects is worthless if the lock's cylinder can be popped out of the door using a claw hammer or a similar prying tool. Or, by using plierlike tools, some protruding lock cylinders can be wrenched out of the lockset with a minimal amount of noise. Consumers Union testers reported that most of the high-security rimlock cylinders they tested were extremely vulnerable to this kind of assault. However, the guarded-rim cylinder models with built-in guard plates were rated from "fair" to "very good," and newer designs with free-spinning collars of case-hardened metal are deliberately designed to resist wrenching. Mortise-type cylinders were also vulnerable to forced separation. Of the ten samples tested, only three rated as much as "fair" and all the others were "poor." To forestall this kind of damage, the testers recommended that a large armored external guard plate be used to interpose another barrier between the typical cylinder and the attacking tool. Guard plates are installed over the cylinder facing so that prying tools cannot be inserted around the edge of the cylinder itself.

Penetration

A burglar may use a drill, grinder, or punch to turn the key plug of a cylinder and release the lock. Consumers Union testers reported that "this sort of attack brought out the weaknesses in most models."

Forced Turning

When a key is turned in a cylinder, it rotates the key plug inside the cylinder, and this retracts the bolt which in turn unlocks the door. The cylinder's housing remains stationary. Burglars can get the same results if they can rotate the cylinder housing by defeating the screws that are designed to hold the cylinder stationary in the rest of the lockset. (Many high-security cylinders have stronger metal plates anchoring the screws and tend to resist this kind of tampering.) Consumers Union found several high-security cylinders on the market that came with armored cover plates and thus provided the necessary protection against this form of attack.

Given the range of hazards to be considered, and puzzled about what degree of security you should be asking of the locks you buy, you may be tempted to defer to local locksmiths' recommendations about the range and complexity of the locks they sell. But the locksmith's judgments may or may not be applicable to your particular home or lifestyle; and even if they are, as with any important purchase, it is wise to familiarize yourself with the basics before you go to the market to buy.

LOCK DESIGN

Warded Locks

Warded locks were in their heyday from medieval times through World War I, and have a keyhole big enough to peep through. They are distinguished by their keyways in the form of an inverted exclamation point and by their keys with long shafts ending in a flag or blade that is cut to match the obstructions or "wards" inside the lock.

Warded locks are still used in some padlocks where exposure to weather, dirt, and sand call for wide tolerances, for cabinet drawers and doors in fine furniture, and for institutional locks in older buildings with extremely heavy doors; but they are useless for front-door security and have not been installed on primary doors in this country since early in the century. If your house predates this changeover and you still use a warded lock as your main security device, you should either replace the lockset or back it up with a contemporary pin tumbler mechanism.

Warded-lock keyhole

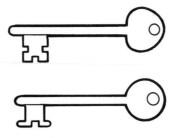

Figure 16   Typical warded keys

Pin Tumbler Locks

The inside of a pin tumbler lock is a kind of puzzle whose pieces fit neatly together when closed. (See Pin Tumbler Cylinders, page 106.) The lock's cylinder is attached to a bolt that can be slid in or out of the door's strike plate when the pins in the cylinder are put in the proper position by the key.

Lockset

A lockset is the entire locking mechanism. It consists of three separate metal parts: the lock body, the strike, and the key.

The *lock body* is a metal casing that encloses the cylinder and holds the protruding bolt that actually fastens the door. The cylinder itself consists of a key plug enclosed in its own barrellike housing, rather like a stopper in the neck of a bottle, and is attached to the lock bolt by a cam at the outer edge of the lock body. The *strike* and *strike plate* together form a separate rectangular metal piece ready to be inserted into the door jamb. The strike plate contains the strike, which is a slot or cavity deep enough to receive the matching bolt attached to the lock body. The *key* is specially factored to match the tumblers in the lock's cylinder and release them from the alignment that normally keeps them in the locked position.

When you go to make your own choice at the local locksmith's shop, though, it pays to consider the parts in relation to the whole. A complex, pickproof lock cylinder with a too-short bolt and inadequate attachment hardware is just as vulnerable as a primitive cylinder with a two-inch throw and a hammerproof guard plate. And if the key control on your lock is poor, the fanciest state-of-the-art cylinder with the longest throw into the sturdiest strike plate still has some vulnerability.

PRIMARY VS. AUXILIARY LOCKS

The "primary" lock on your front and/or back door is the original door lock the builder installed when he built the house, as a first-line barrier against intruders. The primary lock includes the doorknob, and most primary locks hide their locking mechanisms inside the door or doorknob. All primary locks have the strike recessed in the door jamb. "Auxiliary" locks, on the other hand, are added as an extra measure of security after the house has been occupied. Their lock mechanisms are rarely inside the door and they may or may not use bolts that go into strikes in the door jamb.

Because auxiliary locks are often installed to make up for the deficiencies of the original or primary lock, they are often sturdier and more dependable than the locks that they are supposed to back up. But even where the primary lock offers a high degree of security, secondary locks can act as a psychological as well as a physical deterrent to burglars.

PRIMARY LOCKS

Key-in-the-Knob Locks

Key-in-the-knob locks have been popular since the building boom of the late 1940s because they are convenient to use and inexpensive to install. They have an uncluttered "modern" look, and closing the door automatically engages the spring latch. They also have the desirable panicproof feature common to many spring-latch locks today of being easily opened from the inside by simply turning the doorknob. But the doorknob in which the lock cylinder is housed is easily separated from the door and is also vulnerable to picking, drilling, prying, and pulling; and even when the lock appears heavy-duty, the knob can be knocked off, sawed off, or even wrenched free, pulling the interior system of the lock out with it. Once the outside knob is removed, the latch bolt can be freed using a nail file, screwdriver, or any other hand tool. Finally, the short, beveled spring-loaded latch that this lock normally controls is vulnerable to prying, shimming, or "loiding": a flexible steel blade (shimming) or a plastic card such as a credit card (loiding, short for *celluloid*) can be inserted, bent around the door, and made to press against the beveled (slanted) side of the

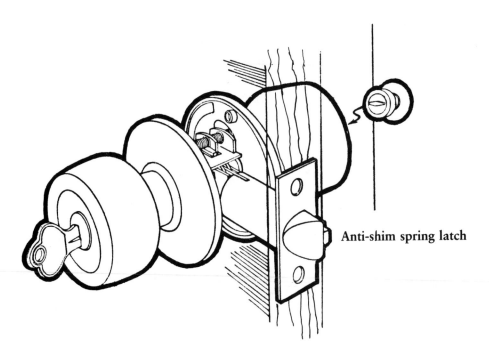

Anti-shim spring latch

Figure 17 Key-in-the-knob lock—widely used because of its convenience and easy installation, it is so vulnerable to attack that it should be used only as a privacy device. Its anti-shim spring latch provides at best only token reinforcement.

spring latch. This forces the latch back against its spring and into the door's lockset, freeing the door to open.

Most key-in-the-knob locks come equipped with anti-shim dead latches (see page 96), but these are no less vulnerable to being knocked off or torn off the door. Any front or back door that has a key-in-the-knob lock as its primary lock should therefore be reinforced or replaced with a sturdy auxiliary lock of a more serious and tamperproof design.

Interconnecting Locksets

To retain the convenience and emergency safety features of the key-in-the-knob locks, and increase your security as well, an interconnecting lockset is the most viable primary lockset. It provides what amounts to two locks in one. On the outside it includes the usual spring latch, with its key cylinder contained in both the knob and the dead bolt above it, both of them interconnected under a single escutcheon plate, and both controlled by the same key. Some models have the lock cylinder only in the deadbolt section. On the inside, the latch and the bolt are controlled by a single knob; when turned, this knob simultaneously withdraws both the latch and the dead-bolt mechanism at the same time, making it ideal for a quick exit in case of fire or other emergencies.

Figure 18   Interconnecting lockset—combines the convenience of the key-in-the-knob spring latch with the security of the dead bolt.

Interconnecting locksets are usually equipped with long horizontal bolts or throws, although some models come with vertical bolts. In its October 1984 issue, *Consumer Reports* discussed nine models of the horizontal bolt and two models of the vertical-bolt interconnecting locksets. The two vertical-bolt locks were vastly superior to the horizontal models in their ability to stand up to such attacks as kicking, punching, prying, wrenching, and hammering.

Dead Latch

To make up for the deficiencies of the standard spring-latch lock, most manufacturers include a dead latch as a supplementary security feature. A dead latch is often called an "anti-shim device," and combines the convenience of a spring latch with some of the security of a dead bolt. It can be found in better-quality key-in-the-knob locks, as well as some models of mortise locks.

In the key-in-the-knob lock, you can recognize the dead latch as a small auxiliary plunger right next to the beveled bolt (the wedge-shaped piece that is extended and visible when the door is opened). When the door is shut the beveled spring-latch bolt enters the strike opening, but the strike plate holds the plunger in the depressed position. In this position it serves to hold the spring latch in place in the strike opening, and makes it resistant to loiding or any other kind of shimming. In some mortise spring-latch locks the dead latch is a smaller beveled latch bolt located above the larger spring latch on the lock body. The same unlocking actions that disengage the primary spring latch also disengage the dead latch's holding action.

A dead latch provides only slightly better security as a supplement to a spring-latch bolt. Although the dead-latch lock cannot be "loided" like the spring latch, the relatively short throw on some spring latches does permit it to be pried out of the strike with a pry-bar or strong screwdriver, unless the door is a perfect fit.

Mortise Locks

The mortise lock was the standard entrance-door lock in most pre-war construction, when the lock assembly was installed by carpenters at the construction site. Mortise locks are recessed in a rectangular cavity chiseled in the edge of the door, opposite the strike case. The key cylinder of a mortise lock is often only anchored to the lock's housing by one or two holding screws, or "set screws," facing the door's edge, and it takes only a bit of muscle and the right tools to pull the cylinder from its housing, allowing direct access to the latch and bolt mechanisms inside.

To replace a mortise lock with a better kind might be more difficult than it's worth. Other locks wouldn't fit into the large door cavity left by the original lock, so this cavity would have to be filled and reinforced before another lock could be put in. Owners of mortise locks would therefore do better to put a protective plate over the cylinder and supplement the original mortise lock with a more dependable auxiliary lock.

Mortise Dead Lock

In a primary mortise lock a spring latch, with or without its accompanying dead latch, is most often found in combination with a dead bolt. The dead bolt is a strong rectangular bolt with a throw that can vary in length from $5/8$ inch to one inch or more. When the door is shut, the spring latch automatically extends into the door jamb's strike receptacle, but it takes a separate operation to extend the dead bolt. To lock the dead bolt from the outside you must turn a key, and from the inside you must either turn a separate thumb knob or (as in the case of a double-cylinder lock) a key. In such mortise-lock combinations the dead-latch mechanism is activated by depressing one of the two buttons that appear on the mortise lock plate, usually just below the spring latch.

A door with a mortise dead lock is supposed to have the security of a dead bolt together with the convenience of a spring latch. But some of these locks are equipped with dead bolts that extend less than one inch into the strike, so that only a relatively minor effort to pry the door away from the jamb causes the short dead bolt to pop out of its strike, allowing

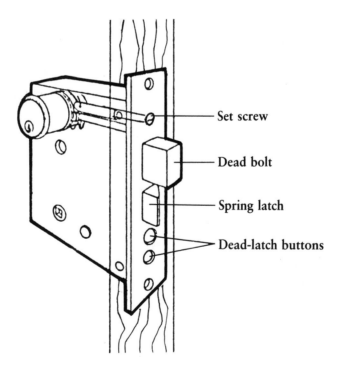

Figure 19 Mortise dead-bolt lock—most models, although they look imposing, are not as strong as they appear.

the door to be opened. The dead bolt should extend one inch or more into the strike in order for the lock to provide decent security.

AUXILIARY LOCKS

Auxiliary locks may come with a single cylinder that requires a key from the outside, or more commonly a double cylinder that requires a key from both the inside and the outside. Some versions of this lock come in the form of a "night latch," or bolt without a cylinder, which is operated by a simple thumb screw on the inside that can be locked or unlocked only by someone already inside the house. The night latch type is generally used for secondary doors on the back porch, a side door, or doors between the garage and the house.

Security experts often recommend installing double-cylinder locks in glass-paneled doors and other places where an intruder can smash the glass to gain access to the knob or thumbscrew on the inside. But such locks make it harder to get out of the house in case of fire or other emergency, and therefore may be prohibited by building or fire codes in some communities. These locks may be a special problem in the case of very young, very old, or handicapped occupants, unless the key is kept close to the door in a reachable place at all times. Even then, finding the key and getting it into the lock may take too much time in an emergency—especially if the house is dark or filled with smoke, hands are shaky with fear, and the key gets dropped or caught in the lock. Whenever a double-cylinder lock is used, it is important for safety reasons to keep an extra key close to the door, or keep the key in the lock when the room is occupied.

Rimlocks (Surface-Mounted Locks)

The most common type of auxiliary lock is the surface-mounted rimlock, where the locking case is mounted on the interior surface of the door and the strike is attached to the jamb. But before you consider adding one, you should be sure that the door is strong enough to accept it and provide sufficient support for it.

If your door is solid-core wood or metal, you have a fairly wide latitude in choosing the lock and positioning the additional cylinder hole and mounting screws. If you have a paneled door the choices may be more limited; but even here the exposed and visible vertical side framing, or "stiles," is usually wide enough to accept an additional lock. In a hollow-core door, however, whether it is made of wood or metal, the interior framing may be so narrow that an additional side piece of framing (or "lockrail") may have been inserted alongside it, to act as a support for the new locking mechanism. You can test for the presence or absence of this piece by drilling or tapping the door to determine if the existing internal framing stile (and its lockrail—if any) is long enough to support the added auxiliary lock.

Cylinder rimlocks are relatively sturdy and easy to install. Their resistance to the typical burglar techniques of kicking, loiding, and prying depends on how they are mounted.

Rimlocks mounted on the inside surface of the door are held in place against the surface with relatively few screws, and most of the screws supplied by manufacturers are so short that forcing the door easily pops them out. This problem can be overcome by substituting screws as long as two inches (depending on the width of the door) for the original screws, although even these may weaken after repeated forcing attempts. In addition, the strike box which receives the bolt or latch is also surface-mounted against the jamb with similar screws, and will therefore require longer screws as well for optimum security.

Vertical Dead-Bolt Rimlocks

The most widely recommended auxiliary lock is the vertical dead bolt. It offers ease of installation, moderate price, and a great deal of security. This type of lock, surface-mounted, has two vertical dead bolts that lock into sturdy metal eyes on the receiving strike in the jamb. This action serves to attach the door to the jamb, making it highly resistant to prying or jimmying, and such locks are often referred to as "jimmyproof."

Because these locks are surface-mounted they are relatively easy to install, requiring only one hole to be bored through the door to receive the cylinder. Most strikes are L-shaped mounting plates, one leaf of which is mortised and screwed into the inner surface of the

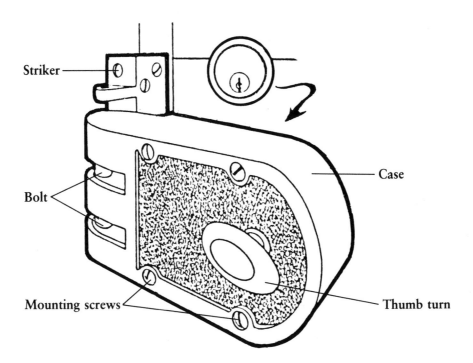

Figure 20 Vertical dead bolt—the most recommended auxiliary lock, it is virtually jimmyproof if installed properly with long-enough screws.

jamb opposite the locking mechanism. The other leaf contains eyes that fit in between the legs of the lock to complete the locking action. The strike usually comes with at least six screws that can be fastened into the jamb from at least two directions. This provides added protection against a horizontal line of force and against most jimmying attempts. As a result, these bolts are hard to kick out of the strike, especially when the mounting screws supplied by the manufacturer are replaced with screws at least 2½ inches long.

Although they are virtually jimmyproof and (with proper screws) kick-resistant, like all surface-mounted locks, their cylinders may not stand up to prying because they are often held in place by relatively flimsy sheet-metal mounting plates screwed inside the door under the lock case. With a minimum of leverage applied to the cylinder, the plate can be split, letting the screws pop through. It is then easy to pull out the cylinder and, with the locking mechanism exposed, use a screwdriver to withdraw the bolt. To forestall this kind of attack, Consumers Union researchers suggest the addition of an armored guard plate or escutcheon plate installed over the lock face on the outside of the door.

Other potential weaknesses in contemporary vertical dead-bolt locks arise from deficiencies in the door assemblies where, given enough play between the door and the jamb, a portion of the lock body can be cut through with a hacksaw.

Horizontal-Bolt Auxiliary Locks

The horizontal-bolt lock comes equipped with a square bolt that penetrates an inch or more into its strike. Although of sturdy construction, these locks suffer from the same basic weakness of any surface-mounted rimlock with relatively fragile screws that fasten its strike to the surface of the door. The holding power of this kind of lock can be improved considerably by replacing the manufacturer's short strike mounting screws with longer, more substantial screws. Another weakness is inherent in the design itself: Because it is parallel to the line of force being exerted, a horizontal bolt is vulnerable to prying or kicking, which can force it from its strike. Horizontal-bolt locks are therefore not jimmyproof, and provide somewhat less security than vertical-bolt models.

Cylinder Dead-Bolt Locks

Although it is used principally as an auxiliary or secondary lock, the cylinder dead-bolt lock hides its locking mechanism inside the door and its strike box inside the jamb, like most primary locks, and is therefore more resistant to forced separation from the door. In some newer construction, you may find that a tubular lock was installed by the builder in addition to the key-in-the-knob or mortised primary lock, as a sort of "primary" auxiliary lock.

Because of the lock's design, the cylinder often protrudes an inch or more from the outer surface of the door, where it is vulnerable to being pried, twisted, or wrenched off. To protect against this possibility, the cylinders in these locksets often have an armored, tapered, free-turning collar. Because of its tapered edges, this collar is hard to grasp with a wrench

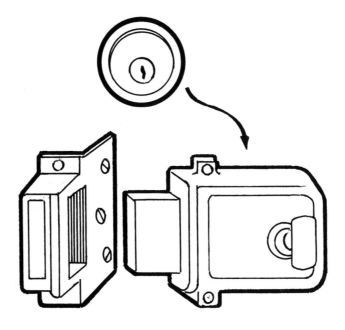

Figure 21 Horizontal bolt—as an auxiliary lock it is vulnerable to prying, kicking, and jimmying.

or pliers, and twisting it merely makes it spin. However, Consumers Union testers found that some of the collars can be crushed with a pair of strong pliers, with the result that the collars could then be twisted off, exposing the protruding cylinder to prying and forced rotation. In addition, some cylinder lock bolts are made of soft metal such as brass or zinc alloy and offer little resistance to the blade of a metal saw—although this is not especially important if the door crack is not visible, as with a tightly fitted metal door and frame.

Keyless Locks

Keyless ciphered (or "combination") locks are commonly used on vault doors, safes, and many high-security sites, and a small but growing number of such locks are now available for residential use.

Keyless locks are advertised as pickproof because there is no keyed opening or other access to the tumblers. Also, without keys that can be copied or distributed, unauthorized access is theoretically easy to control. And manufacturers claim that the usual four-digit sequence used in most keyless ciphered locks offers significant odds against random selection of the proper unlocking sequence, with a seven-digit sequence providing odds of 10 million to one. Four- or seven-digit number combinations written on scraps of paper are easier to

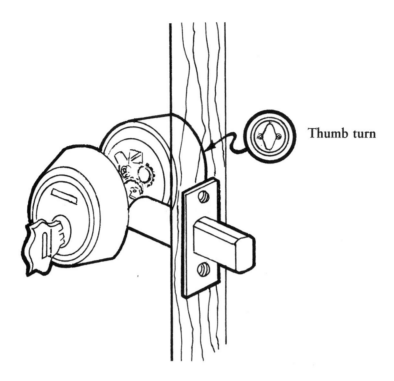

Thumb turn

Figure 22   Cylinder dead-bolt lock—its cylinder protrudes from the outer surface of the door, making it vulnerable to attack.

distribute than authorized copies of a hard metal key. But this can be a drawback when there are large numbers of people to accommodate. To guard against unauthorized code sharing, makers often provide for easy code changes as a convenient method of control.

The market for ciphered locks includes elaborate and expensive models adapted from commercial locks and more moderately priced residential push-button locks that operate along similar lines.

One example of the latter is the mechanical ten-button set. This consists of a digital keyboard mounted on the outside surface of the door with finger-press buttons numbered from zero to nine, and a larger reset or lock bar mounted just below. To open the door from the outside, the user pushes four of the buttons in the proper sequence according to the selected code. This causes the bolt or spring latch to retract from the strike, freeing the door to open. When the door is closed from the outside, the bolt is extended into the strike by pressing the reset or lock bar. The spring-latch models on the keyless locks operate just as they do with other locks, by merely closing the door. To unlock the door from the inside a single panicproof button retracts the bolt or latch. To lock the door from the inside, the button or lever has a lockup capability that in some models is worked by giving the button an extra push and twisting it to the right or left.

The array of keyless locks at locksmith shops and trade shows offers a broad range of variations on the same theme. These include a keyed cylinder that can override its own push-button lockup, and models that reverse the usual design by having their strike mounted in the door, with the bolt or latch extending from the jamb itself, and controlled by an electronic relay. Some come with an electric strike release, similar to the remote control used in intercoms in multiple dwellings, which responds to a push-button code at the door.

Almost all versions of keyless locks come with coded plates that permit the user to change the numbers and sequence as frequently as he wants. Some have a timer that keeps the bolt or latch in an open position for a short period before automatically reverting to the locked position. Still others have a "penalty" capability: if a wrong code is punched in, not only will the lock remain closed, but it will not respond even if the correct code is punched in immediately afterward. The penalty may extend from two to many more minutes. While this provides a safeguard against random attempts at punching in the code, it could seem like an eternity to the homeowner with children or shopping bags in tow who hears the phone ringing inside the house.

Most makers claim that keyless locksets are easily installed and relatively trouble-free, but the experience from institutional installations suggests otherwise. Bolts and strikes on these locks are just as vulnerable to prying, loiding, and battering as they are in all other types of locks. More important, keyless locks are easily vandalized, with their keyboards vulnerable to being ripped, pried, or hacked out of the door. For these reasons, keyless locks should probably not be used for first-line security on any major exterior doors.

SPECIAL LOCKS FOR SPECIAL CIRCUMSTANCES

Fire safety codes in some cities require the doors of commercial buildings to open outwards, where the exposed hinge pins can easily be knocked out, permitting the door to be taken off its hinges from the outside. (See chapter 5, "Doors.") Other weak spots in older commercial and/or residential construction are solid doors that are dangerously loose in their frames, or frames that are old and weak. In addition to repairing the existing structural weaknesses, or as a stopgap until you can do the required repairs, these situations call for special remedies.

Double-Bolt Locks

The framing of a door may be so weakened that it is advisable to bolt the hinged side of the door as well as the side with the lock. To do this, you can install a surface-mounted auxiliary lock on the inside of the door with bolts that extend horizontally into matching strikes on the door jambs on each side of the door. The lock is controlled from the inside by a thumb turn and from the outside by a key. With a high-security cylinder and additional protection from an armored lock plate, this kind of installation offers strong protection, even on old and ill-fitting doors.

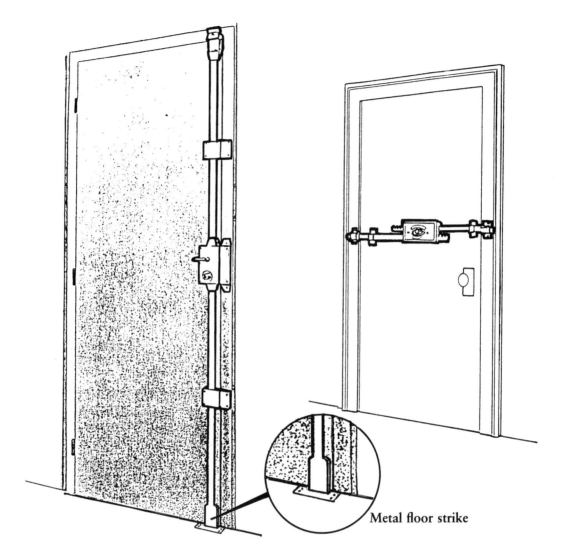

Metal floor strike

Figure 23   Vertical double-bolt and horizontal double-bolt locks

Variations on this theme include models designed so that the bolts operate vertically, locking into the frame at the top and the threshold at the bottom of the door, as well as E-shaped installations, which lock at the top, the bottom, and on one side.

Brace (or Buttress) Locks

Brace locks, commonly called police locks, are especially recommended for use in older buildings where the door is installed in a weak frame. This type of lock can only be used on inwardly opening doors. Rather than securing the door by a bolt between the door and the frame, a heavy steel brace bar is propped up at an angle between the door and a receptacle in the floor. Brace locks are controlled by a thumb screw on the inside and by a key from the outside.

CYLINDERS

The cylinder is the internal part of the lockset that accepts the key and causes the bolt to move in or out of its receptacle in the strike. It consists of a barrellike housing that contains the rotating central "plug." The plug in turn contains the actual keyway.

The plug is normally kept from turning by a series of tumblers or obstructions that project

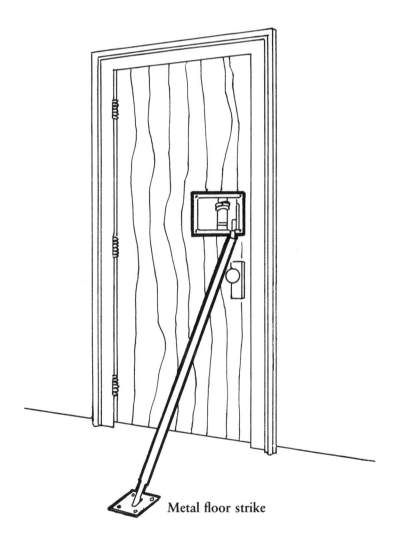

Metal floor strike

Figure 24 Brace lock—provides a buttress against forced entry from the outside

from the housing into the plug, thereby binding the cylinder in its fixed or locked position. When the correct key is inserted into the plug's central keyway, these tumblers are shifted out of the way so that the space ("shear line") between the housing and the central plug is cleared, freeing the plug to rotate when the key is turned. As the plug turns it causes a cam or spindle attached to its outer edge to turn with it, thereby retracting the bolt and unlocking the door.

The tumblers inside a lock cylinder come in various forms. Usually they consist of tiny metal rods or pins; other versions come in the form of disks or wafers that catch the housing along the shear lines. Tumblers consist of two parts—an upper part set into the housing, and a lower part attached to it at the shear line. The pins are driven by springs, or in some cases by magnets, and the lower part can be plain, angled, or magnetized. The magnetized versions can be particularly difficult to pick since they not only lift their pins vertically but can also respond to specially cut keys.

The cylinder mechanism has the added advantage that it can be mass-produced inexpensively, with the code of the tumblers varying almost infinitely. And in most locksets the cylinder subassembly can be removed and replaced at will, or the tumblers can be rearranged to suit a new key whenever the circumstances warrant it.

Pin Tumbler Cylinders

The mechanism of the pin tumbler cylinder is the model for a wide variety of cylinders currently on the market. In a pin tumbler cylinder, a number of paired tiny brass pins are controlled by springs, which force the top pin of each pair to project from a hole in the housing through a matching hole in the plug. When the pins are in their locked position, the top pins project into the plug and keep the plug from turning. When the key is inserted into the keyway, however, the V-cuts in the key position the pins so that the tops of the bottom pins (and the bottoms of the top pins) are aligned flush with the outside of the plug. This is called the shear line. With this alignment, the key barrel is free to be turned, thereby retracting the bolt from its position in the strike.

To lock the door, the same sequence is played out in reverse. When the key is withdrawn from the keyway, the spring in each hole drives both pins down into place, so that the top pin of each pair is once again partly in the housing shell and partly in the key barrel. This pins the housing to the barrel and keeps the barrel from turning.

Key codes vary according to variations in the size, shape, and angle of the bottom pins. The top pins are usually of the same size, and are flat on both the top and the bottom. The lower pins are rounded on the bottom to facilitate smooth key entry and withdrawal. The length of each bottom pin varies according to the depth of the key cut. A well-designed cylinder is one where there are significant differences between adjacent cuts, which vastly increases the difficulty of the would-be lockpicker's task.

Common pin tumbler cylinders have five tumblers and are operated by keys with five V-cuts on their top edge. The five-pin cylinder is the most widely used model throughout the

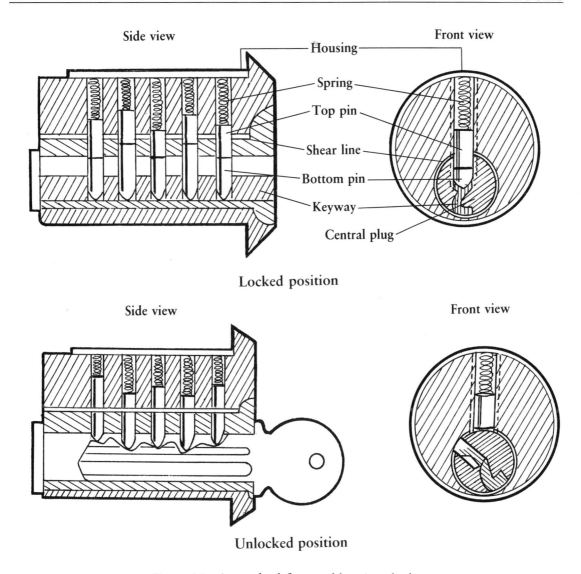

Side view   Front view

Housing
Spring
Top pin
Shear line
Bottom pin
Keyway
Central plug

Locked position

Side view   Front view

Unlocked position

Figure 25 A standard five-tumbler pin cylinder

housing and commercial-building industries today, and in most cases it provides little resistance to picking.

Flat or Disk Tumbler Cylinders

In a flat tumbler cylinder, small metal wafers or disks fit into slots in the key barrel, so that each spring-loaded disk projects partly into the barrel and partly into the fixed cylinder body. When the proper key is inserted, the cuts in the key pull the disks down so that they no longer project above the outer circumference of the key barrel at the shear line. The key can now turn the barrel, causing an attached cam to move the bolt mechanism. When the key is withdrawn, the protruding surface of the spring-loaded disks snaps back into the housing so that the barrel can no longer be turned.

Round Key Cylinders

Another major entry in the cylinder design market involves the use of a round key and keyway. In the keys to these cylinders, varying numbers of key cuts (usually seven or eight) are made around the front edge of the key's circumference. This kind of cylinder is widely used for vending machines, padlocks, and interconnecting dead bolts, and its design, which dates from 1925, calls for the use of special equipment for key duplication. However, round key cylinders are no more difficult to pick than common cylinders. In addition, when round key cylinders are equipped with a soft brass face, as many of them are, the keyway can be cut and the pins can drop out. Cylinders of this type should therefore only be installed if the face is made of hardened steel.

High-Security Cylinders

The cylinder is the heart of any locking system. A lock with a weak cylinder can be improved considerably by replacing the cylinder with one of the high-security types available. Replacing a common cylinder with a high-security one can be accomplished by a reasonably experienced handyperson, but you may want to hire a locksmith if you do not feel comfortable with the task. The cost of the replacement varies from twenty-five dollars to ninety dollars per cylinder, plus labor. Keep in mind, however, that such cylinders are of little use on locks that are weak or unsubstantial in the first place.

There are a wide variety of high-security cylinders on the market that incorporate special keyways and tumbler arrangements designed to thwart drilling, picking, and other mechanical attacks. The following is a brief description of the major categories of high-security cylinders mentioned in the October 1984 issue of *Consumer Reports*.

Medeco Cylinder   The Medeco cylinder has a unique double-locking action that involves not only the cylinder pins but also a sidebar with projections that move into matching slots in the bottom tumblers. The key cuts are made at the exact depth and angle needed to align the pins at the shear line and simultaneously rotate the bottom pins to the precise angle of the sidebar's projections. When the key is withdrawn, the sidebar and its projections are disengaged. The spring-driven upper tumblers depress the bottom tumblers into their chambers below the shear line, thereby closing the lock. The double-locking mechanism makes the Medeco cylinder's action almost impossible to activate without the key designed to fit it, and is therefore highly resistant to picking. Medeco cylinders also provide protection against drilling by virtue of their six hardened anti-drill inserts, including one to protect the sidebar. In addition, Medeco keys cannot be duplicated except by special key-cutting machines that can only be owned by specially franchised locksmiths—thereby introducing a practical element of key control.

Sargent Keso Cylinder   The Sargent Keso cylinder uses twelve pin tumblers, four in each of three intersecting rows. They are distributed along the length of the key barrel. The key to this cylinder is unusual in that it uses circular conical indentations cut into the tip and each side of the key blade. When the key is inserted into the keyway, the three sets of pins align simultaneously along the shear line, permitting the key barrel to be turned in its housing. The manufacturer is said to restrict the sale of key blanks for the Sargent cylinder, with the stipulation that duplicate keys can only be ordered from the factory by authorized locksmiths, but in recent years facsimile blanks have become available, and in 1984 Consumers Union testers found some problems with key controls.

Magnetic Cylinder   This design operates on the same general principle as the pin tumbler lock, with similar metal pins that project partly from the central plug into the fixed housing to keep the key barrel from turning. But the pins in this kind of cylinder are magnetized, rather than spring-loaded, and their magnets are polarized to line up with very tiny magnets similarly spaced and embedded in the matching key. When the key is inserted into the keyway, its magnets repel the pin's magnets and cause them to be pushed out of the key barrel into matching holes in the fixed housing. This in turn frees the barrel to rotate in its housing, retract the bolt, and open the door. The difficulty of duplicating these keys adds to the security value of this kind of cylinder.

These are only a few of the lock cylinders currently on the market. Other locksets are available, but they are too numerous to describe in detail and their omission from this overview is no reflection on their security value.

KEYS

Keys are often overlooked as a factor in the choice of a lock, but keys and key control may be as integral to the security of the locking system as the lock itself.

The critical factor in key design is replicability, and keys are designed—and redesigned—to make them hard to duplicate. Instead of the standard V-cuts on the top of the key shaft, for example, one can find dimples, magnets, and angled cuts that accommodate two or more sets of tumblers placed in pie-cut or even cross shapes within the cylinder. And with the increase in the number of tumblers or pins inside the cylinder, the number of possible different key combinations can expand from thousands to millions.

Keys usually consist of a bow, which is the round or square part of the key that you grip, and the shaft or blade inserted into the keyway. The milled slots running lengthwise along the shaft are (or were at one time) unique to the manufacturer and are cut to fit the shape of the keyway.

V-cuts along the top of the blade are unique to the key, with the cuts corresponding to the pins in the lock cylinder. In most common locks there are five sets of cuts, while in some high-security cylinders there are six or more. The greater the variation in successive cuts, the more difficult the cylinder is to pick; however, a too-abrupt change in consecutive cuts can also result in a sticky key, which is subject to bending or breakage. In addition, locksmiths advise that the deepest cuts should be placed as far from the bow of the key as possible, since such cuts weaken the blade.

A key that does not work smoothly in the keyway, or is bent or has any other observable flaws, should be replaced. A locksmith can readjust or replace existing pins and their combinations in the original cylinder to eliminate the flaws, but it may be more convenient

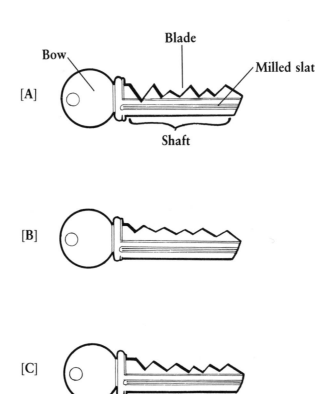

Figure 26   Key cuts

A)   Wrong cut: The changes between successive cuts are too abrupt, and the cut nearest the bow is too deep, resulting in a weakened blade that could bend or break.

B)   Wrong cut: This key shows little variation between cuts; the lock that this key fits is one that can be picked easily.

C)   Correct cut: Although there is variation in the depths of the cuts, there is no abrupt change that might cause the key to stick in the keyhole. The cut nearest the bow is not so deep as to weaken the shaft.

for you to replace the whole cylinder. If so, you might want to consider having one key made to fit all the outside locks by using the same pin code in all of the tumblers.

Master-Keying

Master keys can unlock all the doors in a given house or building. Master-key systems are common in institutions, schools, hotels, and commercial and industrial buildings, as well as in many office and apartment buildings, where they grant landlords and building personnel access to the premises in an emergency. Almost all types of locks can be master-keyed, but since most owners of single free-standing houses will have little need for this convenience, a more detailed discussion of master-keying is offered in chapter 11, "Apartments."

Key Control

Key control refers to the safeguards established by the manufacturer to control or limit the duplication of keys by unauthorized persons. In the security merchandising explosion of recent years, conventional V-cut keys for the common pin tumbler cylinder have proven easy to duplicate and defeat. Key-cutting machines and key blanks are governed by little regulation or control except patent laws. Keymakers, licensed and otherwise, can be found at many supermarkets, shopping malls, hardware stores, or even roadside stands, providing quick and inexpensive duplication of most common keys with no questions asked and no records kept. Even master keys and others that are restricted by law and marked *Do Not Duplicate* can usually be copied with little difficulty. In addition, a would-be burglar needs only a few minutes with your key to have it duplicated either immediately or later from an impression on a bar of soap or some other soft material.

On the other hand, some duplicate keys can only be obtained from factory-authorized locksmiths, and others can be duplicated only at the factory itself. But factory duplication presents problems of its own. Inconvenience and delay are the primary ones; people who have locked their keys into their apartments cannot usually afford to wait for the replacement key to arrive from the factory, and may discover that a local locksmith cannot service such a lock in an emergency. To offset this inconvenience, additional duplicates should be obtained at the time of purchase; some manufacturers will permit you to order up to ten keys at once for an additional cost. But keeping track of so many keys may lead to further key-control problems.

MISCELLANEOUS HARDWARE

Guard Plates and Escutcheons

Where there is a close fit between the door and its frame, the cylinder usually becomes the focus of a burglar's attack because it accesses the otherwise inaccessible bolt. This is especially true for protruding cylinders, but even flush-mounted ones can be chiseled free or wrenched out. To add another layer of security, you may want to add a guard plate that covers the entire cylinder and the area around it, except for a narrow opening that exposes the keyhole.

With a flush-mounted cylinder, the least expensive and most common guard plate is a flat three-by-five-inch plate of heavy steel, held in place by four through-the-door carriage bolts. Polished steel or brass is a more expensive but not necessarily more serviceable alternative. Where cylinders protrude from the door's surface, there are plates that are shaped to accommodate the protrusion and provide the same kind of security. And, although more expensive, some high-security cylinders come with their own heavy guard plates as part of the total lockset.

Guard plates can protect the lock cylinder from hammering and prying, but unless they are constructed of armored steel they may still give way to sawing, drilling, and chiseling. This is especially true for the less expensive models. Even so, they add one more layer of protection to the lock assembly and will discourage, frustrate, or at least slow down a burglar before he can enter your home.

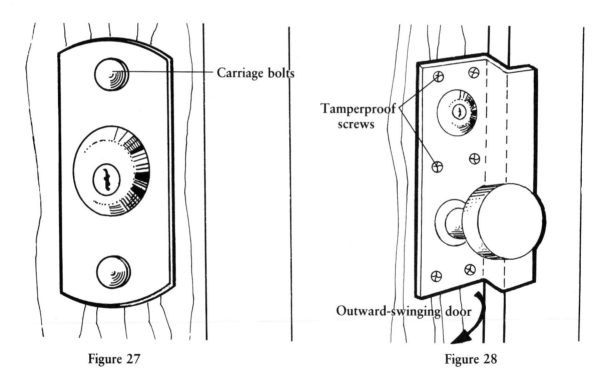

Figure 27   Figure 28

Figure 27 Guard plate—shaped to accommodate and protect a cylinder that protrudes from the door's surface, and is secured by carriage bolts.

Figure 28 Escutcheon for outward-swinging doors—protects both the keyway and the otherwise easily accessible bolt or latch from prying.

Bolts

The bolt is the piece of the lock that actually keeps the door fixed in its frame. It is a rectangular or round metal bar that slides into a receptacle in the strike to lock the door, and it is moved by the turning action of the key.

The security offered by the bolt depends on its resistance to sawing, cutting, prying, or jimmying. While most bolts are made of steel, the relative hardness of the metal varies according to the manufacturer. In 1984, Consumers Union testers found relatively few bolts that could resist a good hacksaw blade for more than a few minutes of sawing. To strengthen the security value of their bolts, manufacturers have tried a number of tricks to make them sawproof. Some use very tough ceramic inserts for this purpose; others use interior rotating metal rods inserted into an inner tube hollowed out of the bolt so that they spin freely when a saw blade tries to engage them. Remember, though, that a bolt's saw-resistance is only relevant if the crack in the door is wide enough to pass a blade through.

Resistance to prying depends upon the overall condition of the door, the frame, and the strike, as well as the bolt itself. A dead bolt should have a "throw" or projection of one inch or more into the strike. Anything less may not hold the door firm against strenuous prying and jimmying.

Night Locks

Not all locks use keys; some consist of simple, keyless bolts that are operated by hand and can be controlled only from inside the house. Otherwise known as "night locks," these bolts can be either surface mounted or recessed into the door and jamb. Another, less expensive version is the sturdy hand-operated sliding bolt with a little knoblike projection on its rod which is used to slide it into place in the strike. For real security, avoid using either the so-called barrel bolts, which are miniature (and much flimsier) versions of the basic hand-operated sliding bolt, or the spring-latch versions, which have all the disadvantages of the usual spring-latch bolt in other, more complex lock assemblies.

Thumb-turned bolts and sliding bolts are often used for back doors, basement doors, and secondary doors; they should never be used on doors with glass panels where burglars can get at them by smashing the glass. To be effective, night-lock bolts should have a throw of at least 1½ inches, and should be fastened to doors and frames with screws that are long enough to anchor the bolt securely.

Strikes

A strike is the receptacle that accepts the bolt and holds it in place, providing the mechanical barrier that actually keeps the door locked tight to the jamb. There are two kinds of strikes currently in use. One is the mortised cavity carved out of the door jamb, which is reinforced by a flat metal strike plate fastened by screws to the inner surface of the jamb. This type is used for locks that are buried inside the door: primary, key-in-the-knob, mortise, and interconnecting locksets, as well as the auxiliary cylinder lockset. Surface-mounted locks come with their own metal receptacles that screw into the jamb to accommodate the accompanying horizontal or vertical dead bolts.

Strikes for surface-mounted locks are only as secure as their mountings on the surface of the door jamb. The least secure are fastened to the jamb flat against only one surface; more secure surface-mounted strikes have L-shaped plates that wrap around the jamb and allow the strike to be screwed in from two different directions with as many as six long screws.

In recently built homes and apartments, the door jambs are usually constructed of relatively soft wood that is seldom more than ¾ inch thick. If a strike is fastened onto such wood with the short screws routinely supplied by most lock manufacturers, one strong kick may be all that is needed either to pop a surface-mounted installation off the jamb or split a mortised strike out of the jamb, carrying a part of the wood with it. If you do substitute such screws with longer ones, be sure the replacement screws are the same diameter, as larger-diameter screws tend to split the wood in the jamb. Also, their heads may not fit properly into the strike.

Strike Reinforcements

Primary locks whose works are buried inside the door itself are also susceptible to being kicked in. Once a door has been hollowed out to accept a cylinder dead bolt or mortised lock, there is less wood left to protect against direct force applied to the area where the locking mechanism is buried. Although a strong kick may not knock out the strike, it may cause the door to split in the hollowed-out area, especially if its core is made of soft wood.

One way to reinforce the mortised area of a door with a primary mortised lock is to install a simple, sturdy metal channel that wraps around the door in the area of the lock, and is held in place with nonretractable screws or through-the-door carriage bolts. While it is possible to do this job yourself, drilling and cutting around the knob, bolt, and cylinder make it a rather demanding project. There is at least one commercially available model that comes in several versions to accommodate different locksets and various thicknesses of doors. It may not completely solve the problem of kick-ins, but it will make the door more resistant.

In surface-mounted strikes, the simplest solution to this problem is to replace the short screws that came with the strike with screws that are 2½ to 3 inches long so that they penetrate the jamb and bite into the wood stud behind it. In addition, make sure that the holes for the longer screws are properly drilled to exactly the right diameter, to prevent any play after they are screwed in.

The solution is a little more complicated for strikes that are mortised into the jamb. In this case, it is a matter of strengthening the sides of the cavity itself. If the existing strike plate is going to be used again, replace its short screws with longer ones so that there is a good bite into the wood behind the jamb. Security can be somewhat enhanced by using a longer strike plate, which can accept more screws and engage more of the jamb. In this case, though, all the screws have to be driven in from the same angle, and a strong kick can bend them out of the way or at least loosen them for the next kick.

A better solution is to replace the flat strike plate with a metal strike box. This box is stamped out to fit snugly into the strike cavity with its deepest surface resting flush against the wood stud behind the jamb, and the lip flush against the surface of the jamb. The deepest innermost surface of the strike box, nestled against the stud, usually has two screw holes that will accept 1½-inch or 2-inch screws anchoring it to the stud at different angles. The outer lip will accept two long screws that go through the jamb and into the adjoining stud.

Other high-security variations on the strike box assembly include one version that fits over the mortised strike box and another that comes with an extra long strike plate and special bolts that anchor the plate to the framing studs. Of all the strike box assemblies tested by Consumers Union, the metal strike box reinforced with an additional strike plate appeared to offer the best security.

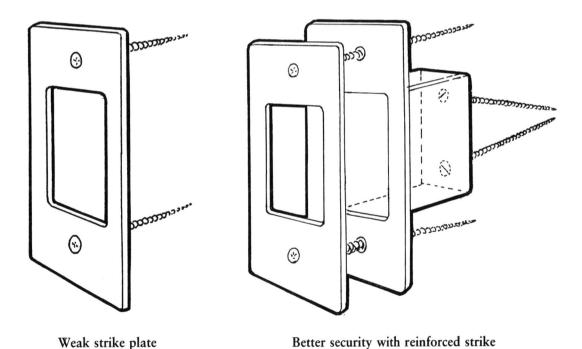

Weak strike plate   Better security with reinforced strike

Figure 29

INTERVIEWING CHAINS

The interviewing chain, or privacy chain, is a length of steel or brass chain mounted on the inside of the door that permits the person inside to open the door an inch or two without letting the person on the outside into the house. It is not a lock and it cannot prevent any willful intruder from entering. Some security experts believe that by giving the homeowner a false sense of security, interviewing chains do more harm than good. While they may provide a momentary barrier to a political canvasser or door-to-door salesman, they are next to useless against an aggressive intruder.

Coat hangers, thumbtacks, or chewing gum have been used to defeat the narrowest chained opening—in addition to bolt cutters or a strong kick. Tests show that most models of interviewing chains can be defeated easily by brute force, and most will snap under a few solid kicks to the lower part of the door. If the chains themselves hold fast, the screws that hold their brackets will probably give, especially in doors that cannot accept more than a 1¾-inch screw. (For suggestions on replacing an interviewing chain, see page 64.)

LOCKSMITHS

A locksmith is an expert in his field, and no matter how well prepared you are, you may be overwhelmed when the expert starts discussing nuts and bolts—or in this case, disk tumblers and retrofits. Even more important than the locksmith's expertise, however, is his reputation and the integrity that goes with it. In dealing with anyone who has access to your home—but especially the person who controls that access at the front door—it pays to remember that you are entrusting him, in a way, not only with your home and possessions but your safety and that of your whole family.

No book or other consumer publication can really help you to make judgments about this person at the level of basic trust, confidentiality, and "chemistry." But there are a few objective correlatives to help you find the most trustworthy locksmith for your needs.

Professional Credentials

The title "locksmith" is often used by anyone from the neighborhood hardware dealer who happens to stock locks to the young man who has been hired to run a key-duplicating machine. A licensed locksmith, however, is someone who possesses certifiable experience and training and must present evidence of these qualifications to the licensing jurisdiction in the area in which he does business. The New York City Administrative Code describes a locksmith in the following terms:

Locksmith: A person dealing in the mechanical actions and the current operation of all locks, key or keyless, or similar devices, and whose trade or occupation is duplicating keys, repairing, servicing, installing, inspecting, opening, and closing such locks by mechanical means, other than with the regular key made for the purpose, without altering, marring, or destroying the original condition or effectiveness of such locks or similar devices in any shape or manner, or a manufacturer of locks, pressure keys, skeleton keys, pass keys, jigs, or any other mechanical device to aid a locksmith in the plying of his trade.

Other major cities and some counties and states have licensing regulations that are modeled on New York's, including Washington, D.C., Los Angeles, Miami, Portland, Ore., Salt Lake City, and Nassau County, N.Y. To be a licensed locksmith in New York City, an applicant must submit documentary proof that he is qualified—usually in the form of attendance and successful completion of a locksmith's training course, and/or affidavits from licensed locksmiths he may have worked for in the past, attesting to his skills and competence. If the documentary evidence is not satisfactory, the applicant is examined by two licensed locksmiths appointed by the licensing agency, who then certify in writing whether the locksmith is sufficiently qualified.

The New York City Administrative Code also describes the licensing of "keymakers," who are permitted by law only to make duplicate keys and not to perform any of the other duties that are reserved for licensed locksmiths. Licensed locksmiths and key makers are also required to maintain books and keep records of all master keys, with written authorization from the building owner ordering the requested duplicates. Apprentices and employees must be licensed, too. And the code specifically forbids anyone other than licensed locksmiths or keymakers to do the kind of work ascribed to these two categories of people.

A number of trade organizations for locksmiths also attempt to establish industrywide standards and codes of ethics. The best known of these is the Associated Locksmiths of America, which is empowered to bond its members. There are also a number of local locksmiths' associations that issue certificates of membership. Look for these certificates when you enter the shop; if nothing else, they are evidence of the individual locksmith's standing in the trade.

Frequently you will see the term *master locksmith* used by members of trade organizations. Some professional locksmithing organizations hand out certificates attesting to twenty years of experience, and award the title of Master Locksmith for such experience. However, this title is not official. Few if any licensing or regulatory agencies award or use the term, and it should therefore not be given any weight when it comes to choosing a locksmith.

Most security experts advise the consumer to check out a locksmith's background and references before engaging him to do extensive work in your home. Visit his shop, inspect his array of products and machinery, and look for evidence of his license and affiliations with professional locksmithing organizations. It also pays to contact the local licensing agency. Is your locksmith licensed? Have there been any complaints? Check him out with the local Better Business Bureau, too, if time permits. Last but not least, find out if the local police are aware of any irregularities in his business.

Try to get the license-holder, rather than his helper or apprentice, to come to your home to do the job. He is the one who has the credentials, and he may be the only one in the shop who is bonded.

These precautions may seem excessive, but not when you remember that a locksmith, by the nature of his work, holds your possessions—and conceivably your actual physical security—in his hands. Anything less than a systematic character check would be inappropriate before you hand him the keys to your house. Besides, there are enough highly skilled, trained, and reputable locksmiths in most neighborhoods to rule out the risk of doing business with those who aren't.

SUMMARY AND SUGGESTIONS

Most locks do not attain their full security potential because they are attached to an otherwise weak door assembly. Shiny brass locks look formidable and are easily purchased and installed, but they may give homeowners a false sense of security and blind them to other vulnerabilities. The lock is only part of the system, and a system is only as strong as its weakest part. However, there are still certain basics about locks and locking systems on which most security experts agree.

- Any lock is better than none. This means that you should use your existing locks as a first step. Locking the door will at least discourage the casual door-shaker or knob-twister. The FBI Uniform Crime Reports, released in 1987, note that of the 3.2 million burglaries that occurred in 1987, two out of three took place in private residences, and 21 percent of all burglaries reported to the police were accomplished without any use of force, simply by twisting the knob or raising the sash and walking in through an unlocked door or window.
- Two locks on a door are better than one. The presence of a second lock buys time, doubles the difficulty of getting in for the intruder, and improves key control. In some high-risk areas, especially in multi-occupancy high-rises, three locks are better still.
- Good locks deserve good cylinders: aim for a high-security cylinder inside a good-quality door lock. This may require a little judicious retrofitting. There are a number of locks on the market today that provide formidable barriers to break-ins except when it comes to their cylinders, which may offer little resistance to picking, drilling, shearing, and prying. If you are not sure about the integrity or reliability of the cylinder in your existing primary lock, have a local locksmith evaluate it. In addition, if this is your only lock, back it up with an auxiliary lockset of your own choice.
- Back up weak primary locks with strong auxiliary locks. Most existing primary locks installed by the builder and controlled by the doorknob are little more than privacy

devices. Among these are the spring-latched locks found in key-in-the-knob locks and some mortise locks. These provide a false sense of security. Instead of replacing them, back them up with a high-quality surface-mounted lock of your choice. Key-in-the-knob locks can be replaced with interconnected locksets.

When you install a secondary or auxiliary lock, make sure to leave at least twelve to eighteen inches between the primary lock and the new one. This helps to dissipate the force of a kick aimed at either one. A good rule of thumb is to place the second lock halfway between the first one and the top of the door.

- Install panicproof knobs for fire safety and ease of exit. Where panicproof locks that open readily from the inside are an overriding factor, install an interconnecting lockset that opens from the inside with a knob instead of a key. These locks combine the panicproof features of a knob-opening lock with the security of a cylinder dead-bolt lock. Look for one with a vertical dead bolt; these are stronger than horizontal bolts because their bolts hook into the strike much the way a hinge pin fits into a hinge.

- Pay attention to the lock-mounting hardware. When you install a surface-mounted lock, remember that the screws that fasten the lock to the door and the strike to the jamb are its most vulnerable points. Make sure that the screws are long enough, and as sturdy as practicable. A number-twelve screw 2½ to 3 inches long is recommended. When replacing screws in existing screw holes, it is suggested that the old screw hole be filled with a tightly fitted wooden peg glued in place with epoxy or wood glue before drilling for and driving in the new and longer screw. Make sure that the new screw is long enough to penetrate both the door jamb and the underlying framing stud.

- Use L-shaped strike plates. Surface-mounted strikes for some auxiliary locks have mounting surfaces that either fit flat against the surface of the jamb or are L-shaped so that they can be screwed into the jamb from two directions. The latter are preferable because their superior gripping action can better resist direct force from a kick or other kind of blow. This type of strike plate adds significantly to the gripping action of the vertical dead bolt.

- Look for a lock with a sturdy bolt. A bolt that ends in a beveled latch offers little security and should be considered merely as a privacy device. A good dead bolt should extend at least an inch into the strike and should be thick enough to resist sawing and other kinds of attacks.

Many bolts are made of a softer metal on the outside with hardened steel or ceramic inserts on the inside to reinforce them. Some of these inserts are in free-rolling rod form. Consumers Union testers found that it didn't take long to saw through the soft outer metal and expose the inserts, which could then be hacked loose. A better idea is a bolt that is made completely of hardened metal. These can still be sawed through, but the process takes much longer and the burglar may be frustrated enough to go elsewhere. To make sure you are getting a hard metal bolt, read all the fine print and be wary when the lock advertises a "saw-resistant bolt."

- Look for a cylinder that fits or can be adapted to fit your existing lock or the new one you intend to purchase.
- Look for special arrangements or pick-resistant features of the tumblers. This includes angled rotating pins of the Medeco with its additional sidebars, and the anti-pick upper pin designs and the multi-series pin arrangements of the Sargent Keso and Fichet, among others. Six or more pins are high security; anything less than five is substandard.
- Internal hardened anti-drill inserts are integral parts of any high-security cylinder assembly worth installing.
- Look for steel-set screws that hold the cylinder in place and resist attempts to rotate the cylinder out of the lock. Holding plates to anchor the set screws should be of at least sixteen-gauge steel.
- While double-cylinder models are recommended for thin-paneled doors or doors with glass "lights," check your local building or fire code to see if they are permitted in your community, and weigh the difficulty they may present in terms of rapid exit in case of fire.
- Cylinders that do not protrude from the surface of a flush-mounted door are preferable to those that do. If the cylinder does protrude, make sure that it is protected with a tapered, armored, or free-spinning ring or collar to prevent getting a purchase on it with a wrench.
- Protect locks and cylinders with metal guard plates bolted through the door so that little more than the keyway is exposed.
- For seldom-used doors, consider installing a hand-operated slide or barrel bolt that can be locked from the inside only. When bolts are screwed securely into the door and jamb with screws of adequate length, they offer a relatively inexpensive and sturdy surface-mounted locking device. However, they should not be considered for doors with glass panels or window lights.
- Be scrupulous about key control. Don't hide keys under doormats or anywhere else a thief might find them. Separate house keys from car keys, especially if you regularly leave your car with an attendant for servicing or parking.
- Keys so unique in their design that they can only be duplicated at the factory may be the best possible protection against unauthorized duplication, but they also present problems when the cylinder needs servicing or you need a replacement for a lost key immediately. Before you install a lock with this kind of key, make sure that your locksmith can service the lock and provide extra keys immediately.

8

PADLOCKS AND OTHER PORTABLE LOCKS

DESIGN

Commercial padlocks come in a wide range of styles designed to secure doors, school and gym lockers, bicycles, boats, trailers, and even skis and ski poles. Whatever their size and intended purpose, all have at least four components in common: a lock case or body; a shackle; a shackle-retaining device; and a release mechanism (cylinder) suited to a key or dial.

The body can be made of almost any rigid metal, ranging from solid or laminated steel down to stamped thin steel plate, as well as brass plate, cast or forged iron, or hammered copper or tin. Most commercial padlocks are made of either brass or steel, but less expensive cast-zinc lock bodies are also still available. The composition of the metal varies as a function of the expected threat. Theft is not the only hazard here; exposure can be a major problem for most large movables like boats and trailers, and the lock in this instance has to be able to stand up to weather and corrosion, as well as brute force, sawing, prying, and picking. While boat owners generally prefer brass locks, no base metal or finish is really impervious to salt air.

The shackle is the metal loop that slides into the housing. In most padlocks the short end of the shackle is called the "toe" and is free-swinging. When unlocked it pivots on the "heel" side—which remains fixed inside the body at all times. In some padlocks the shackle can be removed completely from the body to facilitate locking in tight quarters.

The shackle-retaining mechanism contained in the body is roughly analogous to the bolt and latch in a typical door-lock assembly. It engages the heel, or both the toe and the heel, at slots cut into the shackle, and either holds them fast when locked or frees them to move when the padlock is unlocked. In the case of a double-locking padlock, both the toe and the heel are engaged.

The cylinder is the rotating plug in the padlock's body. When the proper key is inserted into the cylinder's key barrel and turned, it disengages the locking mechanism, freeing up the toe of the shackle.

In addition to these basics, padlocks come with a number of variations. Some use steel ball bearings that lock the shackle, heel, and toe; others provide a key-retaining feature so that the key cannot be removed while the lock is open. Still others offer "shrouded shackles" that are recessed into the body of the lock so that they offer less exposure to saws, files, or bolt cutters. There are also a number of padlocks that use flexible cable instead of the traditional rigid metal loop for their shackles. The variety of available models means that when you go to the store to buy one you are likely to be faced with a padlock for every purpose and at almost any price.

SECURITY

Security experts classify padlocks in three basic groups: high-security, medium-security, and commercial locks. These designations refer to the padlock's mechanical reliability and the resistance of its design features to all known methods of attack. The quality of "commercial" locks is far below those that receive the high- or even the medium-security classification. For a lock to obtain either of these latter headings, it must resist both force and surreptitious opening ("picking"), and use keys that are not furnished to other customers and that cannot be duplicated easily. However, such locks command a high price, which may make them impractical for residential use. At the opposite end of the scale there are many relatively lightweight, low-cost locks that can serve as basic privacy devices but will most likely yield to a burglar's assault.

Padlock manufacturers also have their own classifications, and you may find that what one maker rates as a low-security lock can be another manufacturer's medium-security model, even though both have substantially the same design features and metal components. Many lock manufacturers grossly exaggerate the capability of their products, then place subtle disclaimers in fine print on their brochures. People in the market for a padlock are therefore well advised to use more objective guidelines than the manufacturer's own ratings or literature.

HOW TO JUDGE A PADLOCK

Materials

In judging a padlock, you should be alert to certain features. Body construction is important. For maximum security the lock body should be made of hardened steel. Solid- and laminated-steel padlocks are used for security purposes by the U.S. government. Brass plate, solid brass, and die-cast metal are next in descending rank of security. Stamped metal bodies ("shell locks") or those cast of zinc alloys offer the least resistance to common hand tools and are found in the least expensive locks.

The shackle's level of security can be judged by its diameter and resistance to cutting tools. Hardened steel shackles $7/16$ inch in diameter earn the shackle a high-security rating, while cutting the diameter down to $3/8$ or $1/4$ inch brings it into the medium range. Note, however, that $7/16$ inch may be too wide for some applications. While brass might be the metal of choice in some settings on the basis of its resistance to salt spray and rust, like other models of unhardened steel (and any steel under $1/4$-inch diameter, hardened or not), brass is a soft metal that can be cut with a common hacksaw and would normally rate a low-security designation.

Design

The shackle-retaining mechanism or bolt should be judged on its own by the ability of the fasteners extending from a cam on the key assembly to hold the shackle fast inside the body case. Where the fastener grabs the shackle only at one leg (as in the so-called single-locking mechanism), it provides only minimal security. Instead, look for fasteners that grasp the shackle at both legs (double-locking mechanism); when both the heel and the toe are locked into place with hardened-steel ball bearings, the padlock merits a higher security rating.

Keying Mechanisms

The padlock's keying device or cylinder is the final component that can be judged and graded for its security value. In this case the highest rating goes to the typical pin tumbler cylinder mechanism, similar in principle but smaller in size than those commonly used in door locks. The same warnings about protection against picking, drilling, and separation apply here as with fixed, nonportable locks. On the lower end of the security ladder are the commonly used warded padlocks whose shackles are held in place by a hairpin spring. The keys for such locks can be easily skeletonized to open other locks, resulting in key-control problems at the very least. As with door locks, when the padlock cylinder is keyed for five pin tumblers it offers fair security at best; when it has four pins or less it offers only marginal security. The tubular cylinder that uses a circular key is a rung above those with four or five pins. (See chapter 7, "Locks.")

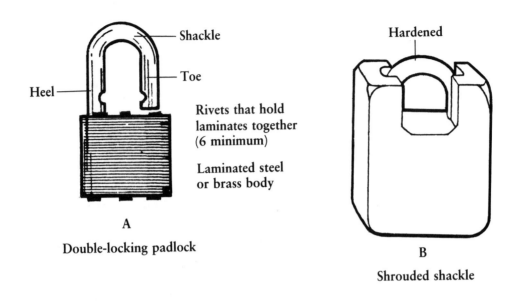

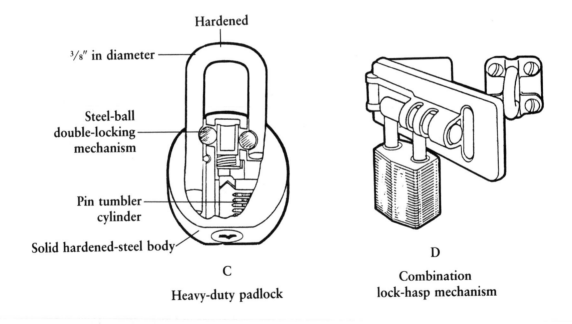

Figure 30   Padlocks

A)   Basic double-locking padlock

B)   Shrouded padlock, whose sides extend to allow limited access to its shackle

C)   Heavy-duty padlock should have a case-hardened shackle ³/₈″ in diameter, solid hardened-steel body, steel-ball double-locking mechanism, and a pick-resistant pin tumbler cylinder.

D)   Combination lock-hasps prevent misplacement of the lock.

Padlocks are often exposed to highly punishing conditions, including sea salt, sand, dust, grime, and industrial contaminants, which adversely affect the fine tolerances of the tubular cylinder's keying device. An alternative under these conditions is the simple warded lock, mentioned above, which has relatively large clearances between fewer internal moving parts. Although warded padlocks offer a low level of security, they may be the only choice where harsh environmental conditions exist.

Combination locks, such as those often used on school lockers, still tend to rate low on most security-performance standards, despite some refinements and upgrading in recent years. They are made of lightweight stamped metal, and the typical combination mechanism can be defeated easily.

The grading of various components may vary within a single lock, depending on its expected use, price range, and the level of convenience it offers. Laminated-steel bodies and hardened shackles that would otherwise give the lock a high or medium rating may nevertheless come with an inferior pin tumbler assembly that is easy to pick or a low-rated locking mechanism to meet production requirements at a certain price level. On the other hand, weather conditions and marine environments on boats and at the shore may require a more expensive brass lock body or even a brass shackle, despite their other medium-rated components. And combination locks may be suitable where security is not a high-priority consideration or where key control is a potential problem.

Padlock Assemblies and Companion Hardware

As with fixed door locks, the level of protection you get from a padlock depends not only on the lock itself, but on the entire assembly of companion hardware, including the hasp, which is the hinged metal rectangle attached to the object or door being locked, as well as the locking mechanism or bolt, and the screws or bolts that attach the lock to the door, lid, frame, or other base. Even high-security locks and hardware cannot deliver the expected performance when they are attached to flimsy sheet-metal doors or weak door frames. The companion hardware on any lock or hasp should always be made of sturdy and hardened-steel components, with fasteners that are hidden and well-anchored. Carriage bolts and inner surface reinforcement plates are recommended for a top-grade installation.

PADLOCK VULNERABILITIES

Auxiliary mechanisms like padlocks cannot promise absolute security, but they help slow intruders down—although, in the case of the common padlock, that time may be only a minute or two. Unlike fixed door locks, where the key cylinder is the only visible component, padlock assemblies are fully exposed. Given the opportunity, a burglar will test their resistance to his bag of tricks.

Shackle Vulnerability

The lock's most vulnerable point is its exposed shackle, which can be separated from the fastening that holds the heel and toe inside the lock body with a lock popper that slips through the shackle. When the handles are pressed together, they build up leverage against both the shackle and the lock body, which pop free of each other. A padlock with only a toe or heel engagement offers only minimal resistance to such tools. A double leg lock that holds both toe and heel offers much better protection, and one that locks both toe and heel with hardened steel balls is the most difficult to pop.

The best protection for a shackle is to restrict access to it in the first place. This is done by choosing a padlock designed to extend the lock body out around the shackle so that it shields or shrouds it from attack by files, cutters, or hacksaw blades.

To protect against sawing and filing, the best shackles are made as thick as possible (generally $7/16$ inch in diameter or more) and are case-hardened to resist cutting and sawing. Case hardening is a metallurgical process which provides a hardened outer shell of a few thousandths of an inch over a more malleable inner alloy core. Without the softer interior core, the metal loop would be too brittle and could be shattered easily by a strong hammer blow. However, while the case-hardened skin may be highly resistant to sawing and cutting, once the skin itself is pierced it may take no more than a few minutes to cut through the much softer core of the shackle.

Hasp Vulnerability

The hasp is the companion hardware for the padlock, analogous to the strike on a stationary door lock, and it can be even more vulnerable to attack than the padlock itself. The hasp comes in two sections: (1) a hinged straight bar that is screwed or bolted to the door (or to one of a pair of double doors) and (2) a plate affixed to the door frame or post (or the other door of a double-door assembly). The plate holds the staple, a U-shaped metal loop designed to go through the slot in the plate's hinged bar and keep the door closed when the shackle is slipped through it. By its very design, the hasp is exposed to tampering, and there are several points of attack that must be strengthened before the hasp can offer more than token security.

As with the lock body itself, the hasp's metal components should be of case-hardened steel to resist attacks by sawing and cutting. The screws or bolts that hold the hinged bar and staple plate should be covered completely by the hinged bar. For increased security, replace the screws with carriage bolts fitting through the door or gate, as well as through a reinforcement plate on the other side. A further precaution would be to deface the threads of the bolt ends on the inside to keep the nuts from being removed or working loose. The hasp's hinges should be attached with headless pins to prevent separation. Finally, the staple, which is generally exposed, should be of case-hardened steel and as thick in diameter as that of the shackle itself, to resist cutting or sawing.

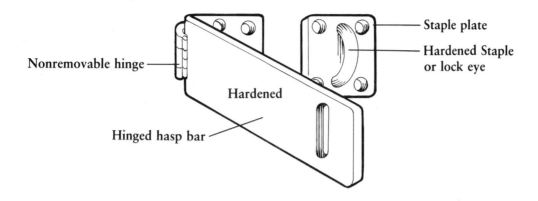

Figure 31A   High-security hasps cover the screws when locked

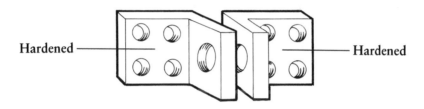

Figure 31B   Vending-machine-style hasps for double doors

For some horizontal cellar doors or even double doors, there are hasps with each side consisting of an L-shaped angle iron, each with matching holes through which a padlock's shackle can be slipped. This vending-machine-style installation provides all the functions of a hasp without the vulnerability of the hinge. And for maximum convenience and security there are a growing number of high-security lock/hasp combinations that come with special shrouded or hooded lock cases covering both the shackle of the lock and the staple of the hasp.

Cables and Chains

In addition to the padlock itself, the chain or cable that is used to fasten a piece of movable property like a bike, moped, or expensive gardening equipment to some nearby stationary object may represent a serious point of vulnerability.

Cables   There are many cable-padlock assemblies on the market with convenient threading capabilities and adjustable cables substituting for the shackles. But the majority of these offer more convenience than security. Industrial-strength cables are engineering workhorses in the uses for which they were originally intended: holding up suspension bridges and pulling cable cars and mine trolleys. But in the lighter thicknesses available on the commercial retail market they offer little resistance to pocket cutting tools.

Cables are made up of many fine steel wires that are twisted into thin strands; the strands are in turn intertwined or braided to make up a specified diameter of finished cable. Cables vary in the number of strands they contain; the more strands there are, the thicker the cable and the more security it provides. Cables come in various grades up to and including heavy-duty and even super-heavy-duty. Some are conveniently self-coiling. Some are exposed; others are coated with vinyl. But either way, unless they are so thick that they are virtually unusable for ordinary locking purposes, they can usually be sawed through with ease: a cable $^7/_{16}$ inch thick requires no more than about one minute's worth of sawing to cut through.

Chains Chains are preferable to cables as movable-lock accessories because they are more difficult to cut. They come in various sizes and qualities; but you should avoid the common chain available in hardware stores and instead look for chains specifically manufactured for locking and security purposes. Avoid chains whose links are less than $^3/_8$ inch in diameter or are twisted rather than welded closed; at a minimum, look for those whose links are made of case-hardened steel alloy, with continuous welded links.

A chain's security level is a function of the thickness of the link and the composition of the steel that goes into the link. A good deal of security is available with a $^3/_8$-inch welded case-hardened steel alloy chain that is looped over, under, around, and through the movable and fixed object. A five- or six-foot length is practical for most purposes; weight may be a factor here, with a $^3/_8$-inch link chain weighing about a pound and a half per running foot. Vinyl sleeves or coverings do not add much in the way of protection but they do prevent the chain from scratching or scraping the objects being secured and are therefore good features to look for.

BICYCLE SECURITY

Although the material presented in the first part of this chapter is applicable to bicycle security, too, bicycles present unique targets. A broad array of hardware has been made specifically for securing them. While the majority of this hardware leaves much to be desired, whatever you lock up with will delay and perhaps frustrate a potential bicycle thief, and is therefore recommended as a substantial improvement over no lock at all.

According to the FBI Uniform Crime Reports, over 440,000 bikes were reported stolen in 1987, at an average value of $172. These are probably conservative figures, since many bicycle thefts are not reported to law-enforcement authorities.

Horseshoe Locks

Horseshoe locks are oversized padlocks designed for bicycles. They consist of special alloys and are constructed to withstand a bicycle thief's tools. The shackle of a horseshoe lock fits into a cylindrical housing to form a closed loop. The shackle is about ½ inch in diameter, with four inches or so between its parallel legs—space enough to secure a bike to the typical parking meter pole or street-sign support.

Most horseshoe locks come with a round key pin cylinder with hardened inserts to resist drilling and forced removal of the cylinder. These models, which weigh between two and three pounds, come with brackets that permit them to be snapped to the bike's frame

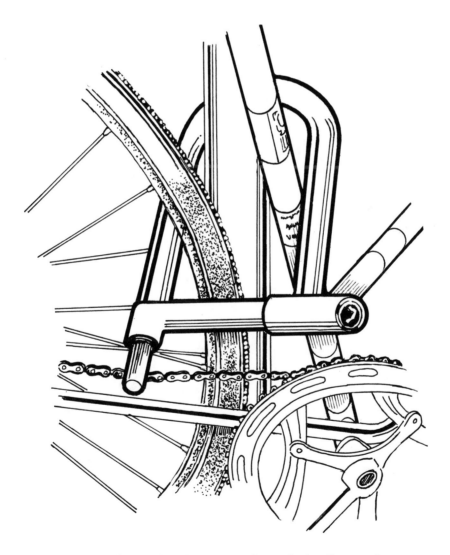

Figure 32   Horseshoe lock—this oversized "D" lock offers good security.

when not in use. The current price of a good horseshoe lock ranges from fifteen to forty dollars.

Horseshoe locks offer the best security currently available against bolt cutters, hacksaws, and pry-bars. Even so, some models can be sawn through with rod saws, but only after great effort, and the time and energy required are usually not worth the effort to most bicycle thieves.

Available Options

Consumer Reports published its findings on 171 tested models of bicycle locks in July 1980, and there have been relatively few design or material innovations since then. Locks tested ranged from the oversized shackle (i.e., horseshoe) lock to chain and cable sets with keyed or combination padlocks either as separate components or as part of an integrated set.

Vulnerability

Consumers Union engineers subjected the tested models to the most common methods of attack, including cutting, sawing, prying, smashing, and lockpicking. They found that more than half of the chain/cable assemblies could be yanked, stomped, or sprung apart without the use of tools. Those that resisted successfully were generally better made, heftier, and of simple design.

Cutting   Whether a cable was susceptible to being cut or not depended on the thickness of the cable and/or the heftiness of the cutting tools. Even the thickest cable could be severed using an average-sized twenty-four-inch bolt cutter; but lock sets with chains and shackles ⅜ inch in diameter and larger tested the outside limits of the big bolt cutters before succumbing.

Sawing   Despite lockmakers' claims of saw-resistant metals, all types and models submitted to a top-quality hacksaw, and a few lightweight models yielded to a common hacksaw blade in less than three minutes. Once again, the large-diameter horseshoe shackle and the hardened chains were the most resistant, taking as long as ten minutes to be cut through.

Prying   Whether a lock or lockset could be pried apart was more a function of design than of actual construction. In this case some cable sets with integral locks held up as well as heavier models because they had no opposing elements to pry apart.

Smashing   A thief may be tempted to use a hammer if the lockset looks vulnerable to a few heavy blows and if he is willing to risk the resulting noise. Here again the smaller cables could be pulverized by a hammer, and some of the harder shackles and chains could be

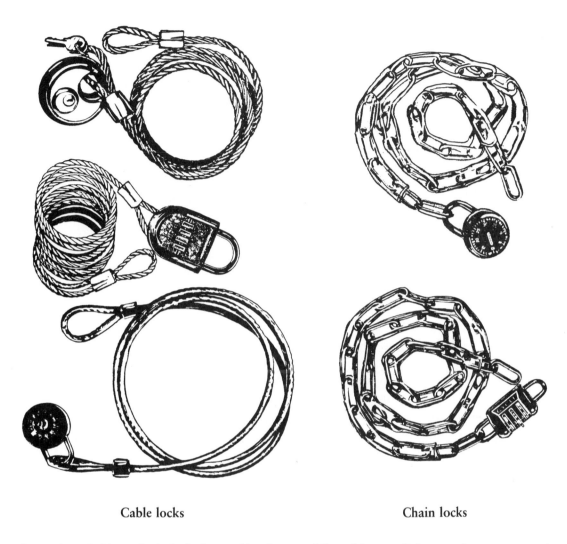

Cable locks   Chain locks

Figure 33   Cable and chain-lock combinations—while cables are lighter and more convenient, a 3/8″-diameter chain offers better protection.

fractured. As in the other tests, the horseshoe locks stood up best, followed by locks with larger-diameter chains and cables.

Lockpicking   Consumers Union found that none of the locks it tested had truly pick-resistant tumbler mechanisms. Some models that would otherwise have received a very favorable rating were easily picked, even by keys that were not made to fit their particular locks. Dial-type combination locks were highly resistant to picking, but other types of combination locks—including those that work by means of spools, tabs, or wheels that had to be aligned before the lock would open—were more easily defeated.

SUMMARY AND SUGGESTIONS

- If you must leave your bike unattended, leave it in a well-trafficked public area, and then only well-secured to a tree, a lamppost, a signpost, or any other immovable object. Never leave your bike parked in the open overnight, even if it is locked.
- Even when the bike is parked at your house, in your driveway or the garage, take the extra precaution of locking it. Any lockset—even the common hardware store chain and wardlock—is better than none.
- If you ride your bike to school or work, try to obtain a secured location for it inside the building where the bike can be locked and someone responsible can keep an eye on it.
- If your bike has a quick-release front wheel, remove the wheel and either take it with you or at least chain it and shackle it together with the rear wheel and frame when you have to leave it unattended.
- If your community has a bicycle-registration program, record your bike with them and engrave the registration or any other identification mark or number in an inconspicuous place on the frame.
- Thieves attempting to shatter a chain or lock will almost always have to use the pavement as an anvil, and people using bolt cutters or lock poppers still have to anchor one leg of their tool against the ground if they want to have both arms free to exert the required maximum force. To make it as hard for them as possible, make sure that the chain, cable, or locking mechanism is wrapped tightly around the post it is attached to, so that there is no slack and it is as high off the ground as you can get it. This makes the thief's job more difficult and the chain more visible to casual passersby.

9

BURGLAR ALARMS

According to a U.S. Department of Justice survey of households affected by crime in 1986, 7 percent of houses nationwide now have burglar alarms, with a somewhat higher percentage for urban and suburban homes. In a June 1978 study in *Police Chief* magazine, it was estimated that there were 1.4 million households protected by burglar alarms, and industry representatives estimate that there were almost five times that number by 1986, based on national sales figures. The same study found that premises protected by alarm systems were only likely to be burglarized from one-half to one-sixth as often as those without alarms. According to figures cited in *Consumer Reports* in its October 1984 issue, police in a wealthy New York City suburb found that during a six-year period 90 percent of the burglaries it recorded occurred in homes without burglar alarms. And in homes that were burglarized despite having burglar alarms, the system either had not been turned on or it provided inadequate protection.

Police, who bear the major burden of false alarms, nevertheless agree that alarms do deter burglaries. Their deterrent value is further substantiated by the fact that insurance companies offer lower premiums to homeowners who install alarms, with the decrease dependent upon the type of system installed.

Do you really need a burglar alarm? What are the odds that by installing strong enough doors, locks, window pins, and lights you will be able to deter or delay a burglar long enough to keep him out of your home? How much peace of mind will an intrusion alarm system add to the security of your home and the safety of your family?

Before you can answer these questions, it may pay to consider the degree of inconvenience that accompanies the installation of an alarm system. People with the most comprehensive state-of-the-art systems must routinely go through a long checklist of switches to be flipped, indicators to be turned on, and control knobs to be set every time they want to leave the house. Some alarm owners describe it as living under a constant state of siege, or as having a permanent and demanding houseguest.

You must also consider the ramifications of false alarms—neighbors wakened by your siren in the middle of the night and police summoned out of their way to respond to your alarm—not to mention fines and other penalties for nuisance calls in many jurisdictions.

This being said, there are almost as many good reasons for having a burglar alarm system as there are for not having one, but to make an intelligent decision on this issue, you will want to consider a number of factors. To a degree, your decision should depend on the kind of target your home or apartment presents, what your budget will allow for, and the level of criminal activity in your neighborhood. If you or some member of your family is home all day, if your home is well-fortified with tight-fitting doors, recommended locks, and strategically placed window-pins, if you have a noisy dog and curious neighbors within easy, round-the-clock sight and hearing of your house, you may decide that a burglar alarm system would be superfluous.

On the other hand, if you live in a house that is easy to get into, or if you are regularly away from home for long stretches of time and do not live within close sight of your neighbors, it might be a good idea to tighten up your perimeter security and install the best alarm you can afford.

Alarm systems range from simple, self-installed, minimal-cost alarms, involving a few sensors and a single alarm horn, to a complex, professionally installed, and expensive system with a wide range of exterior, perimeter, and interior sensors tied in to a central station, or a dial-in connection to the local police and fire departments and even a medical-emergency-response capability. Which system you decide to buy ultimately depends on what risk you anticipate, what you expect the system to do, and what services are available at a price you can afford. There is no single best alarm system. The more complex a system is, the more expensive it is going to be, the more servicing and fine-tuning it is going to require on a regular basis, and the more components it will have that can be expected to go wrong.

PROFESSIONAL INSTALLATION OR DO-IT-YOURSELF

Consumers shopping for an alarm system are faced with the basic choice between buying the parts themselves (either piecemeal or in package form) or of hiring a professional installer to select and install the system's components. Two basic considerations should govern this choice. The first is price; the second is the level of your do-it-yourself skills.

A single system component can cost around fifty or sixty dollars, with the parts for the basic system totaling $250 and up. If you decide to install a system yourself, you will not only save a great deal of money (since most of the cost of a professional installation is labor) but you will also have the assurance that no outsider is privy to the actual workings of the system. Tempering this consideration, though, is the question you may have about your own ability to choose the best system for your needs, or, once having chosen it, being able to install it with your own hands and available tools. And the more comprehensive the system the more difficult it may be to install. Since a comprehensive alarm system should be a once-in-a-lifetime investment, it may pay to leave the installation to a trusted and qualified professional.

Police officials are quick to point out that poor installation and faulty workmanship are among the most common causes of false alarms. In addition to his knowledge and experience, the seasoned professional has access to manufacturers' installation manuals and is in a far better position to steer you to the appropriate options, work out solutions that fit your budget, and eliminate the trial-and-error process that would otherwise be involved in picking and installing an alarm system. A reliable installer will also warranty the system against defective parts and faulty workmanship by thoroughly testing and inspecting it after installation, respond to service calls, and adjust for the blips and glitches that almost always show up following any complex technical installation. In addition, he can work out service contracts and central-station tie-ins that might not be available to you as a home handyperson on a do-it-yourself job. A reputable installer will also train you to use the system properly and will go through a few dry runs with you and your family following installation.

CHOOSING A SYSTEM

In its October 1984 issue, *Consumer Reports* examined seventeen burglar alarm devices and systems that were typical of what was then commercially available for do-it-yourself installations. The engineers didn't rate the systems because they concluded that there was no one best system to cover all kinds of houses, ways of living, and overall levels of installer handiness. However, they surveyed a representative array of the two basic kinds of alarms—perimeter systems and interior-space protective systems—and noted the features they offered, as well as the price and the advantages and disadvantages of each.

The article was devoted to options and advice for both do-it-yourselfers and people considering a professional installation. The material covered in that issue has been expanded on in this chapter, which also includes additional information from other, more recent sources. While the model numbers for most systems have changed in the ensuing years, our research indicates that most of the same manufacturers are still in the market offering current models with almost the same features as those noted in 1984, and at only a slight increase from their 1984 prices.

In selecting a burglar alarm, what counts are certain qualities of design, workmanship, and materials. Before you make your purchase you should keep several considerations in mind:

Effectiveness: Will the system do everything you want it to? Will its presence deter a break-in? Will it alert people already in the house and send out the alarm to others in the vicinity—or, if need be, to a distant off-site response or monitoring agency?

Reliability: Will the system's design and workmanship stand up to time and the environment, so that it works when it's supposed to and rarely triggers an alarm when it's not? What kind of service and warranty do you get with the installation? Are the components rated for safety and effectiveness?

Simplicity: Is the system simple enough to be understood and used by everyone in the house, and still comprehensive enough to perform all the functions needed to provide the level of protection you want? Remember that the more complex the system, the more parts to break down, the more potential glitches to expect, and the more inconvenient to operate.

Impregnability: How will the system stand up to attempts to defeat or bypass it? Is the design and installation such that it can withstand such efforts and still trigger an alarm? Will it automatically reset after it has been deliberately and/or maliciously triggered?

Modifiability: Is the system flexible enough to accept additional or even different components and sensors in the future if they seem to be required? Will the master control unit accept additional zones or the addition of different kinds of circuits if the need arises?

Appearance: Are the components, the wiring, the entire installation as unobtrusive as possible? Do they clash with the decor of the house? Will the more easily installed surface-mounted sensors and wiring be inconspicuous enough for you to live with for a long time?

Legal Requirements: Does the system comply with existing local ordinances? For example, does the audible portion of the alarm automatically silence within the required period of time?

Cost: The more sophisticated and comprehensive the system, the higher the cost. In addition, concealed wiring and sensors are going to be more expensive to install than surface-mounted ones. Add-on features such as automatic telephone dialers or direct line tie-ins to a central alarm station may cost several hundred dollars for parts and from fifteen dollars up for basic monthly connection charges. What about service calls when the warranty runs out? In 1988, labor involved in a professional installation ran from one-and-a-half to two times the cost of parts for a fairly comprehensive concealed wiring system, a little less for a surface-mounted installation.

HOW AN ALARM SYSTEM WORKS

Whatever system you choose, and however much you decide to pay for it, all integrated burglar alarm systems have three basic components: the sensors, the master control unit, and the alerting device or devices.

Sensors act as the eyes, ears, and sentinels of the system. Their function is to detect change in an existing or normal condition inside or outside the house, and send a signal to the master control unit calling attention to the change.

The *master control unit* is the heart and brains of the system. It receives information from the sensors and monitors them for normal conditions. When it gets a signal indicating an intrusion or some other "abnormal" condition, it transmits a signal that sets off the alerting device.

The *alerting device* (A.D.) is the part of the system that calls for human attention and response. The alarm can have one of several different effects. First, it can frighten off an intruder by sheer force of acoustics. Second, it can alert people already inside the house to the possibility of imminent physical danger. Finally, it can summon assistance from neighbors, police, or other responsible authorities.

Some alarm systems can perform all these functions within a single unit no larger than a shoebox, but these are generally "space protectors," designed for interior protection only, and only within a fairly limited spatial range. Systems designed to provide more complex and far-reaching protection take up considerably more space and use separate components widely separated and connected by electric wires or wireless radio transmitters. Either way, most systems are powered by household current with a backup battery designed to take over in case of a power failure, although there are less complex systems available that operate on house current or batteries alone.

Wired, Wireless, or Line Carrier Installations

The alarm signal can be transmitted from the sensor to the master control panel in any of three ways: by direct wiring, by wireless radio transmission, or by using the regular household electrical system. Most systems use only one of these methods, while some may require a combination of both wired and wireless signals.

Hard-wired Systems   In a hard-wired alarm system, the sensors or switches are wired directly to a master control panel, which is in turn connected to the household electrical system for power. Though it is considered the most reliable by security experts, the hard-wired system is also the most difficult to install. It involves all the usual problems of snaking wires through floors, ceilings, crawlways and attics, with the number of electrical connections determined by the layout of the house. Although this makes it less obtrusive and harder to defeat, a concealed wiring system also involves much more labor and skill to install than is required for a surface-mounted system with the sensors attached to the window or door frames and the wiring visibly stapled to the baseboards or floors. Installing concealed wiring may be way beyond the level of a do-it-yourselfer, but if you need the services of a professional installer the additional cost for time and labor can be high.

Wireless Systems   Wireless alarm systems use a battery-powered radio transmitter, located next to or near the sensor, to send a coded alarm signal to a compatible radio receiver located at the master control panel. Despite their name, such systems are not completely wireless because their sensors must usually be wired to a transmitter at some point. In fact, for the sake of convenience and to reduce overall costs, several sensors in a single room or adjacent areas are usually wired into a single transmitter. This eliminates what would otherwise be lengthy runs of wire between sensors and the master control panel, and cuts down on the number of transmitters that would otherwise be needed for a single house. Transmitters are expensive, costing as much as thirty to fifty dollars each, or about ten times the cost of a single wired magnetic sensor. The transmitters require regular inspection and testing of their batteries, but most come with test lights to indicate the status of the battery, and test buttons that permit a test transmission without actually triggering an alarm.

While some alarm-system merchandisers push wireless systems over hard-wired systems, stressing their relative ease of installation, professional installers seldom use them except to save on labor costs or where they permit a remote site or outbuilding to be tied into a system without expensive wiring. In some older houses, where it would be impractical to wire up a remote but necessary sensor, an add-on radio transmitter can also be used for this purpose. But the central control panel in such cases must be adapted to receive the transmitter and react to its signals. This kind of arrangement is often used to connect a separate garage or outbuilding to an otherwise hard-wired primary house system.

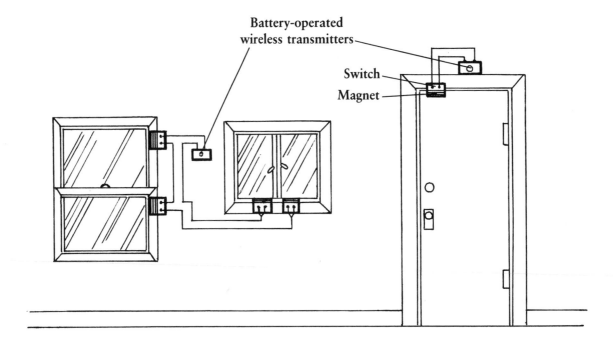

Figure 34   Installation of wireless transmitters and magnetic sensor
(*Note:* One transmitter may serve two or more windows.)

A radio-transmitting wireless system has many inherent weaknesses. If the transmitter's battery fails, the sensors attached to it won't operate. In addition, reception may be blocked in the presence of any large metal obstructions or structural interferences like steel beams, wire lath, metallic decorations, or metal window frames. Furthermore, it cannot be enclosed in metal cabinets or panel boxes. And it is possible for the older system models to interact with other nearby systems or system components, thereby either receiving or transmitting a false alarm. What's more, the individual transmitters may fail and, unless they are tested on a regular basis, you may never be aware of it.

Line Carrier (Plug-In) Systems   There is a third type of system that, since it does not require installing separate hard-wired lines, is also considered a "wireless" system. This system uses the existing electrical wiring lines of the house to transmit and receive the alarm signals, but the sensors operate on one of a number of different principles. In plug-in systems, a single sensor (or several of them), instead of being connected to a radio transmitter, is wired to an encoder, then plugged into an existing electrical outlet. The central control panel is also plugged into another outlet on the wiring system. The power lines not only carry the signals but also serve as a source of power for both the sensors and the master control unit.

While such a simple plug-in system may seem a boon to the do-it-yourselfer, it has several inherent flaws. For one thing, any interference with the regular household power also automatically cuts off the alarm system. For another, if the house or apartment has more than one power line, it is not always certain that individual sensors will trigger the control panel.

Power Sources

House Current and Backup Batteries   Although there are some basic alarm systems that run on regular 120-volt household current, most only operate when the regular household current is converted from 120 volts to six or twelve volts by means of a step-down transformer located in the master control unit. With the sensors, controls, and alarm signals operating on such low voltage, they can continue to function even when the household current fails and a six- or twelve-volt backup battery kicks in. For this reason, a backup battery feature thwarts any attempt to defeat the alarm system by cutting the power lines.

A backup battery feature is a must for any alarm system. The battery system can be as simple as a few C batteries or as sophisticated as an automobile-type battery with its own charger that keeps it at full power. Most residential alarm systems use NiCad (nickel cadmium) or lead-acid gel-type batteries along with an automatic slow "trickle" charger that maintains them at full power.

The period for which a system can operate on battery power alone depends on the power demands of the alarm system at the time it takes over the current supply. If the alarm is in full swing with sirens sounding, strobe lights flashing, and fire bells ringing all at once, the drain on the backup power supply will be much greater and the operational time period will be much shorter than when the system is in the normal, nonactivated mode. Otherwise, without an alarm in progress, most comprehensive systems can operate on batteries alone for no more than twenty-four hours. Floodlights and motor-driven sirens make the greatest demands for power, and these devices therefore require a more powerful automobile-type battery to back them up.

The more sophisticated control units have a battery-status indicator, which signals a "low battery" condition and the need for the service when the battery runs down. No matter what type of battery the system uses, though, all batteries (especially NiCads) tend to deteriorate over time—a frequent cause of false alarms. They should therefore be tested periodically and recharged or replaced when they get low.

Hard-Wired Circuits   A circuit is the wired electrical pathway that loops from the power source at the master control unit to a sensor (or a series of sensors) and then back to the control unit. All sensors, no matter how they are activated, operate by controlling the flow of electricity running through the circuit. This principle holds not only for the simple magnetic or mechanical switches, but also for such sophisticated electronic sensors as ultrasonic beams (which are prone to false alarms) and microwaves. In hard-wired systems these circuits are described as either normally closed or normally opened circuits.

Normally closed circuits: In describing electric circuits, the term "normally closed" might be somewhat confusing. In everyday usage, "closed" means shut or inoperative. However, in describing the flow of electricity in an electric wiring circuit, the term "closed" means just the opposite. It means that the metal circuits at each switch are closed, so that they make continuous contact with each other, providing a bridge across which the current is able to pass.

The word "normally," when it is used to describe electric circuits, refers to the status of the flow of current when the sensors are undisturbed, or in the "default" condition. Thus, a normally closed (NC) circuit is one that permits the current to flow through the switches into the circuit's wiring path and back again without interruption. As long as the current continues to flow, no alarm will be signaled by the processor at the control unit. If the switch or sensor contacts are separated in response to a break-in or other alarm condition, however, the flow of current is interrupted and the processor at the central control unit interprets the interruption as a break-in and sends out the alarm. This type of circuitry has the advantage over a normally opened (NO) circuit of triggering the alarm precisely when there is some interruption of the circuit. If the burglar cuts your wire or your plumber unknowingly cuts it while working, you will know about it immediately.

For this reason, perimeter switches and sensors in most home burglar alarm systems are designed so that they operate only in a normally closed (NC) circuit. On the other hand, most detectors used for interior protection are designed to have both NO and NC connection points. There are some adapters that permit a switch or sensor to work in either kind of circuit, but this is rarely necessary since most master control units are designed to accommodate these differences and have provisions for both types.

Normally opened circuits: In a normally opened circuit, the electrical contacts of the sensors and switches are kept open under normal (nonalarm) conditions, so that no current can flow through the circuit or loop. When the sensor or switch is disturbed and thereby activated, the electrical contacts close, thus permitting the current to flow through the completed circuit. This signals the control unit to transmit the alarm.

This type of circuit has a built-in weakness. If the wire breaks, or the sensor itself malfunctions, no current can flow through it and no alarm signal will be received at the master control unit. This means that any knowledgeable burglar can defeat the sensor merely by cutting the wire. In addition, a break in the wiring or a defective sensor can only be discovered by testing each sensor along the loop individually, and breaks may therefore go undetected unless you make it a point to check each one periodically.

SENSORS AND SWITCHES

Perimeter vs. Interior Sensors

Sensors and switches that detect intrusion come in a wide variety of forms and materials designed to operate under a wide variety of emergency conditions. Basically, sensors fall into one of two main categories—namely, the *perimeter* sensors/switches that are used to guard doors, windows, and other openings; and the *interior* sensors, located inside the house, which are designed to trigger the alarm when they detect intrusion or movement inside a specific area of the house.

Within each of these two main categories there are many different types of sensors designed to meet a range of differing needs. A compact alarm system may use only one type of sensor or switch, while more comprehensive systems will use different combinations of both interior and perimeter sensors.

Perimeter Sensors and Switches   Perimeter sensors set up the home's first line of protection at the most accessible exits and entrances to the house. They are usually installed on doors, windows, skylights, and transoms, while some can even be used to protect against break-ins through the walls themselves.

Perimeter systems are basic to any good alarm system. They detect the intrusion as it is taking place and before the burglar has actually broken into the house. However, to make sure that you have all the possible entry points covered, you may need a number of sensors, sometimes of different types, as well as extensive wiring, with all the labor and expense that this involves. In addition, perimeter sensors must be in contact with the master control unit either by means of electric wiring, as in a hard-wired system, or by radio transmitter, as in a wireless system.

Perimeter systems use one or more of three basic kinds of sensors:

- *switches,* which can be magnetic or mechanical, are triggered into changing their electrical state when they detect the movement of a door or window;
- *metal foil strips,* which are applied to the window glass or wire mesh of protective window screens and work on the switch principle since they "trip" when cut or torn; and
- *detectors,* which can distinguish certain sounds or vibrations associated with the shattering of glass or the breaking of wood or plaster.

Some of these sensors can protect only a single door, or only a single pane of glass. Others can cover a whole bank of windows or an entire expanse of wall.

Magnetic Switches   The magnetic switch is the most commonly used sensor for protecting doors and windows. It is popular because of its reliability and ease of installation. The magnetic switch sensor comes in two separate parts: a magnetically operated switch that usually contains two (NO and NC) or, less often, three (NO, NC, and common) electrical contacts and is installed on or in the stationary door frame or window frame; and a matching magnet, affixed to the door or window sash itself. Each part is directly lined up with its counterpart so that when the door or window is closed there is only a small gap between the two. In this position, in a normally closed (NC) circuit, magnetic attraction draws against a tension-spring-driven metal bar so that it falls across the two electrical contact points, permitting the current to flow continuously between the two contacts. When the door or window is opened, however, the magnet is moved away from its magnetized metal partner and no longer exerts its force over the contiguous metal bar. As a result, under the pull of the tension spring, the bar is pulled back from one of the electrical contacts, thereby cutting off the flow of current and triggering the alarm.

In a normally open, or NO, circuit, the process is just the opposite. In an NO system, the metal bar is held *away* from one of the electrical contact points by the attraction of the magnet, and when the magnet is moved, its spring-driven metal partner is snapped back onto the contact, causing the current to flow and triggering the alarm.

Variations on this theme include high-security magnetic sensors, referred to as "sealed reed" sensors, where the contact points are two thin metal "reeds." In this type of sensor, the reeds are held in the nonalarm position by the attraction of the magnet. Because sealed reed sensors do not rely on the action of a spring-driven metal bar and are thus less vulnerable to being defeated by magnets applied from outside the house, they are considered highly reliable. However, they are considerably more expensive than the ordinary type that uses spring-driven metal bars.

Magnetic switches come in both NC and NO versions, but as a general rule most perimeter

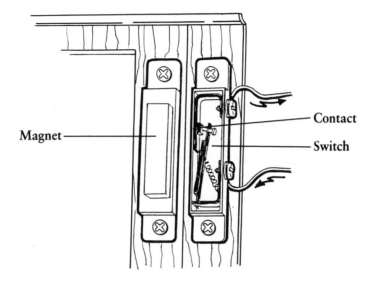

Magnet —

Contact

Switch

Magnet in armed position (using NC circuit)

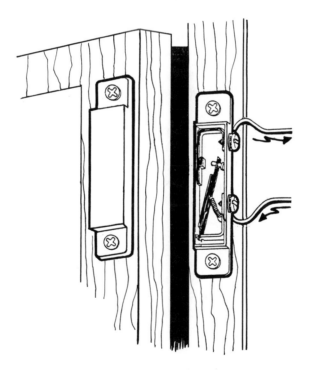

Magnet when alarm is triggered

Figure 35

systems use NC circuits for doors and windows. NO systems can be defeated merely by cutting the wire, while the same action in an NC system immediately triggers the alarm. Either type can be (1) mounted on the surface of the door or window and its respective frame—an installation popular with professional installers and do-it-yourselfers—or (2) concealed in a pair of plastic tubes sunk into the door or window and its respective frame. Similarly, magnetic switches come in various sizes and magnetic strengths for installation on all kinds of doors and windows.

For all their popularity, magnetic sensors have some weaknesses. Like all perimeter system sensors, they must be placed at every accessible opening; but where that opening has two movable parts, as in a double-hung window, a separate switch and magnet must be used for each sash. And if you want to be able to keep the window open while still maintaining an alarm capability, you will have to install an additional magnet at the point to which the window is raised when it is opened.

Another problem with magnetic switches is that when they are surface-mounted the switch is visible and the contact screws are exposed (unless a plastic cover is used to protect them). This means that an intruder can defeat the switch by jumping the contacts with a wire placed across them. And in some older models, a magnet can be used from the outside, preventing the switch from tripping when the door or window is opened.

A third problem is that magnetic switches are prone to triggering false alarms when mounted on loose-fitting doors or windows. There are some "wide gap" models on the market with stronger magnets that are less sensitive to slight motion and vibrations. But these are not recommended in older houses with warped doors and windows, which may have gaps even wider than those allowed for.

Mechanical Plunger Switches   Mechanical plunger switches are often found on doors and windows, gates, hatches, and a whole range of perimeter openings. This type of sensor uses the compression of a push-button plunger to keep the sensor in its nonalarm position. When the door or window is opened, the pressure on an internal spring is released and the plunger button is pushed outward, freeing the switch's electrical contacts to signal the alarm. In doors and some casement windows, the switch is mounted on the hinge side; on double-hung windows two switches are needed, one in the top and one in the bottom part of the window frame.

Mechanical plunger switches are flush-mounted and concealable, with their internal mechanisms buried inside the frame along with the wiring. Positioning this kind of switch is important. If the door or window can be opened even slightly without releasing the plunger, a thin metal strip can be slipped in, compressing the plunger button and thus defeating the alarm. The plunger switch and its spring, being mechanical rather than magnetic, are subject to wear and tear from constant use and shutting or slamming of the door and window. They are also subject to jamming and loss of tension on the spring, and unless weatherproofed there can be corrosion of the electrical contacts. Subsequent painting can cause the switch to stick in the "safe" position, rendering it useless. If there is any amount of play

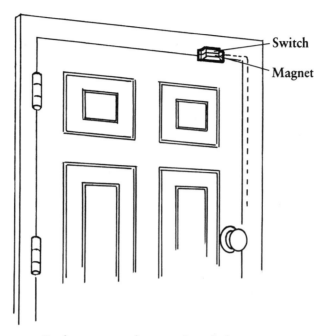

Surface-mounted magnetic switch

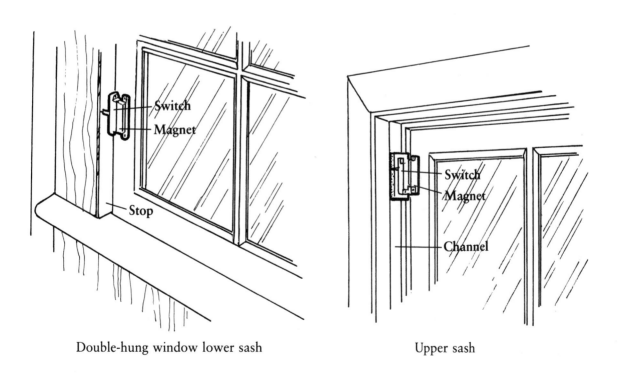

Double-hung window lower sash

Upper sash

Figure 36

between a loose-fitting door or window and its frame, there will also be a greater susceptibility to false alarms. So, like magnetic switches, mechanical plungers are not recommended for old houses with warped window or door frames.

Window Foil   One of the most widely used types of sensors in both residential and commercial security installations is metallic window foil applied to the glass in continuous runs close to the edge of the window pane. Foil strips may be the least expensive and most reliable way to guard the various kinds of window glass that usually represent the weakest part of the house perimeter.

Although installing security foil is hardly a job for the home handyperson, it is very popular with professional installers, not only for its high visibility and the message it sends to would-be intruders, but also because it is easily repaired. The foil, a lead-tin alloy, operates in an NC circuit on a simple flow of electric current through the stripping, which is affixed to the inner surface of the glass without a break from pane to pane.

Security foil comes in long peel-off rolls with an adhesive backing. It is generally applied around the perimeter of the glass. Sometimes, for greater security, it is affixed in a mazelike pattern crisscrossing the entire surface of the window. At the beginning and the end of each loop around the window, there are small tail ends of foil, parallel to each other, which are joined to their own individual connector blocks mounted on the glass abutting a corner of the window sash. The paired blocks in turn are wired to a single sensor, which ties in to the alarm circuit. Any breakage in the glass causes the foil strip to split, halting the flow of current and triggering the alarm. Foil is also good for glass patio doors, and can even be applied to dry wall and wallboard as a continuous-perimeter wall-protection device.

However, foil is not easy to apply. For maximum protection, in multi-paned windows, the strip must run through each pane and over and around the mullions that separate the individual panes. In metal-framed windows the foil will short-circuit if it has direct contact with the metal sash or crossbars, so that insulated crossover stripping must be used to bridge the mullions. Moisture condensation is another cause of short-circuiting, although this can be reduced somewhat by applying a coat of moisture-resistant varnish over the foil. This coat also protects the foil from damage due to everyday wear and tear, and from intentional damage as well; but care still has to be exercised when washing such windows.

A burglar can cut a hole in the glass without disturbing the pane, then reach in through the opening and "jump" the circuit—although security experts maintain that this occurs more often in the movies than in real life. Large panes of glass, like those used in picture windows or patio doors, might therefore make vulnerable targets unless liberally crisscrossed by foil. When applying security foil, some professional installers maintain a mazelike pattern over the whole surface of the window so that no strip of foil is more than six inches from another, in hopes of preventing this kind of break-in; but such a pattern can be very unsightly. Without some kind of webbed network patterning, however, the glass should probably be backed up with some sort of glass-breakage or shock-detecting sensor.

If you have already installed nonshattering or polycarbonate glass instead of ordinary

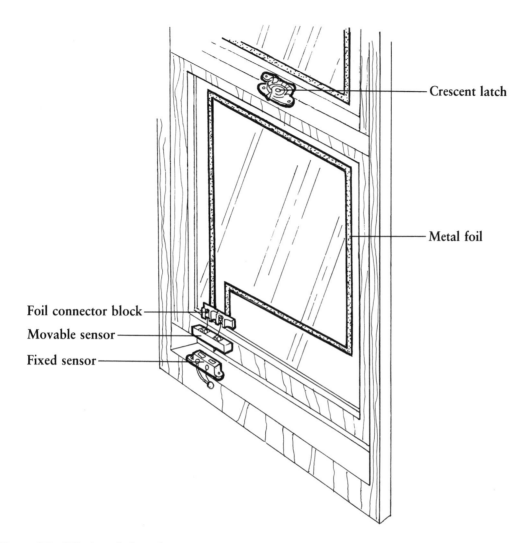

Crescent latch

Metal foil

Foil connector block

Movable sensor

Fixed sensor

Figure 37   Window foil—when mounted on a double-hung window, as with the two-panel sliding window or patio door, requires two sets of switches and magnets, one for each sash or panel.

plate glass for security purposes, window foil is not recommended. Instead, use vibration, sound, or shock sensors to pick up signals of intrusion.

Mercury Switches   Old-fashioned mercury switches are still available for access points like awning windows, skylights, hatch covers, and overhead garage doors, which change their angles from vertical (as in the case of overhead garage doors) or horizontal (as in the case of some skylights or hatch covers) when they are opened. These switches come into play when the opening they are attached to is tilted beyond a certain angle. The typical mercury switch centers on a sealed glass tube containing a small amount of liquid mercury with a terminal wire entering at each end of the tube. This switch is enclosed in a protective housing and is mounted on the movable frame of the opening, so that when it is in the NC position and in a nonalarm state, the electric current can pass from a terminal wire on one end through the mercury and into the terminal wire on the other end, maintaining a normal (nonalarm) circuit. When the door, window, or skylight is tilted open, the mercury in the glass tube flows away from one of its contact wires, exposing it and breaking the circuit, which thereby triggers the alarm.

Mercury switches are rarely used today, although they are sometimes used where magnetic switches are difficult to install, and as an alternative to a magnetic switch where steel in the door or window frame weakens the magnetic field so that a magnetic switch will not operate. Mercury switches are relatively fragile and generally subject to all the disadvantages of the magnetic switch, with few of its redeeming features. They also require flexible connectors between the contacts, which are exposed, unsightly, and relatively easy to defeat.

Wired Window Screens　For people who are concerned about ventilation in warm weather, burglar alarms can be built into special wire-mesh screens that are used like ordinary window screens, to let fresh air in and keep insects out. Security screens are made of fine wire woven into fiberglass screening and framed to fit into the window opening with built-in electrical contacts. The screen is connected to an NC circuit that triggers an alarm when the screen is cut. An additional "tamper" switch, usually magnetic, is installed on the screen frame and can also trigger an alarm if someone tries to remove the screen from the window. Security screens come with a shunt or shut-off switch so they can be removed without sounding an alarm. This is a handy feature when you are cleaning the windows or moving the screens up and down for winter storage.

However, wired window screens should only be considered a convenience and never a real substitute for magnetic window-frame switches or glass-protecting metal foil or breakage sensors. The screens are expensive, and each screen protects only the particular window in which it is installed. To take advantage of the ventilation feature, the other permanent alarm switches that guard the window frame and/or the glass have to be equipped with shut-off switches that make them inoperative while the window is open.

Wired window screens may provide a false sense of security. If you do decide to install them, though, it pays to remember that, with or without such screens, a house should never be left unoccupied with the window open and the primary window alarms shut off.

Glass-Breakage Sensors　Instead of acting on some physical interruption of electric current as in the cases described above, glass-breakage sensors (called transducers) work by detecting the vibrations set off by breaking glass, which they then convert into an electrical signal, triggering the alarm. Glass-breakage sensors are tuned to the unique high frequencies associated with breaking glass while ignoring lower-frequency vibrations. A single breakage sensor can protect up to 100 square feet of glass, depending upon its placement.

The protection of a glass-breakage sensor is limited to the single pane of glass to which it is affixed. This makes it a handy solution for large, single-panel picture windows, but a multipane window would require a sensor for each pane. The sensor must be fastened securely to the glass, and the adhesive used for this purpose should be able to withstand exposure to winter cold and summer heat. A loose-fitting sensor will tend to respond to the lower-frequency vibrations caused by wind, hail, and other acts of nature, and thus trigger false alarms.

Glass-breakage sensors are a relatively new development in the home-protection market, and they are designed to provide protection without the obtrusiveness of metal foil or other surface-mounted systems. Their major disadvantage is that they can be activated only when the glass is broken, so a knowledgeable burglar may be able to cut a hole in the glass or quietly force the sash without disturbing the sensor. For this reason, in any movable window, glass-breakage sensors should always be backed by a protective magnetic or mechanical sash switch.

Trip Wires for Air-Conditioner Protection   Air-conditioning units that are mounted in windows or even inserted through sleeves in the wall offer entry points for intruders just as doors and windows do, and present special problems when it comes to equipping them with alarms. Because air conditioners tend to vibrate when turned on, magnetic or mechanical plunger switches on air-conditioner hatches are prone to false alarms.

One answer is to tie a trip-wire circuit into a normally closed circuit attached to the adjoining wall or window frame, and tie the tension spring into the air-conditioner housing. Any attempt to remove the air conditioner will pull a metal clip out from between the trip-wire contacts, thereby breaking the circuit and triggering the alarm. This type of switch can work with a normally opened circuit, too. However, since most perimeter circuits are normally closed, it is preferable to tie the trip-wire alarm into the normally closed circuit that protects the other perimeter sensors as well.

Miscellaneous Perimeter Sensors   In addition to the perimeter sensors described above, a host of sophisticated sensors and devices designed for high-security purposes in industry, stores, and defense installations are beginning to make their appearance in houses and apartments as well. The glass-breakage sensor is one of them; others include low-frequency vibration detectors that can be tuned to detect the vibrations that accompany break-ins through concrete, wood, and plaster. In addition there are audio sensors or sound discriminators that are essentially miniature microphones to detect the sounds of breaking glass and splintering wood, while ignoring other, more innocent sounds.

The advantage of these newer devices is that they can be set to protect a bank of windows or a whole length of wall without the effort and expense of using a glass-breakage sensor for every single pane of glass, or running a network of metal foil strips along an entire wall. In some instances the installation may be uncomplicated enough for the average do-it-yourselfer, but in most cases these sensors require fine-tuning and constant adjustment to keep them from sounding the alarm for everyday sounds, rumblings, and vibrations. Their weakness is that they don't go into effect until the break-in attempt is already under way

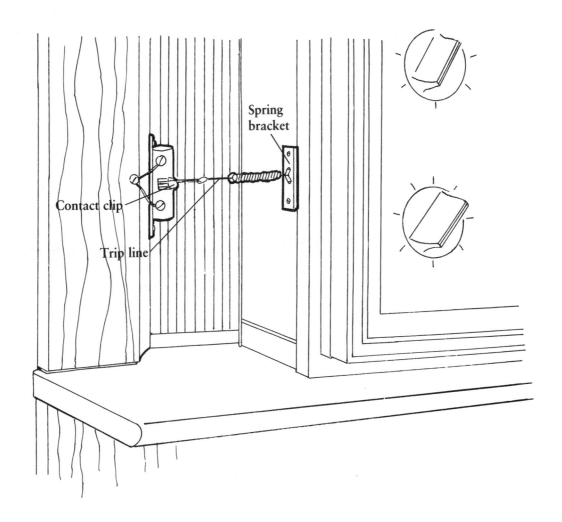

Figure 38   Typical air conditioner trip-wire alarm

or even completed. They are also vulnerable to attack by a professional burglar, who can operate silently, forcing the window, door, or lock, or even bypass them by cutting through the drywall of corridor doors in some multiple-dwelling buildings. In general, impressive as they are, these sensors are more appropriate for high-risk installations such as banks and jewelry exchanges than they are for ordinary houses and apartments.

Tamper Switches   A tamper switch is a sensor that protects the alarm system itself from attack. Tamper switches generally use a magnetic or mechanical plunger that transmits an alarm whenever any attempt is made to open or remove the casings around the master control unit, the alarm bell or siren, or the system's access panel. Tamper switches must be connected to twenty-four-hour circuits that permit them to sound the alarm even if the rest of the system has been turned off.

Tamper switches are also used as part of the regular perimeter and interior protection systems, including wired screens and space protectors. In this case, however, they should be hooked into the regular house circuits, and not the twenty-four-hour circuit, because you may need a shunt switch that allows you to handle the screen, for example, or to shut off one part of the house while the rest of the house stays armed, without running the risk of setting off the alarm.

INTERIOR SENSORS

Interior sensors, often referred to as "space protectors," are used as a second line of detection in case a burglar manages to get past the perimeter system that is your first line of defense. Valuable as they are, interior sensors are limited in that they can only detect an intruder after he has already breached the primary bastions of windows, locked doors, and perimeter alarms.

Interior sensors work on the principle that, once inside the house, the burglar has to pass through certain rallying points, passages, and stairwells to get to the parts of the house where the valuables are most likely to be found. Space protectors are designed to detect his movements as he passes through the house. A single space protector can cover a much larger area than one or even several perimeter sensors. In the more comprehensive systems a single interior sensor may be wired into the central control panel in much the same manner as perimeter sensors. But there are also many types of space protectors on the market that are convenient self-contained units no bigger than a cigar box. These can be plugged into a nearby electrical outlet, aimed, and adjusted to reflect the prevailing conditions of a specific house or apartment. Some of these self-contained units come with a convenient backup battery in case of power failure; others can be hooked up to turn on lights or lamps when the alarm is triggered. Because they are portable and relatively compact, self-contained units are probably the best choice for apartment dwellers who may be limited in the installation options available to them by the terms of a lease.

Protected Zones

In discussing interior sensors, the term "protected zone" is used to describe the area that a sensor can protect effectively. Some sensors provide beams that can fill almost the entire volume of a sizable room, bouncing back signals from the walls, floors, ceilings, and furniture simultaneously. Others project narrow or fan-shaped beams that are effective only within the sight lines of the beam, leaving whole areas in the room that are not protected by the sensors. For this reason, placement of sensors takes careful planning to make sure that the beam will at least cover the points where an intruder is most likely to pass once he has gotten inside the house. Most experts suggest corridors, hallways, stairways, and the approach to the master bedroom as areas that should be covered by the sensor's beam.

Features to Look For

A space protector can be either a component of an entire system (e.g., an infrared unit covering a hallway) and wired into the master control unit, or a totally self-contained "system." A good self-contained space protector can be expensive. Basic units start at seventy dollars and range up to $250; add-ons can boost the cost by an additional twenty dollars to $200, depending on what you choose. But whatever you pay for it, any good space protector, self-contained or otherwise, should have a loud interior alarm, and the following alarm controls:

Exit-entry delay controls. The regular control is designed to sound the alarm the instant any motion is detected. This is an important feature when the system is armed and you are in the house, because you want to be warned the minute an intruder steps across the beam; but it may be a nuisance when you are leaving or entering the house yourself. The better systems give you fifteen to twenty seconds to get out of the protected zone without triggering your own alarm, and the best ones permit you to adjust the timing to meet the unique layout or other conditions of your particular house.

Automatic cutoff and reset. This control shuts off the alarm signal after it has been triggered and a given amount of time has elapsed, then resets itself and is ready to sound again if the intrusion continues or another intrusion is attempted later on.

Testing capability. Since the normal levels of background sound, light, heat, and vibrations vary from house to house, the sensor must be adjusted to distinguish between these normal stimuli and those represented by an intruder. This requires a degree of fine-tuning, and to make the proper adjustments you should be able to test your system without setting off an alarm. A "walk test" feature permits you to shut down the alarm signal while you are adjusting the controls, with an LED light left to signal in place of the alarm itself for the duration of the test. By walking through the protected zone you are not only able to detect whether the sensor is working properly or not, but you can also define the limits and direction of the beam, and readjust it as you see fit.

Concealability. The unit itself should be as unobtrusive as possible. Some models come disguised as books, table lamps, or small hi-fi speakers. But because they have to be located where they can monitor the entire protected zone, interior space protectors cannot be hidden completely from sight.

Add-ons. The better all-in-one models have provisions for additional features which, although they may add to the cost, also add to the effectiveness of the basic model. Instead of the simple on/off toggle switch, for example, add-ons permit the unit to be activated or deactivated by either a key or a code punched into a keypad. Another add-on option is a terminal that permits the connection and powering of an external alarm, in addition to (or instead of) the built-in one. This feature is desirable in a large house or apartment when the built-in alarm might not be heard in another room or on a higher floor. Some models also have terminals which can accommodate remote on/off switches with a separate backup battery supply in case of power failure. Others have a memory capability in which a small indicator light turns on and stays on after the alarm has been triggered, to let you know that the alarm was activated while you were gone. And some units can even be hooked up to sound the alarm outside the house as well as inside.

With all these features loaded on, your interior sensor system is transformed into a complex central control unit requiring extensive wiring to remote alarms, access panels, and status indicators. For the money and effort involved in this kind of upgrading, though, you might want to rethink your project and consider using a conventional central-control-panel unit with wired or wireless remote sensors and alarms—including one which can also accommodate perimeter sensors and hookups to automatic dialers or a central alarm agency, described later in this chapter.

If the system you select has any degree of complexity, you should plan on an initial test period of up to two weeks. This is especially true for systems using space protectors. Even when a system is professionally installed, some subsequent fine-tuning is often required. It's best to give yourself and your family some time to adapt to living with the new system. During this test period the connection to outside agencies (i.e., police, central monitoring station) is disconnected, and the time-out period for the audible alarm set to its minimum. This will enable you to avoid false-alarm fines, if applicable, and the ire of local police and your neighbors.

Active Interior Sensors

There are many kinds of interior-space-protecting sensors on the market for home installations. All of them have been adapted for residential use from such high-security targets as military installations, banks, jewelry exchanges, and nuclear facilities. They come in two basic varieties, known as "active" and "passive." Active sensors project various kinds of waves (radio, sound, light, etc.) that fill the protected zone of the room and bounce back to the sensor continuously. As long as these waves remain undisturbed, the system stays in the nonalarm mode, but any movement through the protected zone triggers the alarm. Active sensors project ultrasonic or radarlike microwaves as well as beams of light aimed across passageways and reflected back to the sensor by mirrorlike devices. Passive space protectors, on the other hand, act only as receivers. They detect changes in such environmental constants as sound levels, temperature, movement, and air turbulence, and react to these changes by triggering the alarm.

Ultrasonic Detectors   Ultrasonic detectors are active sensors that transmit high-frequency sound waves inaudible to humans and most animals, then receive and interpret the signals that bounce back from the surrounding walls, ceilings, floors, and furniture. The pattern in which the waves are received is established as the normal pattern for a given environment, and as long as it remains steady and unchanged no alarm will sound. Any movement in the protected zone, however, automatically triggers the alarm.

Yet despite its sensitivity, there are ways to defeat this kind of sensor. For example, an ultrasonic detector will not react to very fast or very slow movements through its field, and it cannot pick up movements through solid objects at all. If an intruder ducks behind a large piece of furniture, for example, he will not be picked up by the beam, and sound-absorbing materials like upholstery, carpets, and draperies will lessen the system's overall sensitivity.

In addition, the sensitivity to movement and turbulence that is the hallmark of ultrasonic sensors can also be one of their major drawbacks, because it allows many perfectly innocent conditions to trigger the sensor into transmitting a false alarm. These include such everyday noises as a rattling door, a ringing telephone or doorbell, jangling keys, and mail dropping through a slot. In addition, turbulence caused by an air conditioner cycling on or intermittent gusts of air from a hot-air register can have the same effect. Other possibilities are electronic signals from another nearby detector, or from any source (like hi-fi components and TV sets) operating in the same frequency as the ultrasonic transmitter and within close range of the protected zone. Similarly, extremes of temperature and abrupt changes in humidity within the protected zone can also trigger the alarm.

These problems can be offset by careful placement and constant readjustment of the detector's beam, but an ultrasonic detector may need more attention than the average homeowner is willing to give it, and you should probably think seriously about getting another type of sensor if your home is subject to the sort of conditions that call for much fine-tuning on a day-to-day basis.

Microwave Detectors   Microwave detectors operate on the same principle as ultrasonic detectors. Instead of sound waves, though, the microwave transmitter sends high-frequency radio waves into the protected zone, and its receiver monitors the waves of reflected energy that bounce back from it. Once a steady pattern of wave feedback has been established and set for the environment of a specific protected zone, any movement through that zone will change the wave patterns and set off the alarm.

One advantage of microwave detectors is that the zone of protection can be shaped to fit almost any kind of area. By adjusting the microwave antenna, the beam can be made long and narrow for a hallway or wide and fan-shaped to cover a large room. Also, unlike ultrasonic waves, microwaves can penetrate wood, glass, and thin walls, although they will not go through metal or thick plaster walls. This ability to penetrate objects makes it possible for one sensor to extend its zone of protection to more than one room at a time. It also makes the sensor easier to conceal; microwave detectors can be hidden behind a solid wood partition or other nonmetallic objects or screens.

Microwaves vs. Ultrasonic Detectors   Microwave detectors are superior to ultrasonic ones in a number of ways. They are not set off by loud noises or disturbances in air turbulence or sudden temperature changes. They are not muffled by heavy rugs, upholstery, or drapes. When properly adjusted they will ignore the motion of small objects and pets, and respond only to the passage of large bulky objects in motion through their zone.

The secret of an effective microwave detector is the fine-tuning required to adjust the size and shape of the protected zone and limit the waves' penetration to objects and motions inside your home. Unless properly adjusted, a microwave can pass through a window or even a wall, and respond to a person or a car going by outside, or someone walking around in the next apartment. Microwaves can also be triggered by fluorescent lights, rotating fans, and radio transmissions operating at or near the sensor's frequencies. The fine adjustments required to get around these problems are probably beyond the average home handyperson's skills, and for this reason installation of a microwave sensor should be left to an experienced professional installer.

Photoelectric Beam Sensors   Another type of active detector is the photoelectric beam that projects a shaft of light between two points so that anything passing between those points triggers an alarm. Light from the transmitter is projected onto a photoelectric cell in the receiver, and this causes it to generate a current. When the flow of light is interrupted, the current stops flowing and the alarm is set off.

While some industrial models have a transmitter at one end of the protected zone and a separate receiver at the other, most models used for houses and apartments combine both the transmitter and its receiver in a single unit, with a mirrorlike reflector at one end to bounce the projected beam back to the electric eye at the other. It is even possible, by careful placement of additional reflectors, to bounce the photoelectric beam around corners and back again. And with a sufficiently dense placement of reflectors, a single beam can be bounced back and forth throughout the room to creat a latticelike barrier across the entire target area.

Some low-cost photoelectric beam sensors use a special filter to convert the beam's visible light into the infrared spectrum, where it is no longer visible to the naked eye. However, even converted infrared light can be defeated by an intruder shining his own light into the receiver as he steps across the beam. The solution to this problem is a beam that pulses, or flickers, at a predesignated rate, and is coded so that it can be recognized only by a given receiver. This pulsing, which can be set at the rate of up to 1,000 pulses per second, is extremely difficult to simulate. Recently a new light source in the form of a small solid-state device using an arsenide compound entered the market. It produces a pulsed beam of light in the infrared range and is currently being used for certain high-security installations. The advantage of this new entry is that both the transmitter and the receiver are small and therefore difficult to detect.

Photoelectric beams are not volume protectors: they cannot fill a room or a large space with detecting waves. Instead, they shoot a narrow beam of protection across some crucial passageway or area through which the intruder must pass if he wants to get to the rest of the house. They are therefore best suited to protect a narrow hallway, a stairwell, or the approach to a bedroom door. When used for interior protection they can also be set up with appropriate reflectors to cover an X- or Z-shaped barrier across a door or along a wall or bank of windows.

Careful and proper installation is the most important factor in the use of an infrared photoelectric detector. The unit must be properly placed and sharply focused. While adding additional reflectors can increase the thickness of the detection barrier, each added reflector also weakens the beam and increases the possibility of a false alarm. In earlier, steady-beam versions of infrared photoelectric detectors, the alarm could also be triggered by changes in background light or sunlight crossing the floor. On the whole, however, infrared detectors are not as susceptible to false alarms as other space protectors. Nevertheless, loose mountings, smoke, and dust can diffuse the beam or shift it, weakening the light projected back onto the electric eye and triggering the alarm.

In addition, a burglar can spot a reflector and trace its source back to the transmitter. With a puff of cigarette smoke blown across the door or passageway, the otherwise invisible beam hazes up and becomes visible—whereupon an intruder can crawl under the beam or step over it. For these reasons, the photobeam detector should be considered as a special-purpose detector, not as a substitute for perimeter alarms or for other, more efficient types of interior space alarms.

Passive Interior Sensors

Passive Infrared Detectors   The passive infrared space detector is probably the most effective interior space alarm on the market today. Passive infrared sensors are sensitive to rapid changes in temperature within the protected zone. All objects having a temperature above absolute zero (that is, above minus 273 degrees Centigrade) give off infrared radiations to a greater or less degree. This includes all the inanimate objects in the protected zone—walls, floors, ceilings, and furniture—which the sensor can be adjusted to accept as normal. The sensor is programmed to ignore gradual fluctuations in temperature that occur over the course of the day, like those from sunlight, air-conditioning, and winter heating systems. Instead, it reacts only when there is some rapid change in temperature caused by radiation emanating from the body of a person passing through the protected zone.

Passive infrared detectors do not generate or project their own radiation, but react to the radiation they receive from objects in the range of 98 degrees Fahrenheit, or normal human body temperature. The average infrared sensor can protect an area of about twenty by thirty feet, or a long narrow hall up to fifty feet in length. It will not penetrate walls, floors, ceilings, doors, or other solid barriers, so it cannot be set off by objects beyond its sight lines. In addition, it will not be set off by radiation from another detector, so that when two or more sensors are used to cover a very large field, there will be no false alarm where the covered zones overlap.

A passive infrared sensor is also unaffected by the various radio signals, air currents, sudden vibrations, or sharp sounds that plague other sensors. It is therefore almost completely free of false alarms.

Passive infrared detectors are one of the most popular sensors for use in interior-space protection. While they are frequently "hard-wired" into a central control panel, there are also many good self-contained units on the market at fairly reasonable prices. Because passive infrared sensors do not generate and project energy themselves, they use relatively little power and can run for long periods of time on batteries alone when normal house current fails. For this reason they are a good choice for locations where there are few or no electrical outlets. The batteries must still be checked periodically, but not nearly as frequently as with other types of battery-operated sensors.

Passive infrared sensors raise some special considerations, however. Care is required in positioning them. When the sensor is installed, it should not be pointed in the direction of objects subject to sudden heating like radiators, air conditioners, space heaters, or fireplaces. Nor should it be mounted where it will receive direct sunlight or the beam of car headlights at night. By the same token, it should not be mounted in the vicinity of a fan or air duct, because although the direct air current from such sources is unlikely to cause a false alarm, it will still tend to affect the detector's level of sensitivity over time. Also, if you aim the sensor high enough to avoid dogs and cats prowling their way through the room in the middle of the night, it may also theoretically give prowling burglars enough room to slide under it undetected (but only if they know exactly what they are looking for, first of all, and exactly where the projector is positioned as well).

Miscellaneous Interior Switches and Sensors

Pressure Mat Switches   In addition to the interior sensors, both active and passive, which are designed to cover a field of empty space, there are other, more specific indoor sensors that do the same job at key spaces like the threshold of a door. The pressure mat is a relatively inexpensive and reliable space protector, free from most of the glitches that trigger false alarms in more complex and wide-coverage systems. It can be used either as a doormat or as a plastic sheet that is installed under the carpeting or hall or stairway runners. The alarm device involves the use of "ribbon switches" that consist of two thin ribbons of metal, one on top of the other but intermittently separated by some form of insulation. For most residential purposes each switch is about three feet long, but can run to any length desired. The ribbon switches in a pressure mat run the length of the mat, parallel to each other and several inches apart. The switches are hooked into a normally open (NO) house-wiring circuit, but will not make contact unless a sufficiently heavy weight is applied to them. When and if that happens, the metal strips make contact, closing the circuit and triggering the alarm.

Pressure mat switches come as part of an assembly sealed between sheets of plastic that not only protect the electrical switches from moisture and wear and tear, but permit them to be installed unobtrusively under carpeting and other area rugs. Such sheets come in standard widths that can be fitted into most hallways and under most staircase runners. They also come molded into weatherproofed rubber doormats that can be placed at entranceways, and some of them are rugged enough for outdoor use as well. Sometimes referred to as pressure tapes, pressure switches also come in strips that are adjustable for protecting windowsills.

This type of intruder alarm is well suited for installation at entranceways, rooms, and passages where an intruder would be most likely to pass on his way into or through the house. While it can be adapted to fit large areas of floor space, it is best suited for small-space protection. Because pressure mats are fairly easily detected and disarmed, security experts say that they are best suited for places where you are more likely to be at risk from less skilled, impulsive burglars than from those more sophisticated and experienced. In addition, these mats have the defects of any installation that operates on normally open (NO) circuitry, in that they can be knocked out of the running simply by cutting the circuit itself.

In the pressure mat's favor is the fact that it is usually free from false alarms, because the weight that triggers it permits most pets to roam at will. Although the pressure mat usually operates on an NO circuit, it can be converted to an NC circuit to tie it in to the other normally closed components in the interior alarm system. It is therefore recommended as a good supplement to other interior and exterior sensors, but should probably not be used as your only interior protection device.

Trip-Wire Devices   The trip wire is one of the earliest entry-protection switches in operation, but its immediate visibility and easy dismantling limit its usefulness in most environments, and it has long since been replaced on the marketplace by more sophisticated sensors. Trip wires consist of a spring-loaded wire stretched across the door or path that an intruder would normally take after entering a house. The wire is hooked onto a fastening at one end, and to a spring-loaded switch at the other. The switch, when it is armed, is tied into an NC circuit, and any stretching, bumping, or disconnection of the wire causes the switch to trip, cutting off the flow of current and triggering the alarm.

Trip wires are relatively free of false alarms, but because they are visible they can easily be defeated by stepping over or crawling under them. Their most practical use is when they are connected to an air-conditioning unit installed in a window, or in a wall sleeve, where any attempt to remove the unit will trip the wire and trigger the alarm.

High-Tech Sensors and Point Protection   In addition to wide-ranging interior space protectors that cover a whole area or screen, there are many special stand-alone sensors available that send out an alert when specific items like safes, valuable paintings, or antiques are disturbed or even approached. One example is the so-called capacitance-proximity sensor. With this kind of stand-alone "point protector," the object to be protected is given a nonlethal electric charge, as one half of the system. The other half is the floor, which serves as a ground. Together the object and ground act as a tuned electric circuit. Capacitance sensors work in much the same way as the changes sometimes seen in TV reception when a person or some other electrically charged object comes close to the set or touches its antenna, interfering with its electric field and causing the image to waver. The sensor's range can be set for distances between one inch and several feet, and if an intruder comes anywhere within range of the protected object, his own body's electric charge alters the circuit and sets off the alarm. Other point-protection devices include adaptations of magnetic switches, pressure switches, and the whole range of interior sensors described above.

THE MASTER CONTROL UNIT

If the sensors are the eyes and ears of the alarm system, the master control unit is its heart and brain. The master control unit contains all the control equipment that makes the system work. Its basic purpose is to receive, monitor, and take action on the messages that feed through the circuits from its remote sensors and switches along your doors, windows, and walls. It also serves to convert the power from an external source, whether household current, battery, or both, and transform it into the voltage needed to operate the sensors, alarm signals, and other components of the system. The master control unit can also house a range of controls, status indicators, and status-adjustment buttons.

Control units range from the very simple systems that serve one or two intrusion-detection circuits connected to a local horn or siren, to far more comprehensive units with multiple circuits carrying out many additional functions including fire, panic, and medical emergency alarms—in addition to various mechanisms that protect the alarm system itself from any attempt to sabotage it.

While interior space protectors often come as self-contained units with their own controls and power sources, all perimeter alarm systems require a separate control unit that can accommodate a varying number of space sensors and integrate them into a single unified system. The level of security and the types of protection the master control unit provides can best be gauged by examining the number and type of circuits, switches, controls, and status indicators that it contains. A master control unit is usually housed in a metal box with its own door or lid, and looks much like an ordinary electric service box. Inside, the most basic and visible features of the unit are its circuit terminals—pairs of screws that anchor the wiring that leads to the sensors, the alarm, and the other components that the unit services.

Separate circuits are used to carry out separate functions, i.e., perimeter intrusion, space protection, fire and smoke detectors, etc. But in a large house or apartment there are often several circuits that perform the same functions but in separate areas of the house, dividing it into zones for that particular type of protection. Some circuits are electrically live in their nonalarm status, while others are only live when their sensors are triggered into the alarm state. Some independent circuits are designed to remain alert twenty-four hours a day to monitor fire sensors, panic switches, and attempts to defeat the system. Others go into action only when you arm them by pushing a button or flicking a switch at the control panel just inside the door.

Most master control units come with some potential for add-on features that can either be installed before you buy the system or put in at a later date. For this reason, it is probably preferable to install a unit that already has provisions for all the circuits, switches, and controls you may want to add in the future, once you become accustomed to living with the system. It makes sense not to close your options by buying a master control unit that will not handle any future upgrading.

Some of the features that you will want to look for in a master control unit are basic to any alarm system; others provide higher levels of security and convenience.

Switches

In addition to the regular arm/disarm switch (which may be a simple toggle switch, a key switch, or even a coded keypad), various switches, relays, and indicators can also increase the system's level of protection. Among them are the following:

Holding relay: This control is designed to keep an intruder from shutting off the alarm by closing the door or window behind him or running a jumper wire between the contacts once he has broken the glass. Once the sensor switch has triggered an alarm, this relay will continue to send the danger signal to the master control unit even though the switch or sensor has been immediately set back to its normal, nonalarm position by the intruder. In many systems, to make sure that only the owner can disarm the signal, it is necessary to punch a code into a keypad or use a special key to deactivate the signal and stop the alarm.

Manual abort rearm switch: This is used in a situation where the alarm has been triggered by mistake. By one simple flip of the switch the alarm is aborted, local alarms stop ringing, and the automatic holding relay is made inoperative. Later, by flicking the same switch to the opposite side, the entire system is rearmed. However, if any message has been sent to the automatic dialer in the course of the original false alarm, someone at the scene must be sure to call the dial-in center to explain that the alarm was triggered in error.

Automatic alarm cutoff: Most communities require an automatic cutoff built into the master control unit to prevent a local audible alarm from continuing endlessly. This relay will cut off the local alarm after some fixed period of time—anywhere from five to fifteen minutes, according to the setting required by local ordinances.

Delayed entry/exit circuits: Alarm system circuits should have a time-delay feature that lets you leave the house without the alarm being triggered, even after the circuits are actively armed. By the same token, the homeowner should have a brief period after entering the house to get to the cutoff switch and disarm the alarm before its sounds. Such delayed-action circuits are used to service sensors and switches at the main entrance to the house, and even the hallways leading to the entrance. Some delayed-entry circuits have fixed periods,

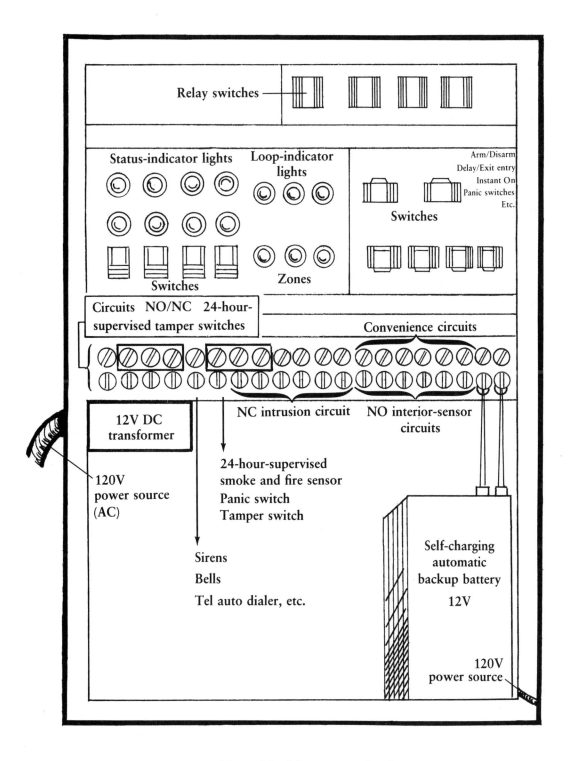

Figure 39   Master control unit

usually of between thirty or forty seconds, for you to get in or out of the house. Others have variable settings of up to a minute or so. These settings can and should be adjusted carefully to meet your specific level of patience or agility, and the distance between the arming switch and the exit door. Exit/entry delay features can be found on many self-contained interior sensor systems as well.

Instant-delay option switch: There are also times when the occupant wants the delayed action circuits to be inactivated temporarily, as for example when he is in the house and doesn't expect to be going out again anytime soon. An instant-option switch converts the delayed-action circuits to the instant-alarm mode, and lets the occupant go to sleep with the knowledge that any attempt at intrusion will set off an immediate alarm.

Automatic alarm rearmer: This device, which usually comes coupled with an automatic cutoff, serves to rearm the alarm system after it has been triggered and then automatically cut off. The disadvantage of this device is that if the switch or sensor is still in the alarm-signaling status, the alarm will go off again as soon as it is rearmed, and continue until a neighbor or the police respond and disconnect the audible alarm device.

Automatic alarm memory: This is usually an LED light that goes on when the alarm has been triggered. Even after the alarm has been shut off, as by an automatic cutoff, the indicator light will remain on to let the returning householder know that the alarm was triggered sometime during his absence. Such indicators remain on until they are manually reset at the master control unit. Sometimes these memory indicators are located at or very near the entrance to alert the returning householder that a break-in has occurred and that the intruder may still be on the premises.

Day/night option control: Most homeowners want the perimeter sensors to be armed at all hours of the day or night, but want only the interior sensors to be armed at night. The day/night option control, which is usually located in the master bedroom or the hall leading to it, gives the owner the option of arming and disarming interior sensors at the flick of a single switch.

Fire-protection circuit: In addition to intruder alarms, many comprehensive hard-wired security systems come with provisions for fire and smoke detection, too. A fire-protection circuit is a supervised twenty-four-hour circuit that will go on functioning as long as it is hooked up to a power source of some kind. Such circuits cannot be switched off, and all heat- or smoke-detecting sensors in the house should be hooked up to this circuit. In these systems, the local alarm is distinct from the intrusion alarm (it might ring a bell, for example, instead of sounding a siren). If the system includes a telephone dialer or digital-dialer hookup, the dialer will similarly distinguish between the fire and intruder alarm messages when it sends them out.

Twenty-four-hour circuit: As noted earlier in this chapter, not all twenty-four-hour circuits are NO. Some are NC, with power flowing continuously through the loop, so that the switches and sensors connected to the circuit will be armed even when the rest of the system is shut off. This type of circuit can be used for normally closed magnetic switches connected to valuable objects or paintings in point-protection alarms, and can even be used to provide protection to the covers and lids that protect alarm sirens, bells, and other exposed controls.

Supervised twenty-four-hour circuits: For sensors that operate on an NO circuit and are therefore on twenty-four hours a day, like fire and smoke sensors, panic switches, medical alerts, and tamper switches, any failure of the circuitry can have potentially disastrous, if not fatal, results. Nevertheless, a break or loose connection in the ordinary NO circuit can go undetected for hours. To forestall this possibility, a self-supervising feature can be built into the circuit itself. This feature monitors the NO circuit for breaks and loose connections by means of an end-of-line (EOL) resistor installed at the last sensor on the circuit. An EOL resistor permits a weakened electric current to trickle continuously through the circuit. Too weak to trigger an alarm, it is just strong enough to signal the master control unit that the circuit is intact. When some break interrupts the current running through his loop, the master control sends out a signal (usually a buzzer or flashing light) that calls attention to the condition.

On the other hand, if the sensor is triggered by a fire, the NO circuit operates as it normally would. The switches close, and a much stronger current flows through the loop, signaling the control unit to send the appropriate alarm. Most acceptable, comprehensive master control units provide for such a separate alarm circuit to serve fire sensors, plus one or two other independent circuits for tamper switches and panic alarms.

Status indicators: These visible signal lights are used to indicate the status of the alarm system and its various circuits, zones, detectors, and power sources. For the sake of clarity, different colored lights (LED) are usually used for this purpose—i.e., green if all the sensors are secured and the system is ready to be armed; red if the system is armed; and amber if the system is in a test status. If the green light doesn't go on it may be an indication that a door or window has not been properly closed, and a reminder that the condition must be corrected before the system can be armed.

Alarm status lights can be found on the door or lid of the master control unit, and also on some access panels near the doors or at remote control panels like those in master bedrooms. Status-indicator lights are often installed near windows or doors that have been equipped with shunt (shut-off) switches, as a reminder that the sensor at that spot has been deactivated. Master control panels may have a whole series of lights, flags, or even audible beeps or buzzers to spell out the status of specific zones, controls, and even individual sensors throughout the house. Lights and beepers are used to indicate low-battery status of battery-powered sensors as well as that of the backup battery used in a hard-wired system. Some automatic dialers come equipped with status indicators of their own.

Hybrid control units: There are some self-contained interior-space protector units that, in addition to providing all controls, power source, and alarm capability for the principal infrared or ultrasonic sensors, also have the capacity to serve as a master control unit for other add-on components as well. A growing number of systems on the market come equipped with several extra terminals, which enable them to accept such additional features as a perimeter sensor circuit, an external on/off switch, external alarm devices, and even an automatic telephone dialer. Such a hybrid unit may be all that a small apartment needs, and can be installed by the average home handyperson.

Emergency alarms: In addition to the sensors and switches that automatically detect an intrusion or other emergency condition in their field, there are also a wide range of alarms and transmitters that are manually operated and allow the occupant the option of immediately transmitting the alarm himself in an emergency situation. These push-button devices are connected to twenty-four-hour supervised circuits so that they will operate even if all the other alarms are turned off. They can send a local alarm signal to scare off an intruder or call for emergency medical help, and they can also activate and transmit special messages through an automatic telephone dialer or digital hookup to summon aid. They can be installed at fixed locations around the house and hard-wired into the master control unit, or can be hand-carried or worn as wireless portable transmitters sending their messages through a receiver at the master control unit.

Panic switches: These switches are for use in such emergency situations as when an intruder rings the front door bell and starts to push his way in, or when you suddenly hear the unmistakable sounds of a prowler either inside or outside the house. Situations like this call for immediate alarms, and you should therefore have a switch as close by your bed, front door, or favorite chair as possible. Panic buttons can either trigger a local alarm outside your house to alert neighbors and/or passing cars, or they can be hooked up to an automatic telephone dialer that transmits the message to a police or central control station. Ideally, there should be at least two fixed panic buttons in every house: one at the front door, and the other close to the head of the bed in the master bedroom so that you can reach it without getting out of bed. (If you don't have a panic button beside the front door and are the victim of a push-in, the next best advice is to push past the intruder and run to the nearest neighbor, yelling to summon help.)

Panic switches come in hard-wired and wireless versions, and add-on radio signal receivers can allow you to carry a wireless receiver all over the house. Wireless panic transmitters are similar in size and shape to the remote control devices used in many TV sets. They can be carried into the yard and cellar, but like all such transmitters their range is limited and there can be metal blocks to direct-line-signal transmission. Panic-alarm circuits can be found on even modestly priced master control units. Panic buttons are such important features of any security system that they should probably be viewed as a necessity, not just another add-on option. In larger houses, in addition to the front door and the master bedroom, there should be additional panic buttons at other easily accessible locations.

Medical alert buttons: These are special-purpose panic buttons with automatic-dialer connections to a doctor's office, a trusted relative or neighbor, or a hospital, as well as or instead of an immediately audible local alarm. Medical alerts are high-priority items when some member of the household suffers from a chronic condition that may require immediate medical response. If that person lives alone or spends long hours alone in the house, pressing the alarm will activate the telephone dialer or digital hookup to call the appropriate number with some pre-recorded message. Medical alert buttons can even be programmed to summon the local paramedic ambulance service, depending upon local ordinances. A wireless transmitter that the owner can wear or carry around is preferred for this purpose.

Remote Controls

Living with an alarm system can be uncomfortable and inconvenient. Without an accessible remote-control unit to activate and deactivate the system, every time you want to turn it on or off you would have to go to the master control unit, which is usually concealed at some locked and purposely out-of-the-way location. By installing remote control units at convenient locations throughout the house, the user can arm and disarm the system at the most frequently used doors, at the master bedroom, and at convenient windows or doors that can be disarmed occasionally without disarming the whole system in the process.

Access Panels   Access panels in convenient places allow you to control the alarm system at the door or doors you use most when entering or leaving the house. The access control unit is therefore best mounted within close range of the door and connected to a time-delay control, so that you can switch it on, set the controls, and make your way out the door with twenty or forty-five seconds to spare before the alarm is armed. The access control unit works much like a wall switch for overhead lights except that it is either operated by a key or a coded digital keypad, which usually permits the owner to change the code at will.

Outside Access Panels   A few homeowners opt for an outside access control unit because of its presumed convenience and because it does not require a time delay to operate the door's switch. But these conveniences are easily outweighed by the disadvantages of such placement. Outside access control units are not only exposed to the weather but are vulnerable to attack by intruders. If key-operated they should be mounted high enough on the exterior wall to make it difficult for the burglar to pick the lock—but this will make them equally hard for the legitimate homeowner to reach. If the panel is controlled by a keypad, the installation should include a hood to prevent an outsider from reading the code while it is being punched in. All access control units should have their protective covering plate equipped with a tamper switch to set off the alarm if an intruder attempts to remove the plate and jump the wires.

Additional Features   Some access control units serve as mini–master control units in that they also have status indicators (LEDs) that not only report on the status of the door's alarm switch but on that of the entire system. (Status lights are not recommended for outside access control units.) The indicator lights also serve as a convenient reminder to disarm the system when entering, and rearm it when exiting the house. Some units use an audible beeper or buzzer as a reminder.

Shunt Switch   A shunt switch is a simple form of access control unit. It is used to take a particular alarm sensor, or switch, out of the coverage of the main system without turning off the other switches or sensors in the circuit. By installing a shunt switch beside a door or window, that particular exit can be opened while the rest of the house is still on alarm status. This kind of arrangement can come in handy when you expect a lot of coming and going on a busy weekend or during a party, and don't want to have to disarm and rearm the whole system every time you let someone in the house. The same thing applies to a window that you may want to use for ventilation—assuming the screen is protected by a sensor alarm of its own. Shunt switches should be key-operated and have an indicator light to remind you to reset the alarm when you leave the house or turn in for the night. Shunt switches are sometimes installed outside the house or on a garage door as a simple, convenient access control unit. If so, they should have the same protection as other outside mounted access-control units.

Bedside Control Units   For convenience and safety it is probably a good idea to have a mini-control unit beside the bed in the master bedroom. This allows you to keep an eye on the status of the alarm system all over your house or apartment and activate the interior sensors' circuits from your bedside. In the morning you can deactivate the space sensors so that you and other members of the family can walk around without setting off the alarm. Bedside control units can also include a panic button, fire alert, and medical alert. Having these controls at bedside makes the usual "countdown" procedures unnecessary and greatly improves the overall comfort and convenience of living with an alarm.

ALERTING DEVICES

After you have pushed the panic button, or a burglar has tried to jimmy your door or break your window, the alerting device—which we will call the alarm—takes over. This is the voice of the system, and it should be a formidable one.

Alarm devices can be wailing sirens, clanging bells, ear-rending beeps, or flashing lights. These signals act both as a beacon for responding police and/or as a hue and cry designed to send the intruder running. In more sophisticated systems, the alarm signal will also silently cause an automatic phone dialer to send out a pre-recorded message to the appropriate monitoring agency. In fact, alarms can do almost anything you want them to, according to the type you select and the service you want it to perform.

Local Alarms

The local alarm, whether a siren, horn, light, or bell, is the basic first-line attention-getter, sending out the message that someone is trying to break in and alerting everyone in the vicinity to what is taking place. At the same time (and perhaps most important of all), it lets the intruder know that he has been detected and that he is in danger of getting caught if he doesn't leave the premises fast. The so-called silent alarms that advise a distant response agency—police or private—that a break-in is occurring may be good for banks and jewelry stores where the prime purpose is to apprehend the thief and recover the property; but they should never be the only kinds of alarm triggered in a residential break-in. The homeowner's major concern is not just to bring a criminal to justice; it should be first and foremost to scare the intruder away before he has done any harm, and summon help from neighbors and local police.

In free-standing houses, local alarms should be installed both inside and outside the house. An interior alarm lets the occupant know what is happening in distant parts of the house, but it is seldom loud enough to be heard on the outside, and may therefore have a minimal deterrent effect on a burglar once he is already in the house. Some self-contained interior sensor units have built-in alarms that lead the intruder straight to their mounting sites, where they can easily be muffled or disabled. It is almost impossible to totally conceal an alarm device inside a house, especially if you really want it to be heard. The best place to mount an interior alarm is in some central location from where it can be heard throughout the house, and some experts suggest putting it in a corner where the walls meet the ceilings, both for better resonance and for relative inaccessibility by anyone trying to dismantle it. Interior alarms should also be located at some distance from the concealed master control unit, so that finding the first doesn't lead the intruder automatically to the second. In addition to sounding an audible alarm, the system can also be set to turn on specific lights inside the house and trigger a bank of outside floodlights as well; this often requires additional electrical work.

Even more important than an interior alarm in most free-standing houses is the outside alarm, because it can do both jobs at once. An outside alarm should be mounted high enough to be out of reach of the intruder, and facing outward for maximum hearing range on the street. It should be enclosed in weatherproof and tamper-resistant enclosures, because a sophisticated burglar's first line of attack may be to muffle or disable the outside alarm. The lids to such enclosures should have tamper switches hooked up to a twenty-four-hour circuit. All the exposed wiring from the master control unit should be shielded with armored conduits, or at least disguised as ordinary electrical wiring. The best location for an outside alarm is on the street side, under the eaves or at the gables of the house.

Horns, Sirens, Bells

The sound of the alarm should be as loud as possible. It should be almost painful to the ears, and audible for a distance of at least 400 feet. Soundmakers are rated by their decibel levels. A 110-decibel (dbl) scale reading is the very minimum for an outside noisemaker, but 120 is better. Another option is to use several lower-decibel noisemakers to achieve the overall decibel level of a single more powerful one; but the rule is fewer and louder, rather than many with a lesser decibel rating.

Of all the noisemakers currently on the market, bells are the least satisfactory because they are the most vulnerable to tampering. However, bells are still good choices for fire alarms, since there is no threat to the alarm itself by an intruder during a fire emergency.

For burglar alarms, warbling sirens are the preferred noisemakers, and electronic sirens are better than motor-driven ones, since they require less power and will cause less of a drain on the power supply when sounding, especially if the electric power has been interrupted and the system is forced to go onto backup battery power. Many electronic sirens can emit two distinctive sounds, one for burglary and another for fire. (There is no standard as to which sound should be used to indicate which condition.)

Shut-off Features   Almost all communities now require audible alarms to have a built-in feature that shuts them down after some fixed period, with or without an automatic alarm rearmer. Some communities even restrict the decibel level of the audible alarms to no more than 110 dbls measured at a distance of 100 feet. Cutoff time and permissible decibel levels may be mandated by local ordinances and should be checked with your local city or township jurisdiction before you install the alarm.

Lights as Alarms

While indoor and outdoor lights can deter burglars by making the house look occupied and minimizing the areas outside the house where prowlers can hide, they can also be part of the local alarm system as well. Interior lights and outside floodlights that are synchronized to go off at the same time as the audible alarm will probably scare off the average burglar and represent attractive add-on features to a comprehensive perimeter alarm system. They can also be set to flash on and off, alerting the neighbors and guiding the police and other helpers to the exact location of the break-in, which may otherwise be hard to determine from the street. A flashing strobe light or a rotating beacon connected to the twenty-four-hour circuit, much like the lights on the top of most police radio cars, is a good local alarm device and a useful beacon for emergency personnel responding to the scene.

REMOTE ALARM TRANSMITTERS
AND TELEPHONE DIALERS

All the audible alarms, strobe lights, and flashers in the world will be of little use in a remote location where the nearest neighbor may be some miles or acres away, out of the hearing range of the alarm. Even if there are neighbors close by, they may either not hear the alarm or mistake it for a passing ambulance or prowl car. Neighbors may not want to have anything to do with a crime in progress and may simply ignore whatever signals the alarm is sending out.

For these situations, another way to summon help is through a direct hookup to a neighbor, a relative, a central monitoring service, or even to the police themselves. Although most police departments will not accept direct-line connections to residential alarms because of physical limitations on available telephone lines and personnel, not to mention the extremely high frequency of false alarms, some will set aside a few telephone circuits to accept calls dialed in from automatic telephone dialers. These telephone connections are not on the usual emergency 911 circuits and will not guarantee as immediate a response as a first-person call-in would, but they should bring a response.

There are two basic types of automatic telephone dialers used to transmit intrusion and other emergency alarm messages. The most widely used is the one that dials the number of people or agencies selected by the homeowner, and transmits a pre-recorded taped voice message over regular telephone lines to the pre-programmed number designated by the homeowner. The other is the more sophisticated digital dialer, or "digital communicator," which transmits electronic impulses over an ordinary telephone line, for decoding at a central alarm station staffed twenty-four hours a day by people trained to take appropriate action on the messages they receive.

Taped-Message Automatic Dialers

An automatic telephone dialer can send messages to the emergency response numbers of police, fire departments, and medical agencies, or to anyone you choose at any telephone number programmed into the dialer. A good dialer's taping system will accept up to four or five telephone numbers and will dial them in the sequence you select. If one number is "busy" it will go on to the next and then redial the passed-over number and go on dialing it until it connects. The dialer is designed to transmit its message as soon as the sensor is activated. As noted earlier, it can also be activated by a manually operated panic or medical emergency button.

A good automatic dialer will have at least two sending channels, each one capable of sending out a different message. In typical systems, one channel is usually connected to the intrusion-detector circuit and is designed to send out a burglary-in-progress message to police or other responders. The other is usually hooked up to a fire sensor and sends out the emergency message to the local fire department. Panic buttons may be hooked up to the same channel as the intrusion alarm, but often have their own channels and messages. With enough channels, a good dialer can alert anyone you select for any kind of emergency situation that a sensor can detect, including a breakdown in the heating system, a power failure, flooding, etc.

Automatic telephone dialers are priced at about $100 for one with limited features. Models with many features can cost from three to five times as much. But in addition to the kind and number of features to be chosen, there also is the problem of durability and reliability to consider. While there are a few reliable and inexpensive auto dialers (Radio Shack's Duofone Sensor Alert, as reported in the July 1988 issue of *Consumer Reports*, lists for $100 and was judged reliable), there are many inexpensive and unreliable models on the market, and when they are improperly programmed or installed they may malfunction or simply fail to function at all, giving the homeowner a false sense of security that could be disastrous in an actual break-in or other emergency. If you are going to upgrade a local alarm system by adding an automatic telephone dialer, it may pay to avoid the flimsier models with limited features and limited reliability, and install the best that you can possibly afford.

Features to Look for in a Good Telephone Dialer

Multiple channels: The dialer should have at least two input-output channels, so that it can handle at least two different taped messages. The input can come from the intrusion circuits and transmit the break-in message to the police, central station, or agency of your choice, while the other channel is hooked up to the fire alarm circuit and transmits its emergency message to the local fire department dispatcher. Check local ordinances for any restrictions.

Backup battery and charger: Although a dialer is usually located close to the master control unit, it should have its own independent power supply, such as a backup battery. The battery should have its own battery charger as well as a "low charge" status indicator.

Line seizure: When a dialer receives an alarm signal, the line-seizure feature will override all other extensions on the line, allowing the dialer to transmit its alarm message without interference from ordinary incoming or outgoing telephone conversations. This feature can also prevent a burglar from tying up the line by taking an extension off the hook.

Line release: This is an antijamming feature, which cuts off all incoming calls and frees up the line for use by the dialer. It can also prevent the burglar from defeating the dialer by calling in from the outside.

Dialer abort: Automatic dialers generally have a few seconds' delay between the time the alarm signal is received and the dialer begins to transmit its messages. This will allow the householder to abort the message in case the alarm was tripped accidentally. The abort switch should be key-operated and located at a concealed but easily reached location.

Multi-call capacity: This permits the dialer to make several different and successive calls for each channel, to make sure that the alarm message is delivered to at least one of the responders on its list.

Redial capacity: When the dialer encounters a busy signal, it will go on to the other numbers in the series and then return and redial the busy number and keep redialing it until it has reached someone at the other end of the line.

Automatic reset: This resets the dialer to its original standby status as soon as the appropriate alarm messages have been delivered.

Fire-channel override: Since a fire message takes precedence over any other kind of emergency and a dialer can transmit only one type of message at a time, this feature will stop the transmission of another alarm message and switch over to the fire tape automatically. Once the fire call has gotten through, the override will return to any other message the system may have been triggered to deliver.

Telephone line monitor (or cut-line detector): This monitor is a sensor that operates on a constant-"on" circuit so that the line monitor stays on whether the dialer is activated or not. It measures the continuous low voltage on the telephone line twenty-four hours a day. If the line is cut, even though that line can no longer transmit messages, the line monitor itself will still trigger the local audible alarm. Although this feature may be available as a separate sensor hooked into the regular alarm system's twenty-four-hour circuit, it is also a standard feature of most good-quality telephone dialers. Its major drawback is that it can trigger the alarm message and send a false alarm when there is a line failure caused by some perfectly natural or accidental condition, which occurs surprisingly (and frustratingly) often.

High-voltage circuitry protection: Telephone lines generally carry a low fifty-volt current. There is thus a possibility that a bolt of lightning can cause a power surge to back up into the line and thus knock out the telephone dialer connected to it. High-voltage circuitry protection keeps the dialer's circuits cut off from the regular telephone lines, switching on only when activated by an emergency signal.

Listen-in device: This is a form of "bug" that permits the person on the other end of the line to listen for any sounds of intrusion in the house after an alarm is triggered. Intruder bugs will activate when the number is dialed from an outside line, permitting the homeowner or central alarm service to check the house periodically by phone. This bug should have a cutoff switch for use when the family is at home and wants full telephone privacy.

Testing devices: Since a dialer should be tested regularly to see if it is functioning properly, it should have a test switch that will cut it off from the alarm and permit testing of the message's content and clarity through a built-in speaker.

Taping the messages: The typical alarm message can run up to forty seconds or a minute, like the pre-recorded message on an answering machine. The numbers to be called are recorded as electronic blips that activate the dialing feature when the intrusion or emergency sensor checks in. The dialer will transmit the same message to each of the three or more numbers on the channel. A longer tape will accept more numbers, but each channel can accept only its own message for the telephone numbers in its own series.

A typical message may go something like this: "This is a recorded emergency message. A burglary is in process [or a fire has broken out] at the home of [give your name] at [your address and/or apartment number if you live in a multiple-dwelling unit]. Please send the police [or fire department] immediately." The subscriber then repeats the address, or the whole message if there is room on the tape for it. Of course a medical-alert message has to be tailored to the medical needs and specifics of the patient, and the type of medical response required. As mentioned earlier, special-purpose messages require their own input and output channels, unless they are sent to a central alarm station that sorts out all incoming messages and relays the responses to the appropriate agencies.

Locating and Securing the Tape Dialer   Like a master control unit, the tape dialer should be in a concealed location, preferably in a cabinet secured by a key or a digital keypad. It should operate silently so as not to reveal its location to the prowler. Tape dialers need access to telephone lines and to house electrical current. They can usually be plugged into a regular telephone jack, although sometimes permission from the telephone company may be required and special jacks may be needed for such features as line seizure or listening-in devices. When the dialer has a line-seizure feature it should not be used on a party line, because the line seizer can block access to the other parties on the line.

Most telephone dialers come with explicit instructions for programming and installation, but few homeowners have the skills required for this kind of installation—in fact, many professionals may not be up to the job either. With a telephone dialer you are moving into a higher level of technology and protection, at considerable additional cost. Under the circumstances, installation and programming should probably be left to the best professional installer that you can afford.

Some police and fire departments will not respond to taped messages because of their notoriously high incidence of false alarms. In addition, some communities have specific ordinances forbidding the use of dialers that place calls directly to those lines, or at best they give relatively low priority to taped messages of any kind. It therefore pays to check with police or fire departments in your area before programming their numbers into your dialer. Check with the telephone company, too, to see if they have any restrictions or requirements for automatic-dialer use. Keep in mind, too, that if you rely on this system and the phone line is cut, no message can go out until the line is repaired.

If police and fire departments do have restrictions for automatic-dialer messages, the homeowner will probably have to rely upon some independent agency to receive the message and relay it on to police or firemen. For a fee, a central alarm station will assume responsibility for taking action on your message and verifying it with a callback before alerting the appropriate authorities. However, there are two kinds of so-called dial-in systems, the first (and most primitive) being operated from an actual telephone dialer, the second using an electronic message relayed by a digital telephone dialer. Most reputable central alarm agencies will not service automatic voice-taped dialing systems when the message is relayed from a regular dial phone, preferring the more efficient and reliable digital dialers for message communication and verification.

Digital Dialers

By opting for a digital dialer, the residential alarm user has moved into state-of-the-art alarm protection. Digital-dialer communication systems are leased from the central alarm station agency or alarm company, and all alarm messages, other than local, stand-alone alarms, are transmitted through it.

Like the automatic taped-message telephone dialer, the digital dialer sends its messages over ordinary telephone lines. But instead of sending a pre-recorded voice message, the digital dialer uses electronic impulses sent directly over the wires to spell out the information coming from your house. These impulses are in turn received and decoded by a compatible receiver at the central station. When an alarm signal is received at the master control unit in your house, the digital dialer automatically exercises its line-seizure capability and transmits a digitally coded message to a receiver at the central alarm station. Electronically, the receiver acknowledges contact and receipt of the message, and displays it on a computer screen, with or without a printout. The operator at the central station will then wait a brief while for a cancel call or an abort signal before sending out the alarm and relaying other messages to the police or fire department. Some central stations make verification calls to the premises.

In case of a message from a panic-button, intruder-warning, or medical-emergency alert, the procedures are similar. The operator will first call your house to make sure it isn't a false alarm. If there is no answer he will proceed to alert the appropriate authorities and notify anyone else on your pre-programmed list. The operator will then log in the time of the message, its contents, and the times and nature of subsequent follow-up activities for the operator's own records—and yours. In addition, depending on the terms of your contract, some companies will dispatch uniformed security guards to your house to determine what—if anything—is going on.

Digital dialing systems have many features, including listening-in capability, line monitoring, automatic reset, and others. Digital dialers send out a twelve-digit signal. The first seven digits connect with the central station; the next three are to identify the protected subscriber; the last digits act as a suffix to identify the type of message according to classification and priority. For example, on any given system a number-one priority usually indicates a fire alert; number two is for a panic alarm; number three would be for a medical alert; and number four for intrusion. The digital dialer also has an override capacity so that it can bump a lower-priority message in favor of a higher one.

Digital dialers can be used to monitor a greater variety of messages than a taped automatic telephone dialer can, and because of their ability to transmit messages back to the original dialing mechanism, they have often been referred to as digital communications systems. They have the capacity to cross-check the incoming message by requiring the dialer to transmit the status information twice for each message transmitted. The successive messages are then compared electronically and must be the same before the central station will accept them as valid. This cuts down on false alarms caused by some electronic quirk in the line. Since the messages are transmitted in binary digital code, such verification takes no more than three or four additional seconds, and is well worth the time it takes in terms of added reliability.

Because of these features and the scrupulous verification and cross-checking of incoming messages, police and fire departments will often accept messages relayed from reputable central-station services that use digital communication solely, and give them an immediate response with a 911 priority. However, it pays to remember that even with a 911 priority, actual response time may depend on other factors, such as the patrol car's distance from the scene, higher priority calls, and backlogs of other calls.

In addition to burglar alarms, digital dialers and central-response stations can also monitor a wide variety of other emergency and environmental conditions (flooded basement, low battery, too cold, etc.) as long as there are appropriate sensors, circuits, and channels to handle the traffic. And for additional fees, an armed-guard response can be provided, with inspection of the inside of the house permitted only when the agency's guards are accompanied by the regular police.

Other Message-Transmission Systems

There are many other ways to relay alarm messages—through dedicated leased lines, for example, as well as radio transmission, and most recently by using cable-TV lines. Radio transmitters located at the subscriber's premises transmit coded signals similar to those used in digital dialers, and can also transmit commands to a central station. The weakness of such systems is that in most cases they operate only within prevailing line-of-sight distances, so that even with high antennas at both the home and central station they can transmit only over a certain distance, depending upon many variables. Signals can also be blocked by large objects like tall buildings and hills. Leased telephone lines from the home to the central station are another option; but they involve high installation costs, sometimes running into thousands of dollars depending on the distance involved, as well as high rental costs that can run to several hundred dollars a month.

For this and other reasons digital dialers appear to offer the best dial-in transmission system for the money. Most insurance companies will not insure against theft or fire at commercial establishments that use voice-taped message dialers, although they will accept them for residential installations. And because of negative feedback about nondigital dial-in messages from local police jurisdictions, many homeowners have also opted for digital dialers as the most efficient alternative to simple local alarms—a trend that should appease the numerous security experts who have come to regard taped-message dialers with disdain.

CENTRAL-STATION ALARM-MONITORING SERVICES

Although you may not have the option of a direct automatic telephone tie-in to the local police, you can come close by subscribing to a central-station alarm-monitoring service. A homeowner or apartment resident who subscribes to a central-station alarm-monitoring service has taken the first step toward making sure that someone, somewhere, knows he is in trouble, has received the alarm signal to that effect, and is bound by contract to act on it. This type of service is invaluable where police will not accept messages from automatic telephone dialers, and it is absolutely essential if the house is located in some secluded or isolated area where the owner cannot depend on nearby neighbors to respond.

A central station is usually a commercially operated communication center, and acts on much the same principle as a round-the-clock telephone answering service, receiving and monitoring alarm messages and information from many individual subscriber alarm systems twenty-four hours a day. Staffed with specially trained personnel, and operating in a well-guarded and secure location, central alarm-response agencies offer a wide range of services, depending on the fee paid.

At the least expensive end of the scale the central station agrees to receive the dialed-in alarm from the subscriber's automatic telephone dialer and send the message on to the police, fire department, or other designated responder—a service which might cost anywhere from twelve dollars to thirty-six dollars a month at current prices. At the high end of the scale, services run to constant monitoring of the premises with audio detectors, callback or on-site screening for false alarms, and on-site response by armed security personnel. This kind of service could easily run to several hundred dollars a month.

Choosing a Response Agency

Some considerations are unique to the selection of a central alarm-response agency. For example, some may be located too far away to provide a quick on-site response; a number of agencies operate by WATS lines from other states, and use the same lines to make notifications to local police and emergency personnel. Others will accept subscribers only if they or their affiliates have installed the alarm equipment themselves, and still others will not accept subscribers unless the system has at least been professionally installed.

Check the reputation of the central alarm-response service with your local police, Better Business Bureau, and governmental consumer affairs agencies. Check with neighbors who have used the service, too; find out if their experience was satisfactory. Most of the well-known and long-established services can be trusted, especially if they are members of professional security associations. You should avoid fly-by-night services without credentials or track records, no matter how modest their fees and extravagant their claims. You are putting your possessions and possibly your life into their hands; it pays to do your homework carefully.

When you are shopping for a central response station, you don't want someone with a history of breaking the law to know all the ins and outs of your dial-in security system, and one of the first questions to ask is whether the station's personnel are screened for prior criminal records. In the same vein, are the employees bonded? Does the central agency carry sufficient liability insurance to cover you if some accident occurs on your property if and when they make an on-site response to a break-in?

Other checkpoints refer to the usual legal boilerplate. At a bare minimum, for example, will the service describe the terms and conditions for their services in a clearly written agreement? Are they licensed as an alarm and/or guard service? Underwriters' Laboratories, Inc., inspects and grades central alarm services that apply for certification, and grades them according to their equipment, personnel, and response time. Their AA rating is the highest; C is lowest. There are some perfectly reputable and reliable services that for reasons of their own do not choose to be listed or rated by UL; but such a rating is a definite plus for the agency. Unfortunately, you may find that you have little choice in which central response station you use. The majority of alarm companies use major central-station agencies and receive a percentage of the fees for having you, the user, connect with them. Inquire if this is the case and, when it is, apply the same criteria outlined above to judge the quality of the agency. If you are not satisfied by the prospects, go to a different alarm company.

In arranging with an alarm company for central-station monitoring, you should know if the company does its own work or subcontracts for this service. Check their track record. Ask how many accounts they serve, how many employees are on duty around the clock, and where the facility is located.

FALSE ALARMS

According to the New York State Office of Crime Prevention, false alarms (or "nuisance alarms," as they are called in the trade) account for more than 90 percent of all burglar alarms received by law-enforcement agencies. Because of the high rate of false alarms, police officials tend to have mixed feelings about the value of residential burglar alarms. While recognizing their deterrent, detective, and alert value, the police are also outraged at the number of unnecessary calls that these alarms engender.

Most false alarms are easily preventable. The New York State Office of Crime Prevention says that among the factors substantially contributing to this problem, by far the greatest is user error and negligence. Many residential users fail to lock their own doors and windows before turning on the alarm system. Or they or some other member of the household will enter a secured area before an activated alarm has been turned off. Another practice that is particularly galling to police is the habit of "testing" the alarm to see if the police will actually respond, and if so, how quickly.

Following a close second to user error as a cause of false alarms is poor installation and defective equipment. While normal wear and tear can always be expected in any mechanical or electronic system, a regular schedule of inspection and testing should indicate a poor connection or the need for corrective maintenance. Professional installers and burglar alarm specialists can obviously be held to acceptable installation and maintenance standards by licensing, regulation, and inspection by regulating agencies. But this may not be of much help to the homeowner who purchases his equipment through catalogues and retail outlets, and whose knowledge and skills may hardly be up to the level of installing a complex alarm system.

Because the police so often bear the brunt of false alarms, they feel that the only way to control do-it-yourself alarm installations is through local ordinances, penalties, and fines. As a result, many jurisdictions have enacted such ordinances. Some require an installation permit and an inspection certificate to assure that various building and safety codes have been observed. Others require a license or some kind of annual "user's fee" for any alarm system that is designed to elicit a direct police response. Permits may stipulate that they will be revoked automatically after a certain number of false alarms, and almost all major jurisdictions have regulations stipulating that no tape-dialer type of alarm can be programmed to dial the police or fire emergency numbers in the area. Sanctions for chronic false alarms include an escalating schedule of fines and the institution of public-nuisance suits—or, as a final blow, the threat that there will no longer be any police response to an alarm at the offending location. Ordinances like these are currently in effect in New York, Denver, Seattle, San Jose, and Pasadena, California.

While a reputable professional installation and/or burglar-alarm service company will or should want to comply with local regulations, one of their most valued services is the actual instruction they give you in the proper usage of the system and in regular servicing of the system once it is installed. If the system is a do-it-yourself project, you should make sure you are not only minutely knowledgeable about the way the system works but are also aware of the various permits and licenses you may have to get and the regulations you may have to comply with, as well as your jurisdiction's overall policy in responding to alarms. You should also train yourself to inspect and test the system according to a regular, perhaps bimonthly, schedule. Above all, you should make it a point to instruct all members of the family and any houseguests in the proper use of the system and ways to shut if off when returning to the house or moving into a protected area from an unprotected one.

SOME FURTHER REMINDERS

Telling the Neighbors

It is always a good idea to tell your immediate neighbors that you have installed an alarm system. Let them actually hear the different kinds of alarms you have so that they will be able to distinguish among them and take appropriate action when they go off. If your system does not have automatic dial-in hookups, ask your neighbors to call the police or fire departments when they hear the alarm. Give them your home and business phone numbers and the number of a friend to be contacted in case of emergency. Other than that, you don't need to, and you probably shouldn't, spell out any major details of your alarm system to anyone except the immediate members of your household—and they in turn should be encouraged to keep the system's workings confidential.

Before programming their numbers into your automatic dialer, check with the local police, fire, and other emergency response agencies in your neighborhood to see if they will accept your calls. You should also get your neighbors', friends', or relatives' permission before you add them to your list of dialed numbers, and find out in advance how likely it is that they will be home to respond to your taped calls during the times when you and your family are away. Let them know what you would like them to do in the event they receive a taped message from your dialer.

Buying vs. Leasing

Alarm systems can be either purchased outright or leased. Whether you buy or lease should depend largely on how long you expect to be at your current address, and whether you think you will be able to recoup the cost of the system when you leave.

If you either own your own home or plan to live in rented quarters for longer than five years, it is probably better, and less expensive in the long run, to buy. While prices and service charges vary from company to company, after a five-year period the total leasing costs usually add up to more than the cost of the original purchase, service, and maintenance. Short-term leasing is not economical, since the alarm company has to amortize its installation costs over a correspondingly shorter period of time and therefore adjusts the monthly payments upward accordingly.

By purchasing the system outright, an alarm system can be considered a capital improvement. It increases the resale value of the house and can be capitalized for tax purposes like any other major improvement to the home. Alarm installations have financing advantages, too. Most banks consider an alarm system a major home improvement, with correspondingly better mortgage and interest rates than would otherwise be available.

Alarm Stickers and Signs

While there is some disagreement on this point, most experts advise a homeowner with a burglar alarm system to advertise the fact to potential intruders. Most burglars, given the option, would probably prefer to tackle a house without the distraction and menace of an alarm, and alarm stickers should therefore act as a deterrent. Whether or not the impression it gives is warranted, a home with an alarm is also more likely to have stronger locks, doors, and other target-hardening devices that would either complicate the break-in or at least escalate the risk of a burglar's being caught in the act.

A few suggestions are in order. It pays to remember that some thieves may be familiar with the ins and outs of certain specific alarm systems, so when you post your sign or sticker don't identify the equipment or even the central alarm service by name. Do post the sign conspicuously so it can be seen from all accessible approaches to the house. If you are tempted to post a sticker when you don't in fact have an alarm, remember that even unskilled burglars have probably learned to look for other visible indications of a functioning alarm system, like horns and sirens or the metal foil of sensors on your window glass.

DO YOU REALLY NEED A BURGLAR ALARM SYSTEM?

A burglar alarm is not a substitute for other target-hardening measures like strong doors, good locks, and constant attention to good home-security practices. An alarm system is ever-present and demanding, and may require you to change your daily habits and/or lifestyle to accommodate its conditions. If it is subject to false alarms, be prepared to face the annoyance of your neighbors and the censure of local authorities when it goes off by mistake. And be prepared to educate your family regarding its workings. Unlike other target-hardening measures, where even a minor reinforcement is better than none at all, an incomplete or misadjusted alarm system will play such havoc with your habits and routines that, like almost half of current owners, you may end up never turning it on at all. Thus, to minimize the headaches involved in "adaptation," it pays to plan ahead.

To decide whether a burglar alarm system makes sense in your household, look at your home the way you think a reasonable, thoughtful burglar would. Look at all the obvious access points and decide whether they can be protected adequately without alarms. Are accessible windows barred or otherwise unbreakable? Are your primary and secondary doors invincible or easily reinforced? If so, would the cost of reinforcing them equal or outweigh a good alarm system? There are other critical points to consider. Are the occupants regular enough in their habits to live by the demands of a reasonably comprehensive alarm system?

Assuming the answers to these questions still argue for installing an alarm system, there is still no one system that can possibly meet the needs of every home, and under the circumstances it would be foolhardy to try to describe the perfect system. Throughout this chapter we have attempted to describe the equipment available in the broadest descriptive terms, together with the advantages and disadvantages of each type, so that you can make your own decision about what is best for your particular house and your particular style of living. What kind of system you will eventually choose to install depends on how you rank your expectations for the system. Do you want it mostly to protect you while you are at home? Scare off intruders while you are away? Bring the police with or without scaring the intruder off? Alert neighbors and or passersby so that they can contact the police in your place?

RECOMMENDATIONS FOR A BASIC ALARM SYSTEM

In some ways buying an alarm system is very much like buying an automobile. There are certain basic features that no system is complete without, and then there are various accessories that make the system more convenient to operate. Listed below are the features of a good alarm system that can be considered basic. Others, described earlier in this chapter, can improve the level of security and/or convenience, but can always be added on later.

- Battery backup with a self-charging feature. Get one that can power the system for at least twenty-four hours or more. The backup should come with a "low battery" indicator to tell you when it is time to recharge or change the backup batteries.

- At least four NC circuits to accept the perimeter and other NC sensors and components of the system. This permits "zoning" of sensors, for better control and testing. In addition, the system should have at least two NO circuits for interior-space protectors and pressure mats.
- No fewer than three NO supervised circuits for fire sensors, panic alarms, and medical and environmental protection circuits.
- An appropriate number of LEDs of different colors to let you know the status of your system and its sensors and other components. LEDs take the guesswork out of the alarm system and do some of your basic inspection and testing for you. And LEDs, as opposed to light bulbs, do not require frequent replacement.
- An automatic alarm cutoff, which terminates the audible alarm after a fixed period, usually five to fifteen minutes. This is required by local ordinances in many communities.
- A holding relay. Once the alarm has been triggered, the holding relay will keep it going, even though the sensing switch may have been reset to normal by a knowledgeable intruder. Holding relays are found in virtually every panel.
- A manual abort/rearm switch. This comes into play when the alarm has been accidentally tripped. The manual abort/rearm switch cuts off all alarm signals with a manually operated key or keypad, which also permits instant keyed rearming.
- An adjustable exit/entry delay circuit, which gives the owner time to enter or leave the house through specific doors without triggering the alarm.
- Panic buttons, hooked up to a supervised twenty-four-hour circuit. As a minimum there should be one panic button by the front door for protection against a push-in attack. Others can be located in the master bedroom and at other strategic points throughout the house. Portable wireless panic button hookups are also available.
- Alarm memory indicator. This LED light warns the returning homeowner that the alarm has been triggered during his absence.
- Shunt switches, which permit you to cut off the alarm at frequently used doors and windows while keeping the rest of the system fully armed.
- Tamper switches, which are hooked up to a twenty-four-hour supervised circuit and sound the alarm if any of the system's components are tampered with.
- Local alarms, with both exterior and interior sirens. Interior sirens should be at least eighty-five decibels; exterior sirens should be no less than 110 decibels. Electronic warbling sirens use less power and draw the most attention.
- A different alarm—either a horn or a loud bell, both inside the house and out—for fire alarms.
- Strobe lights or police-type flashers mounted on the roof or at an outside window to serve as beacons for police and other responders.
- If your budget allows it, a digital dialing communicator hooked up to a central alarm-monitoring agency.

10

FIRE ALARMS

A comprehensive alarm system need not and probably should not be limited to sounding the alarm in case of attempted break-ins. Nationwide, fire causes far more damage and financial loss than burglary does. With very little extra expense, a burglar alarm system can be adapted to include a fire-warning system, too. If not, there are small self-contained smoke detectors with a built-in horn or buzzer for an alarm. If you have no intention of installing a burglar alarm system, these local stand-alone units are inexpensive and should be high on your list of household priorities.

INTEGRATED ALARM SYSTEMS
VS. STAND-ALONE DETECTORS

The primary purpose of a fire alarm is to warn people inside the house that their lives and belongings are in danger. Two out of three homes in this country rely on wall- or ceiling-mounted smoke detectors to do this job, and when properly installed and maintained these stand-alone units have proven their lifesaving value in warning the home's occupants that there is a fire in progress.

Smoke detectors have their limits. If there is no one at home to hear them, interior alarm horns are usually not powerful enough to alert the neighbors or the fire department to the situation, and help may not be forthcoming until the smoke and flames are already visible from the street—too late to prevent major damage to or destruction of the house and everything in it. This is where a digital dialer with a fire-alert hookup comes in.

As described earlier in this book, a good intruder-alarm system will contain a supervised twenty-four-hour NO circuit that accepts signals from heat and smoke sensors as well as intrusion-detector switches. This circuit can also be programmed to send a special local fire alarm with a different sound than that of the burglar alarm, so that people inside the house are warned to get out of it, instead of barricading themselves in as they might to elude a burglar. At the same time, the circuit will transmit special fire-in-progress messages to the appropriate authorities at the other end of a dial-in line. A good system is designed to stay on fire alert even when the rest of the system is turned off; and when the rest of the system is turned on, the fire alarm and the dial-in fire-alert message should override any other alarm message being transmitted at the time.

Stand-Alone Smoke Detectors

Stand-alone smoke detectors are the simplest form of fire-alert mechanisms available, and they come in two versions, based on the different kinds of technology they use: ionization and photoelectricity (or, as a more recent option, some combination of the two).

Ionization Smoke Detectors   Ionization detectors rely on a tiny amount of radioactive material installed in a small sensing chamber. This material ionizes the air in the chamber, permitting a small electric current to flow continuously between two electrodes in the chamber. When smoke particles enter the chamber they interrupt this flow, whereupon the electronic circuitry senses the interruption and interprets it as a signal to trigger the alarm.

Ionization sensors respond quickly to the virtually invisible smoke particles from a fast-burning fire fed by paper, wood, or fat—materials that give off relatively small amounts of smoke and contain the least visible (but most lethal) gas products of combustion. For a wide variety of ordinary household fires they are effective alert systems, and more than warrant their widespread popularity with fire-safety experts and other concerned officials. Their radioactivity is negligible; according to the Nuclear Regulatory Commission (NRC), close proximity to an ionization smoke detector eight hours a day for a year would net you only as much radiation as you would be likely to get from one round-trip cross-country airline flight per year.

Photoelectric Detectors   Photoelectric sensors detect the large smoke particles that result from slow-burning, smoldering fires like those that start in upholstery, mattresses, and rugs. In a sense, the photoelectric sensor "sees" the smoke as it passes through its sensing chamber. It uses a tiny LED as a light source, and projects a light beam across the chamber angled so as to avoid a light-sensitive photoelectric cell on the other side of the chamber. When smoke with large particles enters the chamber, light is reflected off these particles onto the photocell, which generates enough electricity to trigger the alarm.

Combination Models   A recent and highly effective innovation on the smoke-detector

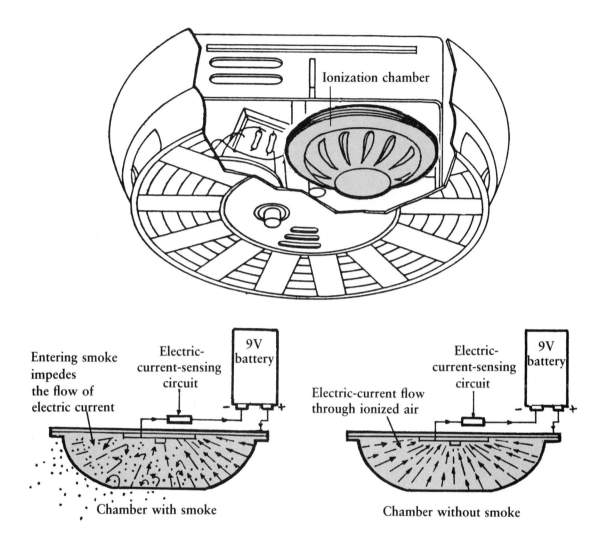

Figure 40   Ionization smoke detector

market is the so-called double-system detector that combines both photoelectric and ionizing sensors in one unit. These were among the best-rated models in Consumers Union's 1984 tests.

Heat Detectors   Most fire deaths are caused by smoke inhalation; but there are many spots throughout the house where normal environmental conditions make a smoke detector either impractical or a recurrent nuisance. In a kitchen, for example, smoke, steam, and cooking fumes will set off the alarm; smoke from a poorly vented fireplace or furnace room, exhaust fumes in a garage, and steam from the washer or dryer in a laundry room can all have the same effect. Unfortunately, these are also the places in a house where fire is most likely to

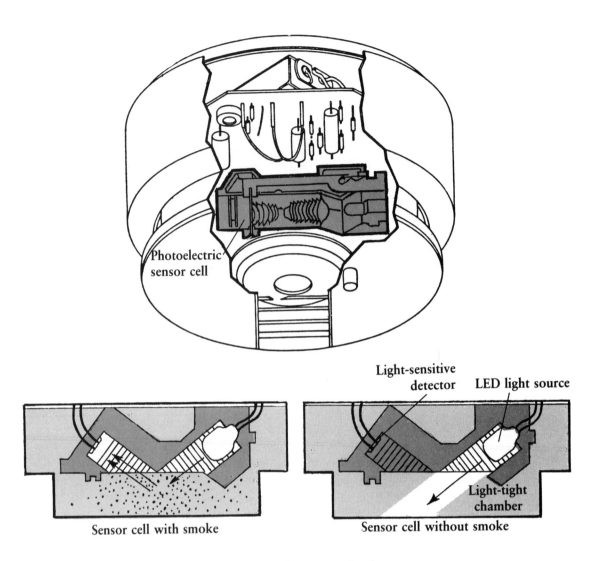

Figure 41   Photoelectric smoke detector

break out. Such trouble spots call for a sensor that reacts directly to temperature, rather than to smoke particles or gases.

There are a wide variety of heat detectors on the market, but almost all work on the same principle. In the typical detector, heat causes an opened switch to close whenever there is a rise in the ambient temperature, much like the basic mechanism of a thermostat. Heat sensors come in two major types for residential installation. The first contains a special kind of material that normally keeps the switch's spring-driven contacts apart. The switch is usually set to close when the temperature reaches 135 degrees, but it should be set higher for an attic or crawl space under the roof, where the summer sun will routinely heat the enclosed air to this temperature or higher.

The second type is designed to sense a rapid rise in air temperature, so that when the temperature rises at the rate of fifteen degrees Fahrenheit per minute—or faster—the contacts close and the alarm signal is triggered. Some heat detectors include both kinds of sensors, as a kind of backup or fail-safe measure.

For residential use, where periodic testing is necessary, the heat detector should have elements that snap closed at the pre-set alarm temperature and return to their opened position as soon as the temperature falls. With this kind of unit, the heat detector can be tested simply by blowing hot air from an ordinary hair dryer across it. Even when a heat detector is regularly inspected and maintained, however, it should never be considered as a substitute for a smoke detector. Smoke is the silent killer in most fires, and can asphyxiate a victim long before a heat detector can begin to react to the actual temperature change caused by the fire. In anything bigger than a closet or a very small one-room apartment, smoke and heat detectors used together form the background of an effective fire-warning system.

CHOOSING THE RIGHT KIND OF DETECTOR

For many years there were clear criteria for choosing the type of sensor best suited to various kinds of residential fires. The usual advice was that the ionization type was best for detecting the lethal by-products of burning plastic, paint, wood, paper, etc. It could detect such chemicals as ammonia, hydrogen cyanide, and prussic acid, and warn you about their existence long before their concentrations became lethal or even detectable to humans. Ionizing smoke detectors were relatively inexpensive, readily available, and required little cleaning. Furthermore, they responded first and fastest to the more intense, fast-burning fires.

Photoelectric sensors were usually more expensive, and for this reason few stores routinely stocked them, making them difficult to find. They also responded more slowly to fast-burning fires than the ionization models did, and the fires they were best suited to detect were the slow-burning ones that seemed less immediately threatening. In addition, because they functioned by means of a light bulb, they drained their batteries quickly and required regular monthly checks and battery replacement. Therefore, if homeowners had a choice, it seemed natural to go with the ionization models, and the sales figures for ionization models rose accordingly.

Most of the thinking on this issue has changed within the past few years. Fire experts tell us that the smoldering types of fires that start in mattresses as a result of smoking in bed or falling asleep on a couch pose statistically graver threats to homeowners than the flash fires that ionization detectors are best designed to sense. In addition, Consumers Union tests show that the more recent models of photoelectric detectors can now detect small-particle smoke and gases just as well as the ionization type, with a response time that is only a few seconds slower, while still retaining their ability to detect large particles from smoldering fires. In addition to these two basic types of detectors, there is now available a unit that combines both kinds of sensors and therefore responds efficiently to both kinds of fires. These combination units received some of the highest ratings in Consumers Union's 1984 testing program.

Remember, though, that no two fires are ever exactly alike. Depending on what goes up in smoke, each fire will present its own mix of fumes, particles, and gases. A multiple detection system therefore provides the greatest degree of safety, and the best current advice is to buy more than one detector. The more detectors there are and the more strategically they are placed throughout the house, the greater your chances of detecting a potential fire disaster in time to do something about it.

In a multiple detection system, experts recommend backing up the primary detector with an ionization unit located at various areas throughout the house. The few seconds' advantage that ionization sensors provide in a fast-developing fire make it a natural for use in the basement and near the kitchen, where furnace explosions and cooking fires are an ever-present possibility. However, if you are going to install only one unit you should make that unit either a photoelectric one or, better yet, one of the newly available units that combine both photoelectric and ionization sensors. These are currently selling for around thirty dollars (as opposed to ten to fifteen dollars for an ionization model). Otherwise, photoelectric models are now recommended as the detectors of choice for bedrooms and living areas.

Testing Features

Some smoke and heat detectors have LED signals, beepers, or flags to indicate various conditions like low-battery status, alarm-volume control, and other self-testing features. These last features are critical. A lot can go wrong with a smoke detector, regardless of its technology; sophisticated circuitry can break down, vents can get so clogged that they prevent smoke from reaching the sensors, the alarm horn or buzzer can go dead, and the battery or other power source can wear out. When it comes to a fire, a false alarm is a nuisance, but the absence of an alarm can be fatal. Fire sensors should therefore be tested at least once or twice a month, and preferably on a weekly basis.

All detectors manufactured after 1979 come with the capacity for spot-testing, including a battery-status indicator, an alarm-status indicator, and a smoke-sensing capacity indicator. The latter may not actually let you know whether the inlet slots are clogged or not, however; experts therefore suggest vacuum cleaning the smoke detector to remove potential blockage. To test the detector's reaction to slow-burning smoldering fires, blow out a match flame or snuff out a burning candle and let the smoke drift into the chamber. If an alarm is in good working order, it should sound within thirty seconds to a minute of the test. For a heat detector, the best test is to focus a hair dryer on the sensor from about a foot away; in a functioning unit it will take a minute or so for the heat detector to sound the alarm.

Other Features

Some smoke detectors not only sound an audible alarm but also have an "escape light" feature. When the alarm is triggered, a flashlight bulb illuminates the area surrounding the detector for several minutes. This is a handy feature to have in a house where the current has been cut off by the fire, since the escape light can help occupants to orient themselves as they grope through heavy smoke on their way out of the house. Such units require two nine-volt batteries, which separately power the alarm and the light.

Response Time

Smoke detectors do not give the instant response that intrusion detectors do, and ionizing detectors and photoelectric models have different response times depending on the kind of fire they are responding to. In tests of ceiling-mounted models conducted by Consumers Union in 1984, the response time of newer models of the photoelectric detectors was virtually equal to that of ionization models, with a lag of anywhere from seventy-five to 240 seconds for both kinds. Photoelectric models took about four seconds longer than ionization detectors overall.

When it came to smoldering fires, it took the photoelectric models an average of forty-three minutes to react, while ionization models took sixty-seven minutes; the closer either type of detector was to the source of the smoke, the faster it reacted under any circumstances. Consumers Union tests simulated the fire conditions of an average home as closely as possible, and the resulting response times are probably as close to a real-life response time as any one homeower can realistically expect. With any kind of fire in the house, seconds count, so it is strongly advised that a pre-rehearsed evacuation plan be instituted for and familiar to all members of the household.

PLACEMENT OF SMOKE DETECTORS

Smoke alarms cannot distinguish between smoke from a broiling steak in the kitchen and the fumes of a house on fire. Smoke from a fireplace, a wood stove, or even the steam from a tea kettle can trigger a false alarm, but the fault is often not so much with the detector as with its placement. Once you have decided what kind of smoke detectors to buy, it is crucial to follow the manufacturer's recommendations about where to place them and how to maintain them.

For maximum protection, there should be at least one smoke detector on every level of the house, including one in every bedroom, in every hallway, and in the basement and the attic as well. The number of detectors you install depends on the size of your house or apartment, the amount of money you can afford to spend, and your willingness to service and test them on a regular basis. Other factors to consider are the physical layout of the house, the number of rooms, the ratio of adults to children in your household, and the presence of smokers in the family.

The first priority should be given to bedrooms, especially if you live in a multiple-story house or duplex apartment. Convection currents carry air upwards, and an upstairs detector will sense smoke wherever it originates. This means that if you are going to buy only a single detector, the best place for it is probably just outside the bedrooms. If you buy two, the second should go in the living room area (at some distance from the fireplace) and close to the kitchen.

The more bedrooms that are covered the better, since the primary function of the detector is to wake up the house's sleeping occupants and warn them of impending danger. If a fire originates in a bedroom and it is the family custom to sleep with closed doors, an individual detector in each bedroom will wake the sleeper before the smoke in the room reaches a life-threatening level. Similarly, if two sleeping areas are separated by any substantial distance, there should be a detector at each location. And if there is a smoker in the family, that person's bedroom should be considered a prime fire hazard area, with its own detector and a loud alarm. In basements, the best place for the detector is on the ceiling close to the stairs, provided this doesn't put it too close to the furnace or any laundry equipment that might trigger false alarms.

Manufacturers suggest that, regardless of what room you install them in, detectors be mounted as close to the ceiling as possible, either in the center of the room or about six inches from a corner. If mounted on a wall, detectors should be between six and twelve inches from the ceiling. Care should be taken to avoid dead spaces and corners where walls meet or ceilings meet the walls, since such places get little direct air circulation and any smoke in the room will therefore take longer to reach the sensor. By the same token, though, steady air flow from a nearby air-supply duct outlet can delay smoke from reaching the sensor in sufficient quantities to set off the alarm. Also, ceilings that are substantially colder or warmer than the rest of the room can act as a sort of thermal barrier that prevents the smoke from reaching a ceiling-mounted sensor. This is especially true on the upper floors of older, poorly insulated houses, or in the ceilings of mobile homes.

FALSE ALARMS

Some people who live with smoke detectors—especially those who are compelled by local fire codes to install them—claim that they sound off repeatedly for no reason or at least from totally innocent causes. To deal with frequent false alarms, owners sometimes remove the battery and then forget to replace it; or in their exasperation they may disable the detector permanently.

There are other, better ways to deal with this problem. One manufacturer equips its models with a "hush button" to minimize the nuisance. If an alarm goes off for no good reason, the owner can push the button, which modulates the strident alarm down to a slow, soft chirp for about seven minutes or so, and then resets itself to its normal alert status. In the intervening seven minutes, you can remove the offending smoke or steam that set your detector off.

Dust and grime can be another cause of nuisance alarms. The detector's sensor is constantly exposed to household air and its daily cargo of cigarette smoke, cooking-oil effluents, and other dirt catchers. Over time, these will accumulate to the point where they cause the sensors to malfunction, and either trigger a nuisance alarm or fail to send any alarm at all. Insects can also represent a problem for older models, and since 1986, Underwriters' Laboratories has required all smoke detectors to come equipped with an insect screen or some other equivalent protection. UL also now specifies the size of the inlet ducts on models it certifies.

Periodic cleaning at least twice a year can help keep the chambers and the vents reasonably free from dirt and grime. Follow the manufacturer's suggestions for cleaning when they are available. Some manufacturers suggest using a vacuum-cleaner wand for this job. On a detector with a nonremovable cover, run the wand across the vents; if the cover can be removed, take it off and carefully vacuum the sensor chambers inside the detector.

BATTERIES

A dead battery in a smoke detector can be lethal. For this reason, manufacturers of smoke detectors have given particular attention to built-in signals that announce a dead or failing battery. Almost all self-contained ceiling units are powered by nine-volt batteries. The useful life of a high-quality battery is about one year; after that it should be replaced, whether it shows signs of failing or not. Replacement batteries are easy to install, and a top-quality long-life replacement currently goes for about $2.50.

Most units nowadays let you know that your batteries are running low well before the battery actually comes to the end of its useful life. Most models use a low-level audible beeper that goes off every few seconds, and some models will continue on this status for as long as seven to ten days, with the better models continuing to signal for thirty days. Some also send a visible warning in the form of an LED light that signals normal battery strength by blinking slowly on and off. When the battery begins to fail, the light stops blinking.

LED LIGHTS IN PHOTOELECTRIC SENSORS

By virtue of its design, the photoelectric smoke detector depends on a steady light source shining across the otherwise lightproof chamber, and triggers an alarm only when smoke deflects the beam onto the corresponding photoelectric cell. Photoelectric sensors use a pulsing LED light as a light source. Most manufacturers claim that these lights drain little power from the battery and have a useful life of about three years. However, the longevity of the LED light may be overlooked by homeowners who have trained themselves to check only on the longevity of the battery itself. LED failure should be checked by periodic inspections, with the same techniques you would use in checking the detector's other workings.

HARD-WIRED SMOKE-DETECTOR SYSTEMS

Hard-wired systems have been used for many years at commercial and industrial installations. Smaller and less elaborate versions of these systems have recently been adapted for residential use. Like their counterparts among intrusion-detection units, they range from single units that plug into regular house current, to multi-unit, elaborately zoned systems with their own fire-control panels and backup self-charging battery systems that can be tied into automatic phone dialers, and external horns and escape lights, among other features. In addition, the more complicated fire alarm systems, like their burglar alarm counterparts, have remote manual-alarm buttons at locations throughout the house, with nuisance alarm shut-offs and other sophisticated features. Central alarm-monitoring stations will also accept digital communications hookups for fire and smoke alarms as well as burglar alarms.

This type of protection is available, at a price, for those who want a comprehensive fire alarm system without a complex intrusion alarm. Cost is usually the limiting factor here; but if you have already contracted for a sophisticated hard-wired intruder-alarm system anyway, the additional cost of a comprehensive fire alert system may be a reasonable add-on option.

SUMMARY

If you decide, like a great many other homeowners throughout the country, to go with a series of strategically placed stand-alone smoke detectors, remember that they should never just be placed on the wall or ceiling and forgotten. Periodic testing is imperative; so are cleaning and other maintenance. Remember, too, that even with proper maintenance, smoke detectors don't last forever, and after four or five years your current smoke detectors may need to be replaced. At an average cost of ten to fifteen dollars for ionization models and thirty dollars for the new photoelectric and ionization combination units, the price is relatively low in terms of potential lives saved and peace of mind.

11

APARTMENTS

There are two schools of thought about apartment security. One says that apartment dwellers are at high risk of burglary and other kinds of break-ins when they live in urban enclaves because they are in much closer proximity to potential criminals than suburban or rural homeowners. In addition, burglars may favor apartment houses as targets because once inside the building they can break into one apartment after another, with relatively little scrutiny from neighbors and passersby.

The other school of thought holds that apartment living is safer than living in a single house because apartments usually have fewer outside doors and windows; with fewer points of entry to defend, people can more readily strengthen the security of the ones they have.

Without controlled experiments it is difficult to say which side has the stronger argument, but in a sense the argument itself is meaningless. Apartment dwellers have just as big a stake in their own security as homeowners do, regardless of the odds for or against them in the search for relative peace of mind.

APARTMENT ENTRY

To their advantage, most apartments are by their very nature limited in access. Individual apartments normally have only one entrance door, or at the most two. If they are also at least two floors above ground level, most of their windows are probably inaccessible from the ground. Vulnerable glass door "lights" are not usually found in apartment corridor doors, and windows facing onto corridors are rare. Target-hardening in most apartments can therefore safely be limited to the entrance door and walls and whatever windows are easily reachable from the street or other outside access points.

Corridor and Other Interior Walls

The security of the walls in older multiple-dwelling buildings can usually be taken for granted; but in newer buildings the sturdiness of the wall between you and the outside world may be worth looking into. In many newer multi-family buildings or newly subdivided older ones, hallway corridor walls are constructed of materials that serve mainly for privacy, insulation, and fireproofing or soundproofing purposes. Interior walls may be made of one or at most two sheets of plasterboard fastened to wood or metal studs. Although it is still a rare method of entry, police officials are reporting more and more cases where a burglar, defeated or delayed by an increasingly sophisticated array of locks and door reinforcements, resorts to breaking through the adjacent wall by chopping, sawing, or brute force.

If the wall between your apartment and the semi-public corridor outside it is weak, one recommendation is to reinforce the area surrounding the door, or even the whole wall, with 1/2-inch or even 3/4-inch plywood nailed to the jack studs supporting the wall. You can buy this kind of plywood in a wide variety of furniture-finished hardwoods to fit most decorating styles. Another alternative is to reinforce the wall on the inside by building bookcases or cabinets on either side of the apartment door with a heavy plywood backing attached firmly to the studs in the corners and at intervals along the wall.

Fire Escapes

Other construction features of apartment buildings that may present security problems are terraces and fire escapes. Both present a greater security hazard if they face the rear of the building, or an unfrequented courtyard, than they do if they face the street.

In newer buildings the fire stairs are enclosed inside the building, or the first flight of stairs is protected by a heavy wire grill with a gate that can only be opened from the inside. In many older buildings, though, the fire escape is a simple iron ladder or stairs attached to the front or back of the building, easily accessible from the ground, the roof, or an adjacent building.

Fire escapes were designed to serve as many apartments as possible, and their landings may therefore span the windows to one or more apartments on the same floor. This means that the same fire escape is often accessible from more than one apartment, and a burglar with access to the roof or to any apartment that opens onto the fire escape may start at the top and work his way down, looking for unlocked or easily opened windows along the way.

For this reason, any windows or doors that open onto a fire escape should always be securely fastened and locked whenever the resident is away or asleep or otherwise engaged. And to strengthen security, locking window grills and gates is highly recommended.

Grills and Gates

Ordinary decorative iron or aluminum gates and grillwork are not the answer here. In most single-house installations, window guards are attached to the outside of the house and are not really designed to be opened. By contrast, window gates for use on fire escape windows are designed to be opened from the inside, so that they are easily retractable or even removable in case of fire. (In most big cities, permanent, nonretractable installations represent serious emergency hazards and can be in violation of prevailing fire codes.)

Retractable "Accordion" Gates Iron accordion gates designed for apartment windows can either swing open from one side of the window frame (like a casement window) or slide open and shut in heavy steel channels at the top and bottom of the window frame. The latter construction is preferable because the gate can't be pried loose at the top or bottom and bent inward to allow someone to squeeze in. Both versions demand a reasonably sturdy window frame, though, and if your frame cannot support the grillwork, you will probably do well to anchor the gate to the masonry wall itself—or to the inner studs in a frame building.

Most retractable gates are secured by padlocks, but some are specially designed to open with boxed-in swivel knobs inaccessible from outside the window. In these gates the "pleats" of the accordion are set so close together that the spaces between them will not admit a human hand, and the knob itself cannot easily be manipulated from the outside by a coat hanger or any other handy leveraging tool.

This kind of locking device is quicker and easier to operate in an emergency than a standard padlock with a separate key, and is actually mandated by fire department codes in some jurisdictions. It may cost more than the conventional gate and may be even less aesthetically pleasing, but it combines safety with security and can therefore pay for itself in added peace of mind.

Shutters Roll-down metal shutters like those used on shop windows in some areas are another alternative to accordion gates. These are designed for maximum protection and are usually operated with a key and armed with some kind of pressure-sensitive alarm. On the ordinary apartment fire-escape window or terrace door, however, such target-hardening may be excessive, and since most of these shutters are designed to be closed from the outside, after the shopkeeper has shut his books and gone home for the day, they would probably have to be retrofitted to make them open from the inside for apartment dwellers' purposes.

Security shutters are much more dense in their construction than gates or grills, and the same density that is responsible for their resistance to attack also makes them relatively impenetrable by air, light, and sound. Ventilation can therefore be a problem with this kind of installation in an apartment that relies on shuttered windows for its major source of light and air.

Another and perhaps more manageable alternative to iron security shutters on vulnerable doors and windows is a heavily constructed wooden interior shutter like those seen in many nineteenth-century townhouses. If outfitted with floor-to-ceiling vertical cane bolts, wood shutters can be extremely hard to breach, especially if they are made of solid hardwood. Louvered versions of hardwood shutters are less resistant to break-ins, but even so they probably offer more resistance to sawing or hammering than the average burglar wants to undertake, and are therefore a reasonably good choice in the trade-off between security, convenience, and aesthetics.

Terraces

Apartment-house terraces and balconies present similar problems, especially if they share a party wall with a neighboring terrace or terraces. Such terraces are usually found as a feature of modern post-war construction, and they are often accessed from the apartment through sliding-glass patio doors or some other variation on the garden-door theme.

In some buildings, terraces are contiguous, and the partition between neighboring terraces may be only waist- or shoulder-high. This means that anyone with access to your neighbor's apartment can easily get on to your terrace and gain entrance to your apartment.

Terrace doors are usually designed on the model of patio doors, and like patio doors they can be secured by the same kind of pins and/or locks designed for other glass doors, and reinforced with retractable gates on the inside if the security situation seems to warrant it. Alternatively, roll-down metal curtains are currently being offered for terrace doors and windows. These roll-downs differ from the kind that are used on shop fronts because they can be locked from the inside, or even installed on the inside; but they carry an equally hefty price tag: about $1,000 installed at 1988 prices. Check your local fire code before you install them, though, because in some jurisdictions they may be a violation. (See chapter 5, "Doors," and chapter 7, "Locks.")

Windows

If you live in a ground-floor or second-floor apartment, you should take the same precautions with respect to window locks or pins that you would in a private house. (See chapter 6, "Windows.") Lower-floor windows that face the rear of the building should be the focus of the apartment dweller's most concentrated target-hardening. Upper-floor windows, except those that open onto fire escapes or terraces, are generally assumed to be relatively free of risk, but this is not always the case. Some upper-floor windows can be reached from the roof, and even those facing the street—visible to neighbors or passersby who happen to look up—have been attacked by the more brazen intruder. In fact, top-floor apartments command top-dollar rentals, so they are considered by many experienced burglars to be richer, more desirable targets.

Skylights

Skylights have all the vulnerability of ordinary glazed windows, but with the added risk factor that they open directly onto the roof. For this reason, any skylight more than a foot wide should be protected with metal bars or grills, unless it is commonly used for access to the roof, in which case it should be outfitted with retractable gates. Where the skylight doesn't have to be used it should be permanently barred with a sturdy iron grill. Decorative ironwork or mesh may be the answer here; but if you opt for simple iron bars, remember that they should never be more than five inches apart, should measure at least ¾ inch thick, and should be inserted in a sturdy metal frame fastened to the underlying studs with nonretractable screws of the maximum possible length.

Doors

In addition to the usual caveats about door security (see chapter 5), there are a few special precautions that apply specifically to apartments. Most apartment doors are constructed of—or faced with—a solid piece of wood or metal; they do not have glass "lights" or side windows from which to monitor the corridor outside. Instead, many come equipped with peepholes or "viewers"—and if they don't, they should.

Security experts recommend that people who live in apartments act as if their corridor doors opened directly onto the street. At the very least, a peephole set into the door will allow apartment dwellers to see who is ringing their doorbell. Some peepholes can monitor a substantial sweep of the visible area outside their door, too, thereby allowing a good view of people at their neighbor's door as well.

If you hear an unexpected ring at the door and you can't see who you are dealing with without opening the door, the best rule of thumb is: don't. Ask the person to identify himself or herself (women and sometimes even children may be used as decoys in some apartment house "push-ins"), and if you have any questions at all about the person's credentials, refrain from opening the door.

Peepholes   Entrance doors from ancient times to the present have often been constructed with portholes or other mini-doors that could be opened to see who was standing outside. Old-fashioned versions of peepholes were several inches in diameter and came with sliding or swinging covers.

These still exist in some pre-war residences and apartment buildings today, but the security they provide is negligible. Old-fashioned peepholes are large enough to permit a wire, a knife, or even a gun barrel to be inserted through the port, and anyone standing with their eye to the opening is at risk of serious injury. Moreover, even when the port is closed it can be forced open from the outside, so that burglar tools can subsequently be inserted and dropped down to open the lock from the inside. If you have this kind of peephole, the best advice is to seal it and replace it with a late-model optical viewer like those described below.

Optical Viewers Modern peepholes are designed to prevent anything except visual contact with the world outside the door. Commercially available optical viewers are small metal cylinders installed in a hole bored through the door; they contain a fish-eye lens allowing for a wide-angle vista onto the space outside the door. Lenses can range from 1/4 inch to as large as one inch in diameter. Although the wider ones permit a better view, they pose the same basic safety hazard as the older-style peepholes, and leave the inside observer almost as vulnerable to attack.

A safe choice for an optical viewer is one with a 1/4- or 3/8-inch lens. While the recommended wide-angle view should be in the neighborhood of 180 degrees, permitting the viewer to see one or more people at the door (including someone pressed flat against an adjacent wall), few on the market actually achieve the promised viewing range. Most commercially available viewers that promise a range of from 160 to 200 degrees have been found to overstate the case by thirty to fifty degrees. Don't rule out a given viewer on these grounds alone, though, because a 160-degree viewing range is perfectly acceptable for most people under ordinary circumstances.

In addition to the difference in their ranges, viewers also vary in their focusing distance, with the majority focusing closer to the door and a few others focusing somewhat farther out. Area of focus is a very personal matter, and buyers should try out the viewer for focus before they have one installed. Information about the focusing distance is often missing from the manufacturer's specifications—or difficult to assess without actually looking through the viewer. Far-sighted people will feel more comfortable with a more distant area of focus than normal sighted or near-sighted people will. The clarity of the lens is another variable to consider, and one that may be particularly important to people with less than twenty-twenty vision. In addition, you should not be able to see in from the outside; even someone outside being able to tell whether a light is on or off may increase your risk.

Most instructions suggest that the viewer be installed from roughly four feet eight inches to about four feet ten inches from the floor. This advice is probably reasonable for apartment dwellers of average size, but it may be too low in a house full of reasonably tall adults, and too high in a house full of small children. While opening the door to strangers is not something that young children should be encouraged to do, there may be occasions when they have to use the peephole. You might therefore think about installing a second peephole somewhere below the first at a height better suited to a child's-eye view of the hall outside.

Locks

It is at least as characteristic of apartments as it is of houses that the residents will change from time to time. In some neighborhoods, and some cities, the turnover in apartment tenancy may average as much as once every two or three years. It should therefore be a rule of thumb for anyone taking up residence in a new apartment to change the locks before he or she moves in.

Landlords may or may not go along with this practice, depending on local ordinances and the terms of the lease. If you do change the lock, and you still feel that you need additional protection, it may make sense to install an auxiliary lock. Auxiliary locks have their own uses as psychological deterrents to lazy intruders or those who are otherwise pressed for time; as noted earlier, doors with two locks double the work of burglars and provide an extra element of key control.

Master-Keying In many apartment buildings the door locks are suited to individual tenant keys and to one or more master keys that can unlock the doors in a given house or building. This practice may involve one group of locks or a whole series of locks in a system. Some master keys will operate only certain doors or groups of doors, as for example all the doors on a single floor. Others may include all doors in the building except certain service areas; and in buildings without doormen or security guards, the locks on the vestibule or lobby door can be suited to operate with tenant keys. Finally, many buildings have installations where one "grand master" key can open every lock in the building.

The principle of master-keying involves circumventing a pre-set series of unique barriers to the unlocking process. Key paths vary in their respective shapes, lengths, and widths, but the master key must be able to enter the keyway by passing through all the existing levels of obstructions. It does so, for the most part, by being thin enough to avoid them. However, to allow the master key to reach the shear line, the tumblers inside the lock must be modified to accommodate all the combinations of pin sizes designed to clear it.

Master Pins Almost all types of locks can be master-keyed, but for illustrative purposes it is probably clearest to explain master-keying as it works in the standard pin tumbler locks.

As noted in chapter 7, a pin tumbler lock is freed for turning when all of the lower pins or plug tumblers are raised so that the line between the upper pins and the lower ones reverts to the shear line as the proper key is inserted. Master-keying is achieved by "splitting" one of the lower pins so that an added line of demarcation is introduced into each pin set. This intermediate pin is referred to as the master pin, or wafer. Its use makes for an additional code of key cuts that permit the master pin to clear the shear line when the master is inserted into the keyway.

This process can be repeated so that an additional splitting of the original master pin can be done among several master key series. In this case it takes one master key to open each of the individual series, but a first-level master of one series cannot open locks in any other series, while the second-level master can open locks in both series, and so on up to three or more series.

The use of master keys is a convenience for the landlord and building-service personnel, but it obviously presents a security problem for the tenant, although he or she may have no choice but to accept a master key system as part of the terms of his tenancy. Master key systems are almost universal in institutions, hotels, and commercial or industrial buildings; and tenants may be the first to appreciate the system when they lock themselves out and are faced with having to call the superintendent or janitor to let them in.

The security problem represented by master keys is threefold. The first is that there is a key in some stranger's hand that can unlock your particular door. The strictness of key regulation and the number of duplications are therefore out of your control, and as the number of such keys increases, so does the threat to your security.

The second problem is the reduction in the odds that your key code is going to be unique. Because your master-keyed lock is now capable of being opened by a number of different keys, the odds of chance duplication of your particular key code increase significantly.

The third problem is that as the additional master pins are introduced, the difficulty of picking the lock diminishes proportionately. As a result, the would-be thief has many more chances in each pin set to reach the shear line on a reasonable number of tries.

As we noted earlier, master-keying may nevertheless be required by the landlord or by housing and insurance codes, in the interests of admitting service and emergency personnel in case of fire or accident, or other representatives of the landlord on their legitimate business. But such codes do not acknowledge the fact that master key systems are also obviously a blessing to would-be intruders, and security-conscious tenants might still consider either replacing the cylinders containing the master key system, or better, adding auxiliary locks for which only they have the key.

Either of these alternatives carries the obvious risk of annoying the landlord or violating city ordinances, and the apartment dweller who takes either course may come home one day to find a door forced open or a lock smashed in the course of responding to some emergency inside the apartment. There are other, less drastic ways around this problem, though. One is to leave a spare key with a trusted neighbor and hope that he or she is available when somebody needs instant access to your apartment. Or, better yet, you may want to leave your unmastered key with the superintendent in a sealed envelope initialed and scotch taped over the flap, with instructions that you are to be notified whenever the key is used. This may not be the ultimate in sophisticated security strategies, but it puts the building's management on notice that you are a security-minded tenant and will take any breach of your apartment's security seriously.

ALARMS

Because most apartments have only one or two doors and a restricted number of windows, wiring an alarm system should be a relatively uncomplicated matter from a mechanical point of view. But for apartment dwellers, the mechanics of installation are not the limiting factor. What is really at issue here is whether you own or rent the apartment you live in, and what your landlord, or co-owners as the case may be, agree on in terms of installing an alarm system.

Building-Wide Alarm Systems

The state of the art for apartment alarm systems is one that is built into the apartment as the building is being constructed. This system can be designed either for response by a doorman at the downstairs front door, or for a front-door buzzer system without a doorman.

In the first case, the building doorman monitors a central console that has wires running to each individual apartment. Break-ins trigger an alarm that is registered by a flashing light on the console, and the doorman either goes to investigate the situation, calls for local assistance, or phones the police. In the second case, consoles are monitored by off-site security offices, which operate like their counterparts in suburban and rural areas, serving as clearinghouses for alarms and false alarms, either by calling the resident at home to see what's going on, then checking the site themselves, or by passing on the news of a likely break-in to the police.

Retrofitting an existing apartment building for this kind of collective alarm system is probably not cost-effective, because the necessary wiring would require tearing out walls or baseboards and snaking new wires past unpredictable obstacles in the walls. To get some approximation of a buildingwide alarm system without going to this kind of trouble and expense, however, landlords might be pressed to install a closed-circuit community antenna system based on a building antenna that carries TV signals from a master antenna on the roof into each individual apartment. This kind of installation is known as community-antenna TV ("CATV" in security business shorthand) and can be monitored either on site—by the doorman, the super, or the landlord himself—or off-site, by an independent security service with a leased phone line into the building's console.

Single-Apartment Alarm Systems

For older buildings without building-wide alarm systems, individual tenants (or co-op and condo owners) may want to consider installing their own stand-alone single-apartment system. In this case, choosing an alarm is not very different from selecting one for a free-standing house. In both cases the relevant variables are the size and layout of the home, the number and placement of doors and windows, vulnerable points like terraces and fire escapes, and the routines and lifestyles of the apartment's occupants. To these factors an apartment dweller would probably want to add the proximity of his or her apartment to the building's exits (either from the street or the roof) as well as the kind of response that might realistically be expected from neighbors, other tenants, and building maintenance and security personnel if and when the alarm actually goes off.

Self-contained alarm systems and components have been discussed in detail in chapter 9. The various power sources, sensing devices, and controls described in that chapter can all be adapted to fit almost any kind of apartment. But although the equipment is identical whether it is going to be installed in a free-standing house or a studio apartment, alarm systems raise certain questions of their own that are unique to apartment dwellers.

Most of these questions are administrative rather than technical. Apartment residents fall into one of three categories: either they are tenants, or they own shares in a co-op, or they own the apartment outright, as in a condominium. In all these cases they are limited by the conditions of their occupancy, including the terms of their lease and/or shareholder contracts or deeds. In addition, other considerations to be weighed range from how long they plan to stay in the apartment, to their relations with fellow building occupants and/or the landlord's willingness to let them install any kind of alarm.

Installation

Whether you rent your apartment or own it, one of the first questions you will want to ask yourself before installing any kind of alarm system is how long you intend to stay where you are. Generally speaking, it doesn't pay to install a hard-wired system unless you plan to remain there for at least five years. Even then, if you are a renter, the standard boilerplate of many apartment leases means that you may be asked to remove the system before you leave, so as to leave the premises in exactly the same state in which you originally found them.

For this and other reasons, in the absence of a built-in buildingwide system, apartment dwellers may want to think of installing an easily mounted wireless system with battery-operated sensors. With three or four rooms, a corresponding number of windows, and no more than one or two doors at the most, the approaches to the apartment can all be easily covered with a few simple sensors. In addition, if the corridor wall is vulnerable it can be fitted with sensors laced across the surface of the wall in much the same way that metallic foil is affixed to glass window panes or panels.

In a large apartment, especially one with long hallways and more than one floor, interior sensors play a definite role; in smaller apartments you would probably do just as well with one or two pressure mats just inside or outside the front door and the threshold to the bedroom. Interior sensors—whether they are ultrasonic, photoelectric, or microwave—are subject to the same limitations in an apartment as they are in a single house, except that in apartments their fine-tuning may be even more critical. Apartment dwellers live in much closer proximity to each other than homeowners do, and may therefore be subject to more than the usual amount of "noise"—both literal and figurative—from their neighbors' comings and goings, electronic equipment and appliances, etc., so sensors should be chosen with an eye for their invulnerability to false alarms. (See chapter 9, "Burglar Alarms.")

Do-It-Yourself Installation The price of an efficient and "noiseproof" alarm system can come high, and to save themselves the cost of labor, reasonably handy apartment dwellers may want to consider the option of doing the installation themselves. If you aren't sure about which elements are compatible and you don't want to choose the components yourself, there are several alarm kits on the market that take most of the guesswork out of the design by providing a switch box, varying numbers of magnetic switches for doors and windows, a front-door switch that you activate when you go out (and deactivate when you come home again), and a siren or bell. Some kits also come complete with panic buttons, and most come with their own wire and mounting hardware.

The hybrid units described in chapter 9 are a good bet for do-it-yourself apartment installations. These units, starting with a single interior passive infrared sensor, have the capacity to serve as a master control unit for additional perimeter sensors, as well as various control switches, interior and exterior alarm-signaling devices, and automatic telephone dialers. Depending on the number of doors and windows to be covered, this job would probably take the better part of a day or two for the determined do-it-yourselfer to install. Since labor costs are generally figured at two-thirds the cost of the hardware, you stand to save yourself a substantial sum by doing the work yourself.

Although you may have reasons not to want a hard-wired system, it should be noted that if you do, hard-wiring the system in an apartment doesn't necessarily entail drilling through walls and snaking wires behind baseboards as it would in a house, where presumably the distances involved would be much greater and the costs more prohibitive. Instead, in the relatively short runs required in an apartment, you can put the necessary wires along the baseboards and door and window moldings, then enclose them in molded plastic or metal channels nailed or screwed to the baseboard or frame. The channels come in two parts. The wire is inserted into the fixed part of the channel attached to the baseboard or door and window frames, and the covering channel is snapped over it in the guise of an unobtrusive molding that can be painted or stained the same color as the woodwork, allowing it to blend easily into the prevailing decor.

Apartment Alarm Signals

One problem unique to apartment dwellers when installing an alarm system is the alarm signal itself. Local exterior alarms cannot be mounted outside your apartment door as they would on the outside of a free-standing house. Most landlords and co-op boards would be equally leery of such installations, not only because they represent major structural changes to common corridor walls, but because the decibels they put out would be acoustically intolerable in the tight space of a common corridor.

But the point of an alarm system is to make as much noise as possible; and if an apartment dweller cannot really broadcast the alarm beyond his or her walls, what is the alarm supposed to accomplish and where will the message ultimately go?

The answer to these questions depends, to some extent, on the occupant's lifestyle and prevailing routines. If an apartment dweller is home all day, probably the most that he or she needs to ask of a free-standing alarm system is that it scare off the burglar before he actually makes the break-in. If the occupant works outside the apartment and has an active social life, he or she will want the alarm to alert immediate neighbors or passing building personnel to the fact that the apartment is being burglarized, in hopes that they will call the police or make some other appropriate response.

Apartment dwellers will be subject to at least the same degree of displeasure and censure on the part of neighbors and other passersby as homeowners are if the system triggers more than its fair share of false alarms. They probably will face even more protest, considering the acoustics and the minimal distances between neighbors in an apartment building. Under the circumstances, it may make sense to pay a little extra for such features as automatic cutoffs and reset relays when you go to buy your alarm kit. And to make sure that someone hears your alarm go off when neither you *nor* your neighbors are at home, the only really practical alternative is an automatic telephone dialer. Most metropolitan police departments will not accept taped messages or will give them very low priority if they do, given the high false-alarm rate for such messages. But a taped voice message to a stay-at-home friend or relative is a low-cost way to get this kind of protection; or better yet, if you can afford it, get hooked up by digital dialer to a round-the-clock central-alarm monitoring station that will agree to receive your message, verify it by calling back, and then call the police or any other appropriate responding agency if action is warranted.

"Buddy Buzzer" Systems

Another simpler and more primitive version of a self-installed alarm system is one that has been used in many community watch and neighborhood security programs for years, and consists of rigging up some kind of "buddy buzzer" system between two contiguous stores or apartments. This can be done with a minimal amount of wiring, and operates by means of a signal with a pre-agreed code (one buzz for the message "I'm going out," two for "I'm back home," and a third, perhaps for "I'm in trouble," to use one common example).

In apartments or shops where people are more or less housebound and can be relied on to monitor the incoming signals closely, this kind of system may be all that's needed for round-the-clock peace of mind. This is a good system for shut-ins or shopkeepers, where there is a reasonable expectation that both parties to the arrangement are going to be on the scene for the better part of the day or night; it is not an effective solution where either of the "buddies" holds a full-time job or is otherwise often away.

Intercoms

A much more exalted version of a buddy buzzer system is the housewide intercommunication system or intercom, as it is popularly known. Intercoms do not usually come with alarms, but they are an integral part of the building's security because they control a front-door latch and thereby limit access to the building by unauthorized people outside the door. As such they act as electronic doormen, and are therefore a must in any building without round-the-clock guard or doorman service. They permit communication between the tenant and someone outside the building's front door, and most of them come equipped with some kind of buzzer operated by the apartment dweller from a small speaker console inside his apartment, which releases the front-door latch by remote control and permits visitors, deliverymen, or other authorized people to come in, even if they don't have the downstairs doorkey.

There are three basic kinds of intercoms: (1) buzzer systems, with or without voice-communication capabilities, which operate over regular house-wiring system electric lines; (2) electronic systems that superimpose voice communications on the pre-existing bell- and buzzer-system lines; and (3) systems that use dedicated telephone lines to transmit conversations between the apartment dweller and the would-be visitor, combined with a simple buzzer system to open the door, or a more sophisticated computer coding device that serves the same purpose.

House-Wired Intercoms   Intercoms with voice communications that use regular house wiring can be broken down into two major types. The first and most convenient permits people to talk to each other and hear each other over the same wire by depressing a single button on the apartment's console. The second kind involves depressing one button for talking and another for listening. This can require fine-tuned timing on the apartment dweller's part and is therefore not recommended.

Aside from this basic message-relay feature, house-wired intercoms also vary considerably with respect to their audio quality and fidelity. Most apartment dwellers will not have much say in the specifications or the quality of the intercom, having inherited whatever system is already installed in the building when they moved in. But if you live in a co-operative apartment building or condominium that does not already have intercoms and is thinking of putting one in, you may want to add to the discussion about specifications for the new system. For example, clarity is important in any voice communication, and if you can, it probably pays to choose your equipment based to some degree on the quality of voice reproduction. Another consideration is volume; adjustability is a desirable feature if it is available at not too high an added cost.

Wireless Intercoms   Another variation on the voice-intercom system is one that uses a direct telephone line, instead of existing or new electrical lines, to hook the apartment up to a central console. In these so-called wireless intercoms, as in ordinary house-wired systems, a buzzer console is installed in the downstairs vestibule or on the outside of the building itself, with either a simple mouthpiece/speaker or a telephone handset for voice communications between the apartment and the street. A speaker recessed behind a mouthpiece is preferable, because telephone handsets are more vulnerable to vandalism. The front-door telephone handset relays voice signals to a local in-house number, which passes on the signal to the apartment in question. If the phone line to that apartment is already being used, a beep overrides the current conversation to notify the tenant that his downstairs door is being buzzed. The tenant then puts his caller on hold and depresses a button on the base of his phone that allows him to speak to the person downstairs. If he wants to admit the visitor he dials a pre-set code, then goes back to his original conversation by hitting the hold button again.

This system has the virtue of fairly trouble-free operation and excellent voice reproduction because it functions exactly like a regular telephone calling system. It is also relatively easy to install from the building management's point of view. Like any other telephone communications system, however, it is subject to the prevailing monthly cost of a leased telephone line.

CCTV Closed-circuit TV (CCTV) intercoms are beginning to appear in more and more high-priced commercial and luxury residential buildings. These systems first appeared in the early sixties, before the advent of solid-state electronics. Early problems in the circuitry and cameras have since been worked out, and they now represent state-of-the-art installations for apartment dwellers.

The main advantage of viewer intercoms is that the apartment dweller can discriminate between friends and strangers on the basis of the person's face. Teleprocessing can distort the sound of the human voice enough to make it difficult to distinguish one person from another; but faces are inimitable and therefore more trustworthy for making such distinctions.

Indiscriminate buzzer-pushers are a problem in most multiple dwellings; there always seems to be at least one tenant who responds to a ringing buzzer by buzzing the outsider in without checking to find out who is at the door, and CCTV intercoms are designed to give such a tenant pause. In buildings without CCTV intercoms, one way to identify indiscriminate buzzer-pushers is to go downstairs yourself and push all the apartment buzzers, one at a time, to see who buzzes back without trying to check your identity. A little judicious peer pressure may then be brought to bear on the guilty person, in the interests of the other tenants.

ELEVATORS

Because nearly all visitors in an elevator building will have to use the elevator, it is virtually impossible to assure total elevator security in a building with an unstaffed front door unless the elevator can be operated only by a key, with the understanding that each apartment dweller personally has to ride downstairs to let visitors or delivery people in. To most apartment dwellers this may seem like overkill, and they will settle for a lock on the elevator at the basement and/or roof level only, to minimize the chances of running into unauthorized outsiders lurking around the boiler room or basement laundry room.

The elevator is a kind of thoroughfare serving everyone in the building, and anything you do to hamper access to it violates its basic function as a route from one place in the building to another. But within the broad limits of this function, there are certain variables that can be controlled without overly hindering the elevator's legitimate users. Elevators have rush hours and, just as in other transit systems, rush-hour users are usually safer travel companions than those who use the elevators at other times of the day or night. Any access controls can therefore probably be limited to the off-peak hours of mid-morning, mid-afternoon, and evening, with even tighter security after eleven or twelve o'clock at night.

Elevator Security Hardware

Elevator security hardware ranges from the simple to the sophisticated. One example of the most simple is the customary concave mirror mounted in the far corner of the elevator to permit people getting on to see who is already there. If tenants or visitors don't like the appearance of the other face in the mirror they need not step in.

A more sophisticated variation on this theme is a wide-angle TV camera mounted inside the elevator, and monitored either by a doorman, the building superintendent, or an independent contracting agency. This is a high-cost alternative and is most practical when the person who monitors the camera is actually free to take immediate steps to intervene in case of attack. However, the camera itself may act as a psychological deterrent to most potential attackers, especially if it features some kind of electronic blinker or LED indicator to remind the intruder that it is turned on and operating, and that there is theoretically someone monitoring it around the clock.

Panic Buttons

Most self-service elevators are equipped with alarms that can be punched if the elevator breaks down or gets stuck between floors. But most elevator muggers act by overpowering their victims, and the victim may never come within reach of the control panel to activate the alarm, let alone ring it repeatedly to signal panic and the need for help.

One solution to this problem is to equip the elevator with one or even a modest series of invisible alarms whose location is known only to tenants. Panic buttons can be recessed behind decorative wood or metal moldings, or under the floor coverings in places not likely to be touched in the course of ordinary elevator usage. Some drawbacks to this kind of installation are the increased probability of false or mischievous alarms, especially if there are a lot of children in the building, and the likelihood that the location of the concealed panic buttons will soon become common knowledge throughout the neighborhood.

"Audio Windows"   Another solution was suggested by architect Oscar Newman in his efforts to capitalize on the apartment dwellers' sense of locally defensible space. (See page 14.) This is the so-called audio window that Newman originally planned to build into the corridor wall outside each apartment as a kind of glorified peephole backed up with two-way voice circuitry.

Another usage Newman envisioned for this window was installing it in elevators to permit passengers to call out for help, with their voices being amplified by loudspeakers mounted in the fixed wall above the elevator doors on each floor. In a heavily trafficked building this might provide anywhere from twelve to sixteen hours a day of coverage. However, unless there was also an audio window built into the apartments on either side of the elevators, it is doubtful that there would be enough people around in the corridors late at night or on off-hours throughout the day to respond to an elevator victim in distress. To make it truly effective, therefore, the elevator audio window should probably be hooked up to a selected apartment, or apartments, whose tenants would have agreed in advance to monitor the elevator on a rotating basis, day and night. In a fully staffed building, this could be a doorman's post or the live-in superintendent's quarters; in other buildings it could be the landlord's apartment, or anyplace else on the premises that has a reasonable expectation of being occupied twenty-four hours a day.

Elevator location is another variable to consider. Ideally, elevator doors should face the main entrance and should be immediately visible from the street and other parts of the lobby. Admittedly, changing elevator door locations is not an option for rental apartment tenants; and unless there has been an unusual crime wave in the building or the immediate neighborhood, even most co-op and condominium boards might be understandably reluctant to tackle the major reconstruction job involved in relocating elevator openings. However, even if elevator doors are hidden or badly placed for daylong surveyability, there are some things you can do to make them more visible. Mounting floor-to-ceiling mirrors opposite and at right angles to the door is one serviceable solution for elevators that open into alcoves; and mirrors should be reinforced with good lighting, day and night. In addition, access to the elevator should also be as open as possible: this is not the place for decorative draperies, fretwork screens, or potted plants.

STAIRCASES

In buildings without elevators, the staircase is the major thoroughfare. In buildings and townhouses where the staircase is unenclosed, it is easily monitored by apartments on each of its landings—but only when the tenants happen to be at home.

Unenclosed staircase landings should, like elevators, be equipped with concave mirrors that permit you to see at least a part of the floors immediately adjacent to yours. Hidden panic buttons on stairways may also be in order in buildings that have frequently been subject to crime. In the normal course of events, however, most old-fashioned unenclosed stairways are probably too "public" for most would-be muggers, and are therefore relatively safe from intruders—so long as you weren't followed upstairs by one and don't actually have the key in the door when he strikes.

The average apartment building mugger aims to force you into your own apartment and raid it—and you—for valuables. These so-called push-in muggings can best be avoided by tight front-door security on the part of all tenants, and a heightened degree of awareness on your part as you follow, or are followed by, a stranger on the stairs. If you find yourself on the stairway with someone whose face is unfamiliar to you (and in a small apartment or converted townhouse building, most faces will be familiar to you before long) and you are uncertain about his or her intentions, one effective course of action is to buzz every doorbell as you go past, and/or call out in a loud voice, to maximize the chances that doors will open and neighbors will respond.

Enclosed Stairways

Enclosed stairways present much the same problems as elevators. They are now required by law in many urban and suburban jurisdictions to provide a smoke-free exit in case of fire, but they also make convenient hideouts for intruders. From the intruder's point of view, they are probably preferable to elevators because they are less frequented and therefore the intruder is less apt to be interrupted in the course of committing a crime.

Buildings designed for multiple tenancy almost always have to accept some serious trade-offs between fire safety and personal security, or between security in one part of the building and security in another. Safety-conscious architects, for example, usually like to design as many fire exits as possible (or as many as local codes require) into the blueprints, while security experts, who are seldom called upon before the building is occupied, prefer to keep access points to an easily guarded minimum, with basement and roof doors rigged to sound an alarm when you open them on your way out.

Either way, enclosed-stairway security typically consists of one-way doors that can be opened only from the outside unless you have a key—thereby effectively trapping unauthorized users once they have somehow breached building security and found their way in. This system is fine in principle, because it keeps intruders out of the building's normal elevator- and corridor-access routes; but it can also be a trap for innocent bystanders who may find themselves dragged into the stairway with an intruder in what amounts to a no-exit situation.

To avoid this possibility and minimize the danger of staircase attacks, the audio window suggested for elevators makes equally good sense in an enclosed stairway, too. Loudspeakers wired into specific apartments as well as the stairway doors on each landing could provide the same kind of round-the-clock monitoring service suggested for elevators or any other enclosed and otherwise unsupervisable space.

In addition, as Oscar Newman suggests, it is a good idea to design stairways so that they exit directly into the lobby, where people entering and leaving are more likely to be seen by people on duty in the lobby or passing through it on their legitimate business.

MAILBOX SECURITY

Security experts suggest that mailboxes be placed either in as visible and easily monitored a part of the building as possible, or in a locked room of their own. The door to the mailbox room should be master-keyed in the same way that the outside vestibule key is; but for security purposes, these locks probably should not be identical.

To hold up to expectable levels of prying and/or battering attempts, mailboxes should be constructed of sixteen-gauge metal—required now by the U.S. Postal Service for new boxes—with tightly fitted doors. The size of the box can vary to accommodate magazines and other printed matter, but the actual door opening should be kept to a manageable minimum. However, the sturdiest mailbox in the world presents an easy target if it is outfitted—as many older models are—with simple, old-fashioned warded locks and keys. To do justice to a sturdy, well-designed mailbox, warded mailbox locks should be replaced with cylinder locks, and even miniaturized versions should have at least five pins.

GARAGE DOORS

In a building where access to the garage is limited to tenants and their guests, garage-door security can probably be managed by some sort of card- or code-access control, much like front-door security in the lobby. But in garages that also serve as public parking spaces during the day, or in which there is an unusual amount of nonrush-hour coming and going, garage security can be a problem.

In unstaffed garages used only by tenants, self-closing doors that permit authorized cars to enter and then close behind them automatically after a delay of about fifteen to twenty seconds may be all the security you need, so long as access from the garage to the building itself is equally tightly controlled. Switches operated by keys or solenoid cards inserted into slots on the driver's side of the garage door can be used by a driver entering or leaving the building to activate the door-opening system. (Keys and cards are usually preferable to radio-controlled door openers, which are easily misplaced or stolen, and which, if stolen, may require replacing all openers on a building-wide basis.)

Doors leading from the garage to the building should be treated like any other major entry to the building, with the appropriate locking- and/or intercom-access systems installed and in good working order. In fact, security at this level should probably be even tighter than at street level, because garages are often totally enclosed spaces without windows or other ways of supervising them from the outside, and therefore provide fewer opportunities for the round-the-clock informal monitoring of casual passersby.

LIGHTING

Everything else being equal, security is a function of maximum visibility and surveyability. Light is one obvious component of visibility, and good lighting is therefore a must in enclosed spaces like apartment building lobbies, corridors, and enclosed stairwells and elevators.

If bulb-breaking is a problem in your building, a wire-mesh covering may not be enough of a deterrent to bulb-smashers, and it may be a better idea to cover the bulb with a translucent bulb protector that does not reveal the outline of the bulb itself. There are several vandal-resistant plastic fixtures on the market that come in a range of shapes and sizes that should fit most ordinary requirements.

In installing lobby and corridor lighting, total wattage may be less important than distributing the available wattage in such a way that there are no dark corners, nooks, or crannies. It is important to provide continuous light throughout a given space, even if it is of relatively low wattage overall.

APARTMENT-SECURITY "SOFTWARE"

Locks, intercoms, access systems, and alarms are the cornerstones of good apartment-security hardware. But probably just as important as the hardware of good building security is the day-to-day "software" of building procedures, tenant organizations, and community and police relations.

In the quasi-community of a modern urban apartment house there is built-in safety in numbers. But the real safety in those numbers arises not so much from the multiplicity of people living in the building as it does from the multiplication of connections among those people, and the likelihood that they will use these connections to reinforce one another's claims on the small territory that they collectively occupy and protect.

To provide these connections, apartment dwellers should get to know each other and negotiate a set of workable dos and don'ts for everyday building operating procedures. This includes front-door and basement-door security, elevator etiquette, and fire and other emergency procedures. In co-ops and condominiums the machinery is usually in place for this kind of small-scale village "government," even though off-site building managers may actually run such day-to-day operations as firing up the furnace, repairing locks, leaks, and electric lines, and ordering fuel deliveries.

The average rental building is usually without a natural political or social organization of its own, and if you live in a building like this you might want to think about trying to establish one before the need for it actually arises in the form of a major emergency, a serious crime, or a rash of less serious offenses and vandalism. A good way to do this is to give a party with a building issue as a theme. Parties seem to draw bigger crowds than meetings, especially if the immediate issue is not one of life or death. Behind their dispassionate façades, most apartment dwellers are at least as curious about their neighbors as their neighbors are about them, and therefore more than willing to meet them face-to-face. A party could be the beginning of a tenant organization, one that can establish rules and regulations and provide the groundwork for exerting a modicum of informal social control if and when the rules are broken.

Procedures

What these rules and regulations should be is a matter of preference and circumstances. Buildings with underground garages will have to establish procedures for their opening and closing; buildings with basement laundry rooms will have security problems not found in those without them. In some modern high-rises there are rooftop gyms and basement swimming pools that may be open to the public, and some way of isolating them from the residential part of the building should be worked out. Other specific dos and don'ts will evolve from neighborhood risk factors and the peculiarities of a given building's design.

Front-Door Security   Good front-door procedures form the backbone of good building security, regardless of whatever other amenities the building or complex may boast. The front door is the major target to be hardened in any building, and security at this point is at least as critical in apartment buildings as it is in free-standing houses.

Front-door security does not begin with round-the-clock doorman service, however; even if the building has a doorman, the front door may have to be locked from time to time—between shifts, for example, or when the doorman is temporarily away from his post and there is no one on hand to relieve him.

With or without a doorman, the front door should therefore have a commercial heavy-duty lock with at least a six-pin cylinder, and if possible it should not be master-keyed, a process that makes a lock more vulnerable to picking. Doormen should be trained to keep the front door locked even when they are on duty immediately behind it, and only unlock it for a familiar face or for a visitor whose legitimate presence has been verified.

Closed Doors   Front doors, side doors, roof doors, and basement doors should be kept closed at all times. This means training tenants—and especially children—to make sure that they close the door behind them when they go out and make sure that it's latched properly when they come back in. One way to enforce this regulation is to arm all outside doors with alarms, buzzers, or beepers that sound until the latch is engaged. This is especially useful on secondary doors that are not under the round-the-clock supervision of a doorman or other security personnel. (Alarms and buzzers can be deactivated when people are moving out, or when furniture and equipment are being brought into the building.)

Elevator Etiquette and Procedures   Paradoxically, good elevator security etiquette requires a reversal of the expected courtesies, and consists of getting off (or not getting on in the first place) if you are apprehensive about someone getting on with you. Don't be afraid of offending the fellow traveler. Go with your own instincts about whom you want to ride with on an elevator. In his study of crime patterns in post-war public housing, Oscar Newman was amazed at the number of women mugging victims whose instincts had correctly warned them that the person on the elevator with them was up to no good, but who were afraid of offending that person by leaving the scene. The rule of thumb should be

"When in doubt, get out." If the person riding with you gets out, too, push the panic button, start screaming, or take other defensive measures.

Another perfectly inoffensive step apartment managers can take to make elevators more secure is to install a key lock on the basement elevator door so that no one can get into the elevator from the basement (or vice versa) unless he or she has a key. This system can be automatic by means of a twenty-four-hour clock set to lock only after certain hours.

Police/Tenant Relations

Today most city and suburban police departments are highly conscious of their relations with the community at large, and have programs to promote greater security among tenants as well as homeowners.

Landlords, tenant organizations, and co-op or condo boards can request a visit from the local precinct's crime-prevention officer, who will walk them through the building floor by floor and give them pointers on the strengths and weaknesses of their present security arrangements, including some indication of crime patterns in their particular neighborhood or on their particular block. These surveys are free and they can be instructive. Where they are available, it makes sense to use them and follow up on the resulting suggestions wherever feasible. Police are by training and experience highly sensitized to the leaks in most security arrangements, and they will be more than willing to share their insights with householders and other ordinary citizens, on the premise that an ounce of prevention is worth a pound of cure.

Tenant Security Patrols

In large apartment houses or projects, one highly effective and virtually cost-free security measure is the introduction of tenant security patrols. Building patrols are misnamed in that they do not actually patrol; more typically they involve a guard stationed at one or more entrances to the building, to sign people in and out, monitor a console for unguarded trouble spots, and stand by for response to an emergency anywhere in the building.

Guards can be paid or unpaid, live-in or nonresident. Their duties can run the gamut from simple guard duty to social service providers (senior citizen escorts, emergency service liaisons, fire wardens, etc.).

Building patrol members may be called upon to act as intermediaries between building residents and the police or other officials if and when the need arises. When patrols operate indoors, where tenants are unlikely to have any contact with the police in the normal course of events, tenants may come to see patrol members as a sort of homegrown stand-in for the police. This raises tricky ethical and legal issues that should be carefully thought out. In addition, the same questions about liability that would apply to a tenant-assessed (and/ or tenant-installed) alarm system or front-door lock are applicable in the case of security guards.

Ideally, as soon as the patrol is organized, patrol members should have a series of informal meetings with local police to get to know the local precinct's community affairs and/or crime-prevention officers and establish mutually acceptable procedures to follow in case a crime is committed or there is some other emergency calling for a police presence in the building.

A national evaluation of citizen-patrol projects by the National Institute of Law Enforcement and Criminal Justice (NILECJ) concluded that building patrols can be very effective components of indoor-security systems, with a corresponding improvement in police/community relations and round-the-clock police coverage of the particular block on which the patrolled building is located. Successful patrols, says NILECJ, have several factors in common, including appropriate personnel, organizational affiliation, and "bureaucratization." According to this evaluation, the best patrols are those where

the personnel are matched to the level of coverage the patrol seeks to provide. Patrols that maintain neighborhood organizational affiliations also tend to operate more effectively. Bureaucratization, involving a paid administrator, maintenance of records, pre-arranged scheduling, and quality control of members' behavior in the field, is a third factor that seems to enhance a patrol's ability to operate effectively.

12

AUTO THEFT
AND PROTECTION

According to the Federal Highway Administration, there were approximately 176.5 million motor vehicles registered in the United States in 1987. Over the same period, the Uniform Crime Reports issued by the FBI stated that there were 1.289 million motor vehicle thefts—up 11 percent from 1986—at a loss of over $6 billion. Of all the motor vehicles stolen in 1987, 77 percent were automobiles, 15 percent were trucks or buses, and the remainder included motorcycles, mopeds, and trailers. Statistics record an additional 2.9 million thefts of auto accessories and contents, amounting to another $1.9 billion in losses in 1987.

Using these figures, the FBI estimates that in 1987 the odds that a motor vehicle would be stolen were one out of 144 nationwide. Broken down regionally, that was one per 107 in the Northeast, one out of 127 in the West, one out of 164 in the South, and one out of 181 in the Midwest. But there are other cogent variables as well. The 1986 Annual Report of the National Automobile Theft Bureau (NATB), an organization founded by the insurance industry to help deal with vehicle theft, stated that six major cities (New York, Los Angeles, Detroit, Chicago, Houston, and Boston) and their surrounding suburbs accounted for 33.7 percent of the nation's total vehicle thefts in the previous year. Both the FBI and the NATB note that vehicle crime remains primarily a big-city problem. But it still occurs in other regions, so suburbanites and rural car owners should not count themselves immune.

RECOVERY OF STOLEN VEHICLES

In recent years about 60 to 70 percent of vehicles reported stolen have been recovered, in one form or another. Data reported by the National Automobile Theft Bureau suggest that recovery rates are improving—63 percent in 1984 and 64 percent in 1985, versus 58 percent in an earlier study by the FBI. In this FBI study of the period 1977–84, 28 percent of the stolen vehicles were found stripped for parts or accessories, 12 percent were damaged in some other way, and only 19 percent were recovered intact—leaving 32 percent that were not recovered at all.

CAR THIEVES

Law-enforcement agencies measure their success by the percentage of crimes that are "cleared" or solved, and car theft is no exception. Often the "clearance" involves an arrest; but in many instances crimes are cleared by some other means entirely—the offender is already found behind bars serving time for another offense, or he is dead, or his arrest for car theft is either impossible or impractical. Many criminals arrested for such crimes as vehicle theft are multiple offenders, and may have been arrested for car theft only after a long string of previous crimes. Since auto theft is a nonviolent crime and rarely draws a long prison sentence, in the course of plea-bargaining the thief will often detail a long list of his previous thefts in return for "consideration" for a lesser sentence. A single arrest for auto theft can therefore result in clearing many crimes.

According to the 1987 Uniform Crime Reports, nationally 15 percent of reported vehicle thefts were reported as cleared, including 14 percent in big cities, 19 percent in suburban areas, and 32 percent in rural counties. The UCR showed that, like most offenders, vehicle thieves were mostly male (90 percent) and young (58 percent of those arrested were under twenty-one and 40 percent were under eighteen).

But the age of the offenders and their similarity to other categories of offenders do not tell the whole story. House burglars are usually independent, operating on their own behalf and answerable to no one but themselves. Car theft, especially as it is emerging in the late eighties, tends to be more institutionalized, with organized crime moving in to establish and enforce guidelines, allocate territories, and set prices. Tremendous profits can be made in operating the so-called chop shops that have come to service a growing market for spare parts. As a result, key crime syndicates are taking increasing control of the auto salvage industry, complete with gang-style violence and "rubouts." The huge profits made from such activities have become major sources of financing for other criminal pursuits, and recent federal prosecutions against top mob figures have targeted auto parts and car theft to almost the same degree as narcotics dealings.

CARS TARGETED FOR THEFT

If the average car owner were asked to guess what makes, years, and models of cars are mostly likely to be stolen, he or she would probably rank late-model luxury and sports cars at the top of the list. But police data disprove this assumption. According to auto-crime detectives, the kinds of cars stolen in any given period tend to mirror the existing mix of cars currently on the road. And since the average car on the road is neither a luxury make nor this year's model, older cars are just as likely to be stolen as new ones. Understandably, the more Chevys there are on the road, the more people there are looking for spare Chevy parts—and the more Chevys there are parked on the streets, ready to be stolen for parts or joyriding or any other illegal purpose.

Older cars are by no means unattractive targets. If anything, the reverse may be true. Owners of older and less exotic cars may be less careful about where and how they park their cars or what kind of anti-theft precautions they take, usually thinking of themselves as relatively immune to car theft. But statistics indicate otherwise. Older models are more frequently involved in breakdowns and accidents than newer ones, and the parts market for older cars is therefore a brisk one. In most cases, insurance underwriters will not pay for a new part for an old car, and finding the right replacement therefore means searching through the inventories of local salvage operations—a time-consuming, tedious, and often unrewarding process altogether.

To make up for the deficit and accommodate the ever-growing market for spare parts, a whole network of local chop shops has sprung up all over the country. At the request of a local dealer, the chop-shop operator sends out his scouts, and soon a corresponding model, year, and make with the desired part makes its way from the street to the chop shop to the repair shop. Replacing a part through a chop shop is less expensive and faster than acquiring it through legitimate channels, and in some cases may indeed be the only way to get a part at all for an older car.

For this and other reasons, the data on cars stolen by make and year often makes surprising reading. The New York City Police Department's Auto Crime Division is considered one of the best in the world. It investigates more auto thefts than any other similar unit nationwide, and maintains a list of top performers on their car "hit parade," a monthly report of the thirty most stolen vehicles. A look at the July 1987 list shows that the 1978 Chevrolet led the hit list and the 1979 Chevy was not far behind, followed by the 1977. Other favorite "hits" were the 1979 Oldsmobile, the 1980 Buick, the 1983 Toyota, and the 1978 Pontiac. Although they may or may not be representative of other jurisdictions elsewhere in the country, New York City figures were not very different from those in New York State as a whole. For the first seven months of 1987, the 1978 Chevy was the state's second most stolen car, and the eleven-year-old 1977 model was third.

FEDERAL MEASURES

To make it harder to get away with stealing a car and/or its parts, a number of measures have recently been taken at the federal level. The Motor Vehicle Theft Law Enforcement Act of 1984 calls for periodic studies and reports on theft and recovery rates; though it may have little or no effect on actual auto thefts per se, it will at least permit law-enforcement authorities to keep better track of existing thefts. In addition, a major movement has been in progress for several years to apply identification numbers to individual parts of cars as well as to the car itself.

The so-called VIN (Vehicle Identification Number) is applied to the car's dashboard at the factory and is clearly visible through the windshield on the driver's side of the car. It is also repeated in concealed places on the car; their location and coding are available to law-enforcement personnel through the National Automobile Theft Bureau. In addition, the federal government now requires all manufacturers to display a safety standard label on the edge of the door on the driver's side, which contains among other data the date of assembly and the car's VIN.

The VIN spells out a code that gives a complete description of the vehicle. VINs were first used in 1954 by some American manufacturers, and the option became a standard requirement by 1981. The VIN consists of seventeen numbers or characters; the first three are designations of the nation of origin, manufacturer, and make and type of vehicle. The next five characters describe the particular attributes of the vehicle, including body style, engine strength, etc. The remaining characters identify the model, year, and plant where the car was manufactured, with the sequential production number. And starting in 1987, as one of the provisions of the 1984 Motor Vehicle Theft Enforcement Act, auto manufacturers selling passenger cars in the United States will begin to mark up to fourteen parts or components including engines, transmissions, both front fenders, both front doors and rear doors, and both rear-quarter panels and decklids, tailgates or hatchbacks, in addition to the prime VIN displayed on the dashboard.

By the terms of the same law, it is now a federal felony with a maximum fine of $5,000 and/or five years imprisonment to "alter, remove, obliterate or tamper" with the resulting identification numbers, with the affected vehicle being subject to seizure and forfeiture. To target dishonest dealers, one provision of the law makes it a crime merely to have knowledge of the obliteration of such identification numbers, and subjects violators to a $20,000 fine and/or ten years imprisonment.

CATEGORIES OF THEFT

Most law-enforcement agencies divide vehicle theft into four major categories according to the purpose of the theft: transportation, parts, resale, and insurance fraud.

Theft for Transportation

Car thieves were once assumed to be out for a joyride—or at most looking for a getaway car to take them to or from the scene of a crime. In most instances a car stolen for transportation was one that had been left unattended, with the keys left in the ignition, and was later recovered blocks or miles from home either intact or minus various crucial parts or accessories.

With improved anti-theft devices, alarms, and locks, together with public awareness of the risk to an unattended car, joyriding has ceased to be the problem it once was—at least statistically, in relation to other types of auto theft. Nowadays this kind of theft accounts for anywhere from 5 to 25 percent of total vehicle thefts, depending on regional factors.

Theft for Parts

Much more common than joyriding nowadays are thefts that involve disassembly for specific accessories or parts. This category of theft includes anything from the loss of a single bumper, tire, or stereo component up to the professional chop-shop liquidation.

The professional parts thief now accounts for at least half of all vehicular thefts. Responding to the growing demand for parts, the parts thief is constantly scouting for the most marketable items needed to maintain a well-stocked salvage operation. He can steal and disassemble a vehicle into its component parts, sometimes in a matter of minutes. The professional can reap huge profits from vehicle parts with little chance of detection, because, with no identifying marks on individual components—at least until very recently—once the parts are stripped from the car they are impossible to trace.

Many chop-shop operations are conducted in repair shops or salvage yards (auto junkyards) in remote rural areas miles from the big cities that their inventories originally came from, making it all the more difficult to match the part to the car. But lawmakers are fighting back. Some states, New York among them, have passed new laws making it mandatory for salvage dealers to keep accurate records of where and when they acquire salvageable parts, and record the final disposition of these parts to presumably legitimate repair shops. In addition to this demand for a verifiable paper trail, the New York City Police Department now has the authority to conduct so-called administrative inspections of auto junkyards, looking into the provenience of both parts and records. According to the NYPD's Auto Crime Division, there has been a noticeable drop in vehicular theft since these inspections began.

Stealing Cars for Resale

Police reserve this category for the professional and the "organization man." Stealing cars for direct resale is a multi-billion dollar industry today. Like auto-parts theft, it requires extensive network connections and the sophisticated organization to go with them. Theft-to-order involves sensitivity to the demands of the market and substantial transportation and distribution capabilities, as well as the necessary paperwork and tools to provide new or otherwise "legitimate" identification of the stolen car—including a new or altered VIN, new or forged title papers to match the VIN, and a plausible registration chain showing previous fictitious ownership.

The name of this game is to deliver a finished product: a specific model, make, and year of car with the requisite documents of title. The buyer is often an innocent consumer who believes that he or she has gotten an exceptionally good buy.

Insurance Fraud

Another and totally different kind of auto-theft entrepreneurship is insurance fraud. This is often a one-shot type of crime and would not bear mentioning in this chapter except that it vastly increases the insurance premiums of all other car owners and therefore adds unnecessary dollars to the cost of driving and maintaining a car.

Insurance fraud represents a major factor in the overall figures for auto theft. It is estimated at a high of 15 percent by the National Automobile Theft Bureau, and most law-enforcement officials think this is far too conservative an estimate. The heads of the Nassau County (N.Y.) Police Department's Vehicle Theft Squad estimated recently that 30 percent of the automobiles reported stolen in that county were actually cases of insurance fraud, and the Police Commissioner of New York City estimates that about 20,000 of the 79,250 vehicle thefts reported in his jurisdiction in 1985 were fraudulent. These figures translate into large raises in comprehensive automobile insurance premiums and a $37 million loss to New York City residents.

This kind of crime can take other forms as well. Car dumping is one of them, and is a popular solution when an older car starts failing and requires extensive overhaul or repairs that would clearly total far more than the resale value of the car. To sidestep salvage costs, the car is therefore often "dumped"—abandoned at some remote location or delivered to a friendly salvage operator who promises that the car will never be seen again in its present form. The car is then reported stolen, and an insurance claim is made.

Methodology

Since the advent of the chop shop and illegitimate resale business, the pros and their agents are always on the prowl for cars to fill existing "orders." The scouts scan city streets and parking lots for the cars most popular with their "clients," and when they find them parked regularly at a given location they record the information in their files. When the "order" comes in for such a model, the entrepreneur consults his index cards and dispatches his "agent" to steal the car.

Understandably, there are strong parallels between burglary and car theft. National statistics indicate that 42 percent of all stolen vehicles were taken with their keys still in the ignition; and an undetermined but much higher percentage were cars whose doors were left unlocked. This figure is similar to the estimated 40-plus percent of home burglaries that occur in houses with unlocked doors and windows.

But even if you routinely take your ignition keys out of the lock and lock your car doors carefully whenever you park it, there are other ways of breaking in, and to the seasoned professional, anti-theft devices like locks and alarms are merely mechanical systems that can be bypassed with a reasonable expenditure of time and energy. Locks can be picked, car windows broken, doors forced, and lock cylinders removed. Or, if all these strategies fail, the targeted car can simply be hooked up to a towtruck and openly towed away.

Tools for breaking and entering cars range from wire coat hangers, screwdrivers, and other prying and "fishing" devices, to the so-called slim jim (a flexible piece of metal strapping about eighteen inches long that can be inserted down along the car's window and maneuvered to engage the lock) or the slap hammer (a lock-cylinder puller in the form of a sliding hammer on a steel shaft with a sheet-metal screw at the end). Other, even more specialized tools designed to extract or break the ignition lock are being used increasingly as well.

Defeating an alarm is a job for a specialist. It generally requires some knowledge of how a particular system works, and how to get at its "black box" or central controls, and trace the wiring back to its power source or siren so that it can be disarmed before the alarm goes off. But unless the car is parked in a very unfrequented spot, many car thieves will be unwilling to devote much time to working this puzzle out and risk being caught in the act—particularly when there are other cars of the same make and model number without alarms easily available elsewhere on the streets.

PROTECTING YOUR CAR FROM THEFT

Despite the billions of dollars involved in car theft, it sometimes seems that the institutions set up to deal with it have been doing little to stem the tide. Car theft is a nonviolent property crime and as such has a relatively low priority in most law-enforcement agencies. Police and prosecutors have trivialized car theft to the point that it often commands little more judicial attention than does passing a red light. Insurance companies that would seem to have the most to gain from promoting anti-theft devices only reluctantly hand out premium discounts for car alarms, and then only when such reductions are mandated by local statutes. From their point of view, it is probably easier to tackle the problem of rising thefts by simply raising the premiums.

Car manufacturers seem to be almost oblivious to the security problem. In fact, in their race to reduce the weight and size of their cars to meet reduced fuel standards, manufacturers have recently been using lighter materials with less resistance to common burglar tools. To date, only a handful of car makers have included security devices as a factory-installed option available to purchasers of new cars.

In the absence of factory-installed anti-theft devices, there are still measures you can take to make your car less vulnerable to car theft, and steps you can take to make a car thief's job harder, more time-consuming, and substantially riskier. Car anti-theft add-ons are currently producing revenues of up to half a billion dollars annually, and they are growing at a rate of 30 percent per year.

There are three basic strategies for keeping thieves out of your car. The first is deterrence (commonsense measures to make the car as unattractive as possible to thieves); the second is classical target-hardening (attention to the condition of doors and locks, and the installation of various kinds of alarms); and the third is the use of immobilizing devices, which make the car impossible to move except at the owner's convenience.

DETERRENCE

Police and insurance officials believe that a substantial number of car thefts could be averted if the owners simply trained themselves to lock their doors and take the keys with them when they leave their cars unattended and parked in a public place.

The next major step in an overall deterrent strategy is to assess your parked car with a car thief's eyes. A car full of interesting-looking packages, a briefcase, or a wallet left out in full view on the front or back seat is an invitation to thievery. If you must leave things in the car, leave them in the trunk and lock it. If your car radio or stereo deck is installed so that it can be removed and hidden when you park the car and leave it (as is increasingly the case on newer brands of cars), take the time to do so.

TARGET HARDENING

Anti-theft hardware falls into three basic categories: alarms that are designed to monitor any attempt to steal the car; system interrupters or car disablers that make it impossible to drive the car away; and improved security and upgrading of ignition locks. As we have done elsewhere in this book, we will describe such devices generically. In addition, we are including the *Consumer Reports* Ratings of auto alarm systems at the end of this chapter.

The kind of perimeter "hardening" that is important to the security of houses and apartments is less relevant when it comes to cars. In the case of a car, for example, there isn't much you can do to "harden" its doors, except perhaps to substitute a tapered door-latch button for the standard mushroom type, so that it cannot be pulled up by a wired loop or coat hanger angled in through a closed side window.

Trunk Locks

Although a locked trunk provides some security by virtue of the fact that it blocks whatever is inside it from view, gaining access to the trunk without a key is probably not much harder for the average car thief than getting into the passenger compartment itself. Thieves who want to break into a trunk can do so, either by drilling a small hole alongside the lock and inserting an awl-like tool to lift the lever controlling the latch, or by pulling or punching out the cylinder of the lock itself.

Several years ago, Consumers Union testers tried out a number of trunk-lock reinforcement plates that were supposed to make trunk break-ins more difficult, and found them only marginally better than no protection at all. The more secure among these devices are hardened metal plates mounted on the trunk lid around the lock and fastened with carriage bolts, installed through the trunk lid with nuts on the inside. Some of the fancier models have an added reinforcement in the form of a rotating disk that covers the entire lock cylinder except for the slot where the key is inserted. While Consumers Union testers found that both kinds of reinforcement could be pried off, thereby exposing the lock, it did take time and additional effort to do so. Such devices may be all that is needed to steer the average thief to easier targets.

Hood Locks

Although car owners tend to think of car security in terms of keeping thieves out of the inside of the car and/or the trunk, it is equally important to keep them out from under the hood. This is the place to find all the electrical components that make an engine start and run; this is also the usual location for alarm components, together with the wiring to switches and the various controls of any anti-theft system the car may have. And latching the hood from the inside is no defense against a car thief who has managed to get inside the car.

There are devices on the market that can prevent a thief from getting under the hood of your car even if he has access to the passenger compartment, including special dead-bolt locks controlled by rods or cables running from the dashboard through the engine compartment and hooking onto the front of the hood. Most of these devices are a bit of a nuisance to operate, though, since they have to be engaged actively each time you leave the car.

Auto Alarms

There are limits to target-hardening when it comes to cars, just as there are with houses, but one way to cover all contingencies is to hook up the car's doors, engine, and trunk to a central alarm, so that when any one access point is tampered with the alarm is automatically activated. The increasing popularity of car alarms is testimony to their effectiveness, to the increasing desperation of car owners, and to the faith that many insurance underwriters place in them in the form of discounts on the owner's auto insurance policy.

The same caveats that apply to house burglar alarms apply to car alarms. A car is primarily a convenience, taking you where you want to go, when you want to go there, without advance notice or planning. If getting into the car requires fumbling around in the dark for the numbers on a digital keypad or groping under the seat and dashboard for hidden switches, driving will sooner or later cease to be a pleasure, and the alarm will cease to be turned on. Testers rate ease of turning the system on and off as a major plus or minus for specific systems. The more convenient it is, the more likely it is that the alarm will actually be used on a regular basis, according to the National Highway Safety and Traffic Administration.

An auto alarm system may not prevent a determined thief from getting into a car, but it will scare off almost everyone else, even with allowances for the prevalence of false alarms on unmolested cars. A car alarm system is like a residential burglar alarm. It has its perimeter sensors and switches at various access points (in this case the car doors, hood, and trunk lid or hatchback). It has a second line of interior sensors that can detect sound and the vibrating motion attending a break-in, including glass-breakage sensors, pressure mats (at the driver's seat), and motion detectors that go into action if an attempt is made to tow the car away. It has a control unit through which the sensors report the intrusion attempt, a power source from the existing auto battery, and provisions for an independent backup battery that can take over if the regular power system fails. Finally, it has its "voice"—the horn, siren, or flashing distress lights, headlights, or taillights that let the world know that a crime is in progress.

With literally hundreds of companies manufacturing either complete systems or separate components, and with installers sometimes mixing components from different systems to meet price, convenience, or special security needs, it would be impossible to judge the overall quality of performance any specific system could be expected to provide as installed in any particular car. At best, the consumer should go into the marketplace for car-security equipment armed with some general idea of system design and components as the basis for what in the end must be a purely individual choice.

Passive vs. Active Systems A passive system goes on and off automatically, arming and disarming at the turn of an ignition switch or the closing of the car door. Since passive systems are the easiest to use and cannot be ignored or forgotten, they command higher deductions on theft insurance than more complicated manual systems do. An active system requires the driver to flip a toggle switch, press a button, punch in a code on a keypad, or even use an additional key to arm and disarm the system. And there are some hybrids that arm the system passively but require the driver to disarm the system actively by turning a key, pushing a toggle, or punching a code into the keypad.

Other controls and features can make the system easier to live with whether it is active or passive or some combination of the two. An adjustable time delay for exit and entry is a plus in a passive alarm system, as is a beeper, buzzer, or LED light that reminds you that the system is armed. A "valet" switch can turn the system off without revealing its inner workings when you turn it over to a parking lot or service station attendant, and can also be a timesaver when you are in and out of the car on frequent brief stops.

Finally, when the alarm misfires and you can't get it to turn off, there are alarm cutoffs under the hood that are designed to bypass the usual arming and disarming mechanisms and silence the siren at the source. Keep in mind, however, that such a feature may be equally accessible to a moderately savvy car thief.

Sensors The most commonly used sensor is the *pin switch,* a spring-loaded mechanical plunger connected to the auto's power supply and through the control box to the alarm. When the door is closed, the plunger is depressed into its housing in the door frame and no electrical contact is made. When the door opens it releases the plunger; electric contact is made, triggering the alarm.

Pin switches are already present in all cars; they are used to operate dome and convenience lights in the passenger compartment when the door is opened. In some models, such convenience lights and their switches are found under the hood and trunk. Where they do not already exist, separate pin switches have to be hard-wired into the alarm system. Some alarm installers make use of the car's existing switches while others recommend installing separate hard-wired switches to serve the alarm sensors only.

Voltage-monitoring sensors: These are the most popular alternatives to the hard-wired pin switch described above. They work by monitoring the voltage usage inside the car. When a door opens, or dome or courtesy lights turn on, there is normally a voltage drop, just as there is when driving lights are switched on or the ignition is activated.

The weakness in this kind of voltage-monitoring sensor is that if for some reason the light does not go on (i.e, there is a defective light bulb or one that is not screwed in properly), there is no voltage change and hence no alarm is sounded. Voltage-monitoring sensors also have to be adjusted to compensate for electronic accessories like self-winding auto clocks that sporadically draw current, and other intrusion sensors (i.e., sonic or vibration detectors that also drain some power when they are switched on).

Intrusion sensors: Many systems have a backup sensor that will sense an attack even when the door, trunk, or hood is closed. Most of these are motion sensors that protect a car from being towed or pushed away by a thief. This kind of sensor responds to shaking, tilting, or bumping of any kind, and is designed to resist any towing or pushing. Motion sensors usually come in the form of a pendulum switch mounted under the hood. The sensors can also be controlled externally, but the most effective ones work on time-delayed exit/entry controls located inside the passenger compartment. Their weakness lies in their susceptibility to being triggered by otherwise innocent bumps and jostlings.

Other car-intrusion sensors include vibration or sound sensors that detect and respond to window breakage, and resonance detectors that respond to both glass breaking and the opening of a door. Ultrasonic detectors like those used in house-interior protective systems project invisible ultrasonic beams inside the passenger compartment, and respond both to the sound of breakage and to actual motion inside the car. Another type of sensor is similar in effect to the pressure mats used inside houses, except that it is mounted on the driver's seat rather than the floor.

Although the sensitivity of such sensors is adjustable, they are prone to false alarms from vibrations and sounds common on any city street. Lightning and thunder, hail, and other natural phenomena have also been known to set them off.

Horns, Sirens, and Lights   The effectiveness of any auto alarm system, like that of a household alarm system, is its "voice"—the noise it makes to attract attention and (you hope) frighten off the thief. Like house alarms, car alarms should be as loud as possible, producing a sound that is instantly recognizable far and wide. And, just like house alarms, car alarms should come equipped with controls and safeguards that permit them to go on sounding even after major efforts to bypass them or turn them off.

Horns: Many low-cost alarm systems use the car's own existing horn as an alarm signal. This is not a very good idea for a number of reasons. Car horns are subject to wear and tear, malfunctions, and breakdowns. In addition, horns that are installed at the factory are fairly easy to get at under the hood, where they can easily be dismantled or disconnected. Finally, the sound of a blaring horn is so commonplace on many city streets that even if it is actually in its alarm mode and not a false alarm, chances are that it will go unnoticed or be written off as a "stuck" horn on its way to a service station for repairs.

Mechanical sirens: These are bulky motor-driven sirens. Although they produce an impressive decibel level, they also have many intrinsic disadvantages. For example, the moving parts become corroded and inoperative when exposed to water, sand, salt, and ordinary road grime; rusted sirens can short-circuit, causing extensive damage to the electrical system. Mechanical sirens also draw substantial amounts of power and can therefore drain the battery after they have been sounding for some time. In addition, these sirens usually send out a steady tone that is hardly distinguishable from factory whistles and otherwise non-alarming urban noises, thus making them easy to ignore on a busy street in a relatively noisy neighborhood.

Electronic sirens: The most effective sirens currently on the market are the electronic "warblers" whose undulating sound is unique, or at least unusual enough to attract attention on the busiest of streets. Although not as loud as most mechanical sirens, most electronic warblers produce anywhere from eighty-seven to ninety-three decibels, which is more than loud enough to be effective. These sirens usually draw little power, which means that they can go on sounding for long periods of time without excessive drain on the car's battery. They are also capable of operating independently of the car battery on a backup nine-volt battery of their own.

Flashing lights: Some systems are designed to set off the car lights as attention-getters in addition to sounding an audible alarm. Some only turn on the hazard lights; others activate all parking lights including front, rear, and side lights. Still others will also flash the headlights. These may be a worthwhile addition, especially if the alarm is triggered at night and in a reasonably public place. Lights will direct attention to the specific car whose alarm has been triggered, whereas the source of a siren's sound may be difficult to locate. However, the flashing of the car's headlights could drain so much power from the battery that they end up closing down the entire alarm system.

Controls Car alarm systems, like household burglar alarms, come with many basic controls that can assist their operation and make them easier to live with. A good alarm system should have the following features at a minimum:

Holding relay: This relay keeps the alarm sounding even though the door, lid, or hood is immediately closed by the thief in his attempt to silence it.

Automatic alarm cutoff and reset delay: This prevents the audible alarm from continuing endlessly, annoying passersby and neighbors and draining the battery. It cuts off the alarm after a pre-set time, varying from thirty seconds up to ten minutes, and some experts suggest the longer the better. The cutoff relay is usually coupled with a companion relay that immediately rearms the system after the timed cutoff, so that the system is once again ready to detect any further attempts.

Manual cutoff switch: This is a hidden switch, usually concealed under the hood, that permits the owner to shut off the siren if it goes off accidentally. Sometimes referred to as the "midnight cutoff," it can disable the siren without turning off such other valuable security devices as engine disablers and sensors. It cuts down on complaints from the neighbors and permits the owner to drive to a repair shop without attracting embarrassing attention from police or passing motorists.

Panic switch: These are as useful in cars as they are inside the house for personal protection, especially if you are driving alone. They are mounted inside the car and easily accessible, within easy reach of the driver's seat, and allow you to sound the alarm independently of door switches and other sensors.

Exit/entry timed-delay circuit: This kind of relay is found in all active alarms of the sort that must be armed before the operator gets out of the car. It gives the driver time to arm the system, get out of the vehicle, and close and lock the doors without setting off the alarm. The arming and disarming switches are usually cleverly concealed and made so time-consuming to operate that a thief unfamiliar with the location or the mechanics of the cutoff will in all likelihood set off the alarm before he can find the relay or defeat it. Generally the delay for exit (five to twenty seconds) is shorter than the delay for entry (forty-five seconds). Both are set by the installer or at the factory. When Consumers Union tested these systems in 1986, it found that some of them allowed too short a time for exit, sometimes as little as five seconds.

Alarm switches on the trunk and hood of a car should be made to operate independently of the exit/entry delay relay, so that they will instantly trigger the alarm in the event that they are tampered with when the system is armed. This can pose a problem, however, unless you remember to turn off the alarm every time you want to look under the hood or open the trunk while the ignition is turned off.

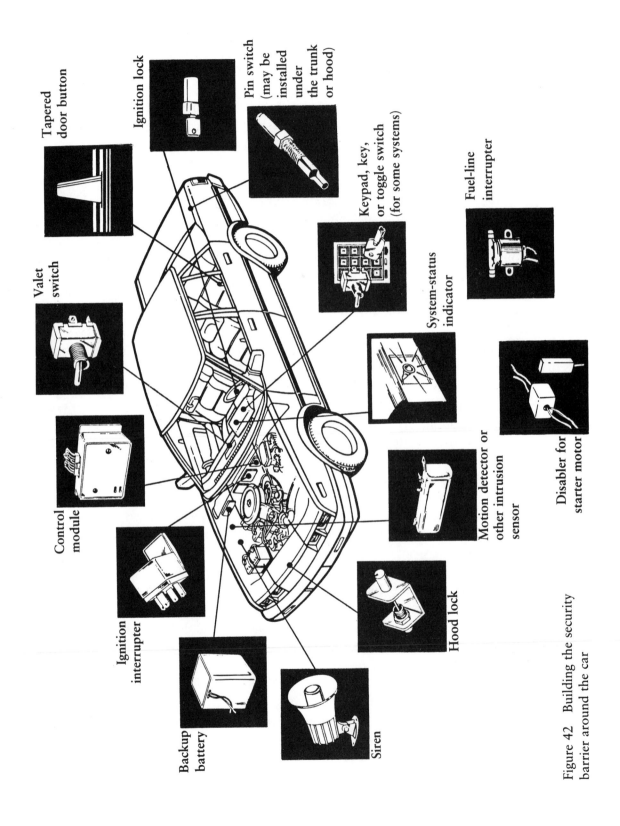

Tapered
door button

Ignition lock

Pin switch
(may be
installed
under
the trunk
or hood)

Keypad, key,
or toggle switch
(for some systems)

Fuel-line
interrupter

Valet
switch

System-status
indicator

Control
module

Motion detector or
other intrusion
sensor

Disabler for
starter motor

Ignition
interrupter

Hood lock

Backup
battery

Siren

Figure 42   Building the security
barrier around the car

Arming and Disarming the System   Arming and disarming systems for auto alarms can be either active or passive.

Passive systems: These are preferable to active systems. They are activated by switching off the ignition, and disarmed by switching the ignition on. The system is fully automatic and therefore impossible to overlook or forget. For this reason, insurance underwriters and the government agencies that regulate them mandate higher rebates for passive systems than they do for active ones, where the driver has to make a separate move to turn the system off or on.

An additional refinement of passive systems is the passive door-arming system. These do not arm themselves until the ignition is turned off, the key is removed, a door is opened, and all doors are then shut—precluding the need for the driver and passengers to rush out of the car to avoid the car's automatic alarm delay period. In addition, some systems on the market only arm themselves passively but are disarmed actively by punching a specific code or turning a key.

Active systems: Some active systems consist of a key-operated lock mounted on the outside of the car—usually a fender. But although these externally mounted locks are convenient to operate, they are also visible and exposed to attack. As a result, active systems are increasingly being designed with concealed toggle switches or numbered digital keypads mounted in the passenger compartment.

In addition to the switches themselves, there are also a wide variety of devices designed to foil any attempts at disarming the system by anyone other than the owner. One of these involves the use of a specially encoded card that must first be inserted into a decoder before the car will start. Another involves a magnetic switch, with one of a pair of magnets concealed behind the dashboard; still another requires the driver to touch two secret locations simultaneously on the dashboard before the car can be started.

Numbered-code keypads: Some of the more sophisticated and expensive alarm systems feature a numbered keypad into which a coded sequence of numbers must be punched to disarm the alarm each time you enter the car. Because these usually come with a passive alarm system that automatically arms itself as you get in and out, the constant punching of keypad numbers may become unnerving. Because of this, many car owners simply do not turn on the alarm. These systems have other inconveniences as well. It can be difficult to get into a car with your arms full of packages and gloves on, then immediately start punching a keypad—especially if it is dark inside the car. In addition, if you let other people drive the car you will have to teach them the code. By and large, keypad disarming should be avoided unless the car is being used only by a restricted number of disciplined drivers.

Remote Controls   The convenience of remote control devices is gauged by the ease with which they are disarmed. Some systems use small portable radio transmitters carried by the operator, which work in the same way as a wireless remote control for a garage door, utilizing coded radio signals.

Valet Cutoff   This gadget cuts off the entire security system by the operation of a special key, punched-in code, or unique manipulation of the ignition key. After the cutoff is armed, the car can be turned over to a parking lot or service station attendant without disclosing anything about the way the alarm system works.

Pagers (Silent Alarms)   These are a kind of alarm similar to pocket paging systems. They use a small transmitter that sends out a coded signal on the Citizens Band (CB) to pocket-sized receivers that the driver carries with him. The transmitter is hooked up to sensors or switches at all the car's access points, and sounds the alarm at the first attempt at tampering.

These systems usually need a specially installed antenna for their use. The single-watt systems have a very restricted range in urban downtown areas because of interference from surrounding concrete and steel structures. They work better in open and suburban areas, where their range may extend to half a mile or more. There are some larger, four-watt models on the market that send out much stronger signals—but even these have a limited range in a big-city setting. Consumers Union testers tried out several models in 1986 and concluded that although they worked as advertised, their limited range and high cost made them a poor buy for the money.

Another important consideration in the use of silent alarms is that the thief himself may be totally unaware of the fact that he has triggered the alarm and is thus not deterred from continuing the attempt to break in. Even if you call the police immediately, it may be some time before they arrive, and the thief may long since have finished his job and driven off in your car. This device may make some sense as an expensive add-on or auxiliary system in a very heavily defended car, but as a first-line alarm system it is probably not a good bet.

SYSTEM INTERRUPTERS

A system interrupter (often referred to as a "black-box security system") acts as a final line of defense against auto theft once a thief has broken into the car. System interrupters act by disabling one or more of the vehicle's vital systems, so that the car can't start or, if it does, can travel only a very short distance before coming to a standstill.

The concept of disabling devices started in the late sixties, when the federal government mandated the installation of steering and transmission locks. With the steering wheel and shifting lever immobilized by such locks, it would be almost impossible to drive off in the car, even if it had been "hot-wired" to get the engine started. Since then, other system interrupters have been designed and refined. The newer versions can either cut off the ignition, the starter, the fuel supply, or in some instances they can even lock the brakes.

The original system disablers were active devices that required separate controls and switches to activate them; but many of the later models are engaged automatically merely by turning the ignition key. They therefore qualify as passive devices for insurance-rebate purposes.

Types of Interrupters

Ignition Interrupters The ignition interrupter is a small relay that cuts off the flow of current to the ignition when it is activated. In active systems it takes a special key or toggle switch to turn on, while in passive systems the interrupter is turned on simply by turning the ignition key. While one kind of ignition interrupter will not allow the engine to turn over, there are some models that allow the car to get started but will stall the engine after about ten seconds of operation. Ignition interrupters won't work on cars with diesel engines; they are also not recommended for newer-model cars with computerized ignition systems, since attaching an ignition interrupter can void the warranty of the car.

Starter Interrupters These interrupters cut off the current to the starter motor relay. They work on diesels as well as normal engines, and are recommended for newer-model cars with computerized ignition systems. For this reason, they are among the most highly recommended for all kinds of cars.

Fuel Line Cutoffs This cutoff disables the car by cutting off the fuel to the engine and carburetor. In some active systems the cutoff is manually operated by a control reachable from the driver's seat. In the more sophisticated passive models, turning the ignition key activates an electronically operated fuel valve. With a fuel cutoff system the car will start up as usual, but it can run only for a short time before the gas remaining in the fuel line and carburetor is used up. Then the car stalls out, usually just a short distance from where it was originally parked. To restart the car with this kind of cutoff you have to disengage the valve, usually by means of some hidden toggle switch or key. This system can be used with an ignition or starter cutoff device to provide a further layer of security.

Brake Disablers In addition to systems that cut off the fuel flow and/or disable the ignition or starter, there are devices on the market that can lock the brakes as well. But these systems are difficult to install and may so completely immobilize the system that when they malfunction they can make roadside repairs impossible and towing to a repair shop difficult.

Override Switch The best disabling systems come with an override switch that turns off the disabler in case of malfunction. Overriders can also serve as the parking lot "valet" function when necessary.

All delayed-action disablers have certain built-in disadvantages in that they permit the car to be driven for a short distance before stalling out. This is all very well and good if the driver is a car thief, who can simply abandon the car wherever he happens to be at the time of the stall; but if the car's legitimate owner inadvertently fails to disengage the disabler before entering traffic, it can bring disastrous results. The car's owner also incurs civil liability for any accident that might result from a thief's abandoning the car, because this can be construed by the courts as an event the owner should have foreseen when he installed the disabler in the first place.

Protecting the Ignition Lock

Most alarms and system interrupters are controlled by means of the ignition key, but the critical role that the ignition plays in arming and disarming a car's security systems seems so far to have elicited little attention from car manufacturers, who as a rule do not focus on the weakness of the original ignition lock. Despite an increasingly sophisticated arsenal of ignition-lock breakers in the hands of car thieves, most ignition locks are primitive by the standards of household locks and cylinders, and as a result are highly vulnerable to manipulation and physical assault.

Replacement Locks   Faced with these obvious oversights on the part of car manufacturers, the lock industry has come up with a seemingly impregnable replacement lock completely recessed into the steering wheel column, where it is inaccessible to any kind of existing lock puller. It resists the screw tip of the slide hammer and the lock puller by surrounding the keyway with a hardened-steel face guard. Dead-locking retainers and stress-displacement rings add to the level of protection. The cylinder is a high-security design with superior pick and drill resistance, whose specially cut keys can be duplicated only by factory-authorized dealers.

While this device at first glance might seem to solve the problem of weak ignition locks, its theft resistance is ultimately a function of the strength of the steering column's housing. Until recently, such housings were routinely constructed of sturdy cast steel. Lately, however, as part of a mandated downsizing and weight reduction on the part of car manufacturers, designers have switched from metal to plastic steering-wheel housings, and as a result the value of this kind of replacement lock has been seriously undermined. Consumers Union testers found that locks in plastic housings could be knocked or pulled out in just a few minutes, using common tools. But for older cars or even some current top-of-the-line models that still feature metal steering-wheel housings, it is an excellent choice; and there is cause for hope that the National Highway Safety Board's anti-theft equipment standards will encourage a return to metal steering columns as an approved security feature in all standard cars.

Mechanical Ignition Lock Cuffs   Ignition lock cuffs are designed to provide an added layer of protection for original-equipment ignition locks. These cuffs surround the ignition lock and protect it from assault. There are several brands currently on the market. Some models face the keyway away from the dashboard and the driver for added pick resistance. Although the inconvenience of access may seem a small price to pay for the added security, Consumers Union testers found such cuffs vulnerable to head-on physical assault, and therefore hardly worth the effort and expense of installing them.

Cane Locks Cane locks are designed to hook the steering wheel to the brake pedal and thereby immobilize both of them at once. They are constructed of a telescoping rod with J-shaped bends at either end, adjustable by means of a sliding lock. Consumers Union testers found that cane locks can be knocked apart easily by simple hammering, and therefore offer little real protection beyond slowing down the would-be car thief.

Protecting Stereos and Tape Decks The high-priority targets of an increasing number of car burglars are the stereos and tape decks that have become a common accessory in many new cars. There is always a brisk market for such items on the street. While there are various kinds of metal plates or covers designed to make a car's stereo equipment more secure, most offer only limited protection.

ANTI-THEFT PRECAUTIONS

There are many commonsense precautions that can be taken to reduce the odds that a car or its contents will be stolen. Some require a minimal outlay of money and effort. The National Auto Theft Bureau recommends the following measures as a means of deterring or deflecting car theft or burglary:

1. Park in well-lighted areas, preferably where there are other cars parked. Try to park on a busy street or at least near occupied homes or buildings. Avoid parking on deserted streets or in remote and isolated parts of a parking lot.

2. Try not to park at the end of a line of cars. Park between two other vehicles, with your front wheels sharply turned to the right or left, and put on the emergency brake before leaving the car. This way, it will be difficult for a thief to push or tow the car away.

3. Use a garage with a door that locks if one is open and available, especially when parking your car at night or in a high-crime area. Then remove the keys and lock the car and the garage, taking the keys with you. Some of the larger city garages are considered high-crime areas, particularly when they contain many unattended levels, and should therefore be avoided whenever possible.

4. Take the same precautions when parking the car in a driveway. Lock all doors, keep all the windows rolled up, and lock the glove compartment.

5. Take the key with you every time you get out, even if you are leaving the car for a very short time. In some jurisdictions, you are liable for a summons if you leave the keys in an unattended vehicle.

6. Don't leave ignition keys concealed in the car or in magnetic boxes stuck under the dashboard or fender. Car thieves are on to this ploy and are always on the lookout for such hiding places.

7. Leave only the ignition key with the attendant in a parking lot. If necessary, separate it from house keys and other keys. Parking-lot attendants have been known to duplicate such keys and get the owner's house address from the registration papers, as a step toward a future burglary.

8. Never use an identification tag bearing the car's license-plate number with your keys. If you lose your keys and a thief finds them, he will know what car to look for.

9. Always know the license number, make, and model of the car you have parked, whether it is your own or someone else's. That way, if the car is stolen you can give the relevant information to the police, even if you don't have the registration with you.

10. Don't keep the driver's license and vehicle registration in the car itself. If the car is stolen, the thief could use these papers to impersonate the owner. Always keep important documents on your person.

11. Don't leave money, checkbooks, wallets, or credit cards—or anything else of value— in the car at any time.

12. When leaving a car unattended, keep packages and other portable and valuable items locked in the trunk out of sight. Hiding them under blankets and other paraphernalia doesn't fool the vast majority of thieves.

13. When returning to your car after parking in an unfamiliar area, check to see if it has been tampered with, and scan the back seat to see if someone is hiding inside the car.

14. If you do park in an unfamiliar area and discover that your car won't start when you come back to it, be very wary of the stranger who wants to help. He may be setting you up for a crime.

15. When you leave the car parked and unattended, even in a familiar area and even for a very short time, be sure to activate all anti-theft devices and alarms.

Identification of vehicles after they have been stolen is difficult for all parties to the theft, including police, car owners, and insurers. Even with VINs, ownership may be difficult to trace because sophisticated thieves are adept at erasing or altering the original manufacturers' codes. Owners are advised to make identification easy by placing their own "brands" on their cars. To do so, officials advise using engraving tools available from most local police as part of the "Operation ID" program to engrave the VIN in several hard-to-get-at locations. Another suggestion is to use dye markers for the same purpose at inconspicuous spots on the interior dome or less-visible spots on the car upholstery. Write your name, address, and VIN under the hood or the trunk lid, using a dye marker or a white touch-up brush. Hide business cards or home address labels in window channels or on the bottom of floor mats and under the seat.

HOW TO PROTECT YOURSELF FROM BUYING A STOLEN CAR

As part of its crime-prevention effort, the NYPD's Auto Crime Division regularly sends expert detectives into the community with advice on auto theft. They offer the caveat that there is no absolute way of guaranteeing that a used car for sale is not stolen. But to reduce the chances that it is, they recommend the following precautions:

1. Buy a car only from a reputable car dealer. This way there is a better chance of recovering some, if not all, of your money if the car you bought turns out to be a stolen one.
2. Pay by check or money order. Never pay cash. This way you have your check as your receipt.
3. Be wary of bargains and "sad stories." Car thieves will play on your greed and/or your sympathies to sell you a stolen car.
4. Require identification from the seller. Always make sure that the seller is actually the person named on the title paper, registration, and transfers.
5. Be very cautious of out-of-state documents of registration and title. Some states require very little proof of ownership to register a vehicle.
6. Get a notarized bill of sale. Make sure that the bill of sale also shows the actual price you paid for the car.
7. Register the car yourself. Never let the seller register the car for you, since as one of his techniques a professional thief will often register a car other than the one he is selling you, then give you the stolen car with fraudulent documents.
8. Be careful to check the VIN on the visible VIN plate and make sure that it is exactly the same as the one that appears on the registration and title papers. The VIN plates

can usually be found on the dashboard or on the driver's door-hinge post. A further check can be made by examining the federal safety sticker at the edge of the driver's door. It contains the VIN of the vehicle in addition to other information.

9. If in doubt, don't buy the car. Auto-crime experts say that if the car you buy is actually a stolen vehicle, you as the buyer stand to lose the car and everything you paid for it if the police trace it to you.

Auto alarm systems

Guide to the Ratings

Listed by types; within types, listed in order of estimated quality. Closely ranked models differed little in quality; models judged equal are bracketed and listed alphabetically. Except as noted: all have sirens that produced between 92 and 96 decibels; all do-it-yourself models lacked minor installation hardware.

① **Brand and model.** These are component systems and sometimes require purchase of more than one part. In such cases, we note multiple model numbers.

② **Price.** What we paid for dealer-installed models; what the manufacturer suggests for do-it-yourself models. Includes any parts bought separately.

③ **Convenience.** Our judgment of how easy a system was to use.

④ **Entry/exit.** How long a system gives you to get in or out of the car before the alarm goes off. Some systems allow too little time for entry—5 seconds to get in (as on the *Pioneer PAS 100*) is not enough. Adjustable times are usually set by the installer, not the user.

⑤ **Arming/disarming.** Systems with a **passive** mechanism usually arm when you turn off the ignition and disarm when you turn it on. Because you don't have to take extra steps, they're the easiest kind to use. Best are passive systems that don't start to arm until a door has been opened, and all doors are shut (**passive door**, in the table). They don't make you race a timed exit delay. Some systems arm passively, but require you to actively disarm them. **Active** mechanisms include a special **key**, a numeric **keypad** into which you punch a code, or a **toggle switch**. The toggle is less secure than the other types—there are only so many places to hide such a switch within the driver's reach.

⑥ **Integral disabler.** Engine disablers are often an integral part of the system. They're easier to use than disablers that have to be activated separately. A disabler, generally an electronic switch that interrupts current to the starter motor or the ignition system, keeps the car from being started. The installer often decides which system to interrupt. Attaching it to the starter is generally preferred, especially with late-model cars that have a computerized ignition system; attaching the disabler to the ignition can void the warranty on such a car. One system (*Automotive Security Products*) disrupts the fuel supply; even if a thief started the car, it would go only a few blocks.

⑦ **Intrusion sensor.** Most systems have some way to sense an attack even if the door, hood, or truck is left shut: a **vibration** or **sound** sensor to sense a window being broken; a **motion** sensor to tell if the car is being moved. A **resonance** detector can tell if a door has been opened or if a window is broken; **ultrasonic** sensors do all that, plus sense any motion within the car. Several systems require you to buy sensors separately as options. Their sensitivity can usually be adjusted—important if you are to avoid false alarms from a careless parker, say, or a ball bouncing off the hood.

⑧ **Hood lock.** Typically comes as part of a separate engine disabler and must be actively engaged each time—a nuisance. A dead bolt operated by a key in passenger compartment.

⑨ **LED indicator.** Many systems have a little light-emitting diode that shows whether the system is armed or not. LED indicators are much more convenient than systems whose sirens chirp when arming (see Comments).

⑩ **Valet mode** lets you leave your car at a service station or parking garage without revealing the mysteries of the car's security system. It turns the system off—with a switch, a punched-in code, a special key, or a maneuver with the ignition key.

⑪ **Panic switch.** This allows someone in the car to sound the alarm without opening the door.

⑫ **Backup battery.** Integral to *Multi Guard*, an option with the rest. It supplies power to the alarm should an intruder disable the car battery. Good, especially if car's electrical system can be reached from below.

⑬ **Comments.** Other features and performance peculiarities.

Company names and numbers
For top-rated products: Crimestopper Security Prod., Inc., 805-526-9400; Clifford Electronics Inc., 800-824-3208; Alpine Electronics of America Inc., 213-326-8000; MaxiGuard of America, 800-323-6601; Vehicle Security Electronics Inc., 800-932-9999.

Ratings

Auto alarm systems

As published in *Consumer Reports*, October 1986.

Better ● ◐ ○ ◑ ● Worse

Brand and model	Price	Convenience	Entry/exit sec.	Arming/disarming	Integral disabler	Intrusion sensor	Hood lock	LED indicator	Valet mode	Panic switch	Backup battery	Comments
	②	③	④	⑤	⑥	⑦	⑧	⑨	⑩	⑪	⑫	⑬
Professionally installed systems												
Crimestopper HP2501	$399	●	0-28[1]	Passive door/passive	✓	Vibration	—	✓	✓	✓	✓	C,D,E
Clifford System III	550	●	30[1]	Passive door/active remote	✓	Vibration	—	✓	✓	✓	✓	A,B
Alpine 8101	400	◐	0-45/5-45	Passive door/active keypad	✓	Vibration, motion	—	✓	✓	✓	—	E
Maxiguard P-1000; Maxi-Lok L480	370	◐	5-30/60	Passive/passive	—	Motion	✓	—	✓	✓	✓	F
Techne Ungo TL1600	485	◐	[2]/32	Passive/active remote	✓	Vibration, motion	—	✓	✓	✓	✓	B,I,R
Thug Bug Avenger 1001; 0825, 0826	450	○	0-24/40	Passive/active keypad	✓	Motion	✓	✓	—	—	—	A,F
Paragon K6550; KPS9200	550	○	13/65	Passive/passive	—	Optional	—	—	✓	✓	—	—
VSE Digi-Guard VS8200	450	◐	5-30/60-180	Passive/active keypad	✓	Motion	✓	✓	✓	✓	✓	P
Code Alarm CA1085	325	◐	3-30/3-60	Passive/active keypad	✓	Optional	✓	✓	✓	✓	✓	A
Chapman-Lok Generation III; System 400	375	◐	11 or 18/60	Active key/active key	✓	Motion	✓	✓	—	—	—	A,G
Multi Guard MGB II	300	○	0-21/60	Active toggle/active toggle	✓	Vibration	—	✓	—	✓	✓	A,G,H,P
Watchdog Trooper[3]; BM707R	260	○	12/55	Passive/passive	—	Vibration	—	✓	—	—	—	A,G
Anes Pro 900; HL Pro 10	472	◐	15/110	Passive/passive	—	Sound	✓	—	—	—	—	A,K
Pioneer PA200	324	●	2-25/30	Active toggle/active toggle	✓	Ultrasonic	—	—	—	—	—	A,F,J,R
Harrison 7119; 7828	281	○	17/70	Passive/passive	—	Optional	—	✓	✓	✓	✓	G,I
Automotive Security Products K400FS	455	○	16/45	Active keypad/active keypad	✓	Optional	—	✓	—	—	—	G,L
McDermott AKO12; KP-1	467	●	13/30	Active toggle/passive	—	Motion	—	✓	✓	✓	✓	G,J

Do-it-yourself systems

Model	Price		Ratio	Arming		Sensor				Comments
Crimestopper CS9502; CS8003	221	◑	0-28[1]	Passive/passive	—	Vibration	—	—	—	M
VSE Theftrap VS7810; SureStop VS3600	170	◑	11/15	Passive/passive	—	Vibration	✓	✓	✓	—
Auto Page MA/07S	165	◐	[2]/46	Passive/active remote	✓	Resonance	✓	✓	✓	B,N
Audiovox AA9135; AA7007	140	○	13/60	Passive/passive	—	Ultrasonic	✓	✓	✓	G
Sears Cat. No. 5980	100	◑	10 or 18/45	Passive/passive	—	Motion	—	—	—	G,I,Q
Anes KD5000	99	●	14/55	Active toggle/active toggle	✓	Motion	—	✓	—	A,G
Pioneer PAS100	100	●	5/30	Active toggle/active toggle	✓	Vibration	—	✓	—	G,J
Wolo 612-XP	82	●	15/150	Active toggle/active toggle	✓	Motion	—	✓	—	O

[1] Unlimited—arms when last door closes.
[2] Unlimited—disarms by remote control.
[3] Also sold as do-it-yourself model.

Key to Comments

A - Hood and trunk switches are an extra-cost option.
B - Has remote transmitter to arm or disarm system from outside car.
C - Needs battery to power memory; inconvenient to replace.
D - Parking lights flash when alarm is tripped.
E - Has override switch that allows car to start should engine disabler malfunction.
F - Headlights flash when alarm is triggered.
G - Alarm stopped too soon, after only one cycle, if entry point was left ajar.
H - Comes with backup battery.
I - Siren emits chirp at start of arming cycle.
J - Siren perceptibly quieter than most.
K - Paging device beeps when alarm is tripped.
L - Has fuel-line cutoff and ignition cutoff as engine disablers.
M - All installation hardware and wire included.
N - Siren emits chirp at end of arming cycle.
O - Once alarm is tripped, it runs until stopped or until battery is drained.
P - According to manufacturer, model discontinued but may still be available.
Q - According to manufacturer, model discontinued.
R - Disabler was optional extra.

13

WHAT TO DO
IF IT HAPPENS TO YOU

In 1986, the average U.S. household had a 5.3-percent chance of being burglarized, and indications since then are that the risk is rising. Burglary rates vary from year to year; at the time of this writing, they were in a mild upswing following a seven-year downward trend. But the yearly figures may give a false sense of security by deflating any one individual's specific chances of being victimized in any one particular year. Stretched over a lifetime, research conducted recently at the U.S. Bureau of Justice Statistics suggests that your household's overall chances of being hit by burglars are much higher than previously suspected.

"At 1975–84 victimization rates, over a period of twenty years almost three out of every four households will suffer a burglary," writes statistician Herbert Koppel, and "three out of eight will suffer more than one." There is a one-out-of-five probability that someone in your household will lose a car to theft, and a somewhat higher probability that you or some member of your household will be the victim of an automobile accident. Clearly, then, there is a much better than fifty-fifty chance that you will become the victim of a burglary over the course of your lifetime.

In a study of 274 New York City crime victims, criminologist Kenneth Friedman found that whether or not a given crime involves actual personal contact between the victim and the offender, for the victim it is still invariably interpreted as a crime against the person. This means that, assuming you were in the house when the burglary took place, you will probably have gone through some of the same fear and trembling, the same escalating terror and paralysis that many rape and other assault victims experience in the course of the crime.

If you come back to a house that has recently been attacked by a burglar, the sense of violation may be equally acute. Researchers at the National Institute of Justice rated victims of "intrusive" crimes like rape, assault, robbery, and burglary on such measures as fear, anxiety, stress, "dismay," and overall adjustment one month and again two months after the crime, and found that there were no significant differences among victims on these measures.

Crime victims can now count on a growing range of services to see them through the aftermath of the crime. A new consensus on victims' rights seems to be building, and with an ever-increasing number of people who have been victimized at one time or another in the past, "victimology" is becoming a respectable sub-discipline of social psychology and criminal justice studies.

AFTERMATH OF A BURGLARY

Calling 911

After a break-in has occurred, a first step for most victims is—or should be—to call the police. If you are in the house when the intrusion occurs and the telephone is within reach, call your city's central 911 emergency number (if it has one) or your local operator, and have him or her contact the police for you. Dialing the precinct number may be more than a frightened tenant or homeowner is capable of in a darkened room in the middle of the night. If so, dialing 911 or 0 is a feasible shortcut and may be the best that the anxious victim can manage. Police in most jurisdictions tend to respond quickly and with real urgency to reports of a burglary in progress.

If you come home and find something amiss—an open door, an unexpected car or truck in the driveway, or some more subtle sign that things are not quite right—don't go into the house; run to your nearest accessible neighbor and call the police from there. Do not attempt to enter a house where there is a burglary in progress.

Train yourself to enter your own house cautiously, with all your senses alert. This may go against the homeowner's natural psychological grain, since most people are inclined to let down their defenses the closer they get to home, but having all your antennas up and well-tuned as you enter your own front door can pay off in terms of security in the long run.

Dealing with Police and Courts

Calling the police may be a reflex reaction for victims of a crime. But what exactly can you expect at the hands of the criminal justice system? Victims and critics of the system may disagree on the answer to this question. Research suggests that your first contact with the police may be a relatively reassuring one. In a study supported by the National Institute of Justice, Kenneth Friedman and his coauthors found that two out of five people in a cross-section of assault, burglary, and robbery victims reported that the police had lent "significant" help, and one in five reported that the police "had gone out of their way" to be helpful. The officer who responds to your call may have had some formal training in the art of crisis intervention; if not, years on the force will have given him or her considerable on-the-job training in that area, and most police officers will treat you with at least a modicum of compassion.

The police officer may not pursue your case, however, with anything but the most perfunctory entry in his or her patrol journal. Sociologist Sally Merry studied crime patterns and responses in a large urban-housing development and found that police were willing to investigate cases only where the burglar was easily identified, with his name and address already known to the complainant or a witness. Otherwise, the odds of finding the offender are slim, and (rightly or wrongly) it is the unofficial police wisdom in most urban and suburban jurisdictions that under such circumstances they cannot afford the time to do more than a cursory investigation.

If the police do recover your stolen property, it may take weeks of paperwork and hours on the phone to get it back. And if you want to press charges and prosecute the offender, you may be up against an even more formidable bureaucratic jungle.

The victim has been called the forgotten person of the criminal justice system. This situation is changing, but it is changing slowly. Court systems are entrenched and intricate bureaucracies. Offenders get shepherded through the system by defense attorneys and corrections and parole officers, but complainants tend to get lost in the shuffle. Delays are common and witnesses may be reluctant to come to court. Defense attorneys are trained to do everything they can to subvert the prosecutor's case, and this can include making you as uncomfortable as is legally possible on the witness stand. In the meantime, prosecutors may or may not be able to shield you from the resulting insult and/or trauma.

Repairs

A significant part of crisis intervention consists of helping the victim to deal with the physical aftermath of the crime. Doors and locks may need to be repaired, windows may need to be replaced. In research cited earlier, government statistician Herbert Koppel estimates that over a lifetime any particular household has a 23-percent chance of being burglarized twice and a 14-percent chance of being burglarized three times, so there is no guarantee that a first-time victim has "paid his dues" to the crime statistics and can afford to let his or her guard down.

Start out by strengthening the security of your house or apartment at the point of break-in. The burglar has shown you where you are vulnerable, assuming you didn't already know it yourself. If your lock was picked or loided, install a pickproof auxiliary lock and a sturdy 1 to 1½-inch bolt. If the intruders came in through an open window, drill for window pins and make it a point to train yourself and other members of the family to close all windows before you leave the house. Then go over your living quarters with a burglar's eyes and decide what points need target-hardening next. The measures you take are not only dictated by the immediate need to set things right, but are also a way of bringing matters back under your own control—an important psychological mechanism for coping with the aftermath of any trauma.

Victims' Services Agencies

With the rising recognition of victims' rights in recent years has come a concomitant rise in the number of institutional resources available for victims of various kinds of crimes. In 1975 the National Organization for Victim Assistance (NOVA) was founded in Washington, and many large jurisdictions now have some kind of locally administered victims' service agencies. NOVA helps find funding for local victim-assistance programs, including rape crisis centers and prosecutors' victim/witness programs, while services provided by other agencies run the gamut from replacing broken front-door locks to actual cash payments compensating the victim for property or money that may have been lost in the crime.

A good victim-assistance program will provide guidance on getting information about your case from the police or the courts, and help with recovering your money or your property if it was found by the police. It will also steer you to appropriate therapy if you have trouble handling the thoughts and feelings generated by the crime. In addition, it will help you negotiate days off work for court appearances. It may also provide transportation to and from courts, police station houses or central bureaus, and medical or psychiatric appointments. In New York City, the municipally funded Victims' Service Agency even puts up the money to replace broken locks and windows for victims who can't afford the cost of these necessities on their own.

INSURANCE

Homeowner's Coverage

After you've made the necessary repairs and security tightening, find your homeowner's (or tenant's) insurance policy, if you have one, and see what you are and are not covered for. Most policies cover burglary among their basic market basket of insured disasters or "standard perils," which also include fire and lightning damage, explosions, vandalism, etc. But the extent of coverage varies from policy to policy, ranging from "basic" to "comprehensive" according to the cost of the premium. The top of the line is the so-called all-risk policy, which, instead of listing specific standard perils that are covered for, is worded so that it covers *all* perils except those specifically excluded in the fine print. These policies were once routinely available to anyone who was willing to pay the price, but the industry is now phasing them out in favor of policies with more limited coverage, at least for household belongings; so if you are a new buyer, an all-risk policy may not be available to you.

Cash Value vs. Replacement Value

Indemnification for a burglary has two major purposes: the first is to allow you to replace the stolen object; the second is to give you the cash to repair any damage the burglars may have caused in the process of breaking into the house. Most policies will cover both contingencies; the question is, at what *level* will they cover them, and how do you as an insurance buyer decide what level of coverage you need, both for burglary and for other "standard perils"?

If you insure your home for what you think you could get for it on the present housing market, you may be paying too much for insurance; if you insure it for what you originally bought it for, you could be paying far too little. The best way to insure your home is to figure out how much it would cost to replace the house, and if you can afford to do so, insure it for 100 percent of replacement cost.

To determine replacement cost, take the square footage and multiply that figure by local building costs. The resulting figure may be a bit startling, especially to people who have not bought or built a new house in the last twenty years; but whatever that figure is, insurance should cover at least 80 percent of it. Coverage at anything less than the replacement cost will affect the level of payouts for all kinds of less far-reaching claims. As a result, in some cases you could end up getting only the current "cash value" of your loss—meaning the original cost of the stolen item, minus depreciation for the age of the item. In the case of elderly electronic equipment and furniture this "cash value" could be negligible, and well below the price of whatever you bought to replace it.

Riders

The level of homeowner's insurance coverage you opt for will depend on a number of personal considerations, including what kind of a house you have (masonry? wood?); geography (do you live in a flood plain? a hurricane belt?); and your budget.

One other variable that should be factored into this calculation is the prevalence of crime in your neighborhood. The cost of your homeowner's policy will reflect the insurance company's assessment of its own risk, and this figure will be factored into your overall premiums. The high cost of insurance can be offset to some degree, however, by installing dead-bolt locks, burglar alarms, and fire and smoke detectors. Most insurance companies will reduce premiums by anywhere from 5 to 15 percent overall on houses with these items.

If you live in a neighborhood where insurance rates for an acceptable level of coverage are prohibitive, it may pay to insure individual items of special value at a higher rate than your blanket homeowner's policy allows. Most homeowner's insurance is targeted at fire or storm damage to the building itself, and puts rather stringent limits on payouts for luxury items that few homeowners may actually possess. If you have one or two items of expensive jewelry, for example, or an antique silver tea service, you should consider covering each of these items with its own mini-insurance policy, or "floater," under your general policy.

Typically, the most you could expect to get for the loss of such items under the average homeowner's policy in 1987 was $200 on cash, gold, silver, or platinum; $1,000 on securities, deeds, and other valuable financial documents; $2,500 on silverware or silver-plated flatware; and $2,000 on guns and firearms. Floaters will cover you for the full replacement value of all these items (minus whatever deductible your overall insurance policy demands), and they will cover rented property as well as your own possessions. They also cover the protected item for a wide range of clearly nonstandard perils—like the accidental melting of a gold ring in a hot oven, or its loss in a grinding garbage disposal, for example. To get a floater on any specific item you will need a receipt from the original bill of sale, or at the very least a detailed description, preferably with color photographs.

Another way to deal with this problem is to negotiate for a different rate on the contents than the one covering the actual structure of the house. You can do this by insuring the contents at their full replacement value as opposed to their actual cash value. This kind of split may only cost you an additional 10 percent if you live in a free-standing, single-family house, or somewhat more if you are a co-op or condominium owner. Two-level coverage may be a good bet in a neighborhood where the crime threat is high in relation to the risk from the standard perils of fires, explosions, and storm damage.

Before you sign up for this kind of split-level coverage, though, make sure that the limit on the replacement value of your house is realistic. Typically, insurers will calculate that limit at four times the cash value of the house's contents. Insurance consumer analysts agree that anything less would probably not be worth it to you as a buyer, if and when you go back to your insurer to file a claim.

Mugging and Robbery Coverage

The point of a floater is that it "floats" with the object, meaning that you are insured for its loss wherever it—or you—happen to be at the time of the loss. With or without floaters on individual items, you may be insured for things you lose in the course of a mugging or robbery even if you were miles from home when the incident occurred. This kind of indemnification can come in handy, especially in a mugging or a purse snatching, where the victim may be out hundreds of dollars after adding up the costs of the items stolen, including cosmetics, gloves, prescription glasses, sunglasses, calculators, scarves, and keyrings. With proper documentation in the form of a report from the local police, such losses are usually covered at their full replacement value, minus the prevailing deductible on the policy as a whole.

Federal Crime Insurance

For high-crime neighborhoods where private insurers either refuse to write burglary coverage into their homeowner's policies or charge astronomically high premiums for doing so, federal crime insurance has been an available stopgap for the past twenty years. Administered by the Federal Emergency Management Agency (FEMA), the Federal Crime Insurance Program is headquartered in Rockville, Maryland, and is currently offering rates of $120 per year for $10,000 worth of coverage. Federal insurance pays a maximum of only $1,500 for any one item and is available only in areas where private crime insurance is difficult to get. As of 1987 it was limited to twenty-two states, including Alabama, Arkansas, California, Connecticut, Delaware, Florida, Georgia, Illinois, Iowa, Kansas, Louisiana, Maryland, Massachusetts, Missouri, New Jersey, New York, North Carolina, Ohio, Pennsylvania, Rhode Island, Tennessee, and Virginia, as well as parts of Washington, D.C., Puerto Rico, and the Virgin Islands.

Inventory

Although the cash value of the average burglary has been rising over the past ten years, the burglar's normal objectives are still relatively limited, and most burglaries are still restricted to portable items like jewelry, furs, cameras, portable TVs, and other electronic equipment. However, another kind of heist is becoming increasingly popular, especially in more affluent suburbs. Sophisticated burglars will back a van into the driveway, break into the house, and remove everything that strikes their fancy, whether it's "portable" or not. In the aftermath of such a crime, the owners may be hard put to figure out exactly what was and was not taken, unless they had the foresight to prepare a room-by-room inventory of the house's contents.

Inventorying a large house can be a tedious process, and if you have accumulated many valuable possessions you may want to hand the job over to a professional appraiser, who will not only list the house's contents for you but also put an estimated cash value on every item. If so, be certain that you are dealing only with a reputable appraiser—preferably one who is listed by the American Society of Appraisers or the Appraisers Association of America.

If not, and you decide to tackle the job yourself, your best bet is to set aside at least a day for the project and make a photographic record of every item in every room of the house. These photographs serve to back up your written inventory with a pictorial one and work as memory aids in case of a major burglary. Inventories should be photocopied, with one copy kept in a safe-deposit box and another in a file at your office, or someplace else off-site. Such lists, together with brief descriptions and the original sales tickets if you can find them, are also invaluable documents to have on hand in case of fire, flood, or any other household disaster.

Safe Rooms

One way to obtain maximum peace of mind in your home is to set up a "safe room" inside the house—usually the master bedroom—and lock or bolt yourself into it at night. However, a room that is difficult to enter may also be difficult to leave, and too "safe" a room can be a hazard in an emergency situation such as a fire.

The master bedroom should always have a lock, and most do. But the locks on many bedroom doors are simple spring-latch mechanisms with short, wedge-shaped throws, which can be easily retracted with simple tools or a celluloid card. To feel completely safe at night, it makes sense to install a more serious lock and, if you are at especially high risk of burglary or are easily unnerved, add a police lock and/or a portable door alarm that creates a loud piercing beep whenever the door handle is moved.

Other features that a "safe room" inside a house could have include a telephone with its own underground phone line, so that you can use it to call out even if the other phone lines to the house are cut, and a self-contained signaling device—either a flashing strobe light or a loud horn alarm that you can work manually from your bedroom window. The decibel level should be at least as high as the standard hard-wired alarm siren, so that it rouses the neighborhood if and when you use it. Remember always to keep an extra set of house keys in your "safe room" so that you can throw them down to the police when they respond to the scene. A flashlight is a good bet, too, in case of fire, electrical blackout, or both.

In a house with a well-designed automatic alarm system or sufficiently tightened security, none of these stopgaps should theoretically be necessary. But the reassurance of this additional layer of protection may be just what a particularly uneasy homeowner needs to get a good night's sleep—especially if he or she has been traumatized by a break-in in the not-too-distant past.

However, setting up a "safe room," complete with police lock, strobe lights, and extra keys, is not and was never meant to be a substitute for a properly hardened target. It is a last resort, not a first one, and whatever you do or don't do to fortify the master bedroom, your first step to discourage a burglar should start at the property line, with well-maintained hedges or fences, regularly mown lawns, and appropriate outside lights, so that your house projects a look of round-the-clock occupancy. These stage effects should be all that are needed to dissuade the most opportunistic burglars and send them looking for other, easier targets.

Another level of target-hardening, at the outside perimeter of the house, will screen out a second level of intruder—the kind who may be bold enough to try a doorknob or an unsecured window, looking for a way in, but who may then not be up to the strenuous task of battering down a door or breaking a window. Tightfitting doors in strong door frames, sturdy locks with long throws, and strategically placed window pins will stop most nonprofessionals, and if you add an automatic alarm system to the mix you will probably screen out 80 to 90 percent of burglars currently in the business. The other 10–20 percent are probably not worth worrying about, unless your house has a trove of unusually high-priced and easily resellable items, and someone out there knows that it is, and knows the price your possessions would be likely to command on the current resale market.

Bibliography

Adams, Robert C., ed. *Fire Safety Educator's Handbook*. Quincy, Mass.: National Fire Protection Association, 1983.

Alth, Max. *All About Locks and Locksmithing*. New York: Hawthorn Books, 1972.

Bard, Morton, and Diane Sangrey. *The Crime Victim's Book*. New York: Basic Books, Inc., 1979.

Barnard, Roger L. *Intrusion Detection Systems*. Boston: Butterworth Publishers, 1981.

Bennett, Georgette. *Unlocking America*. New York: Commercial Insurance Companies Association, 1980.

Bennett, Trevor, and Richard Wright. "Constraints to Burglary: The Offender's Perspective." In R. Clark and T. Hope, eds., *Coping with Burglary*. Boston: Kluwer-Nijhoff Publishing, 1983.

Block, Richard. "The Impact of Victimization, Rates, and Patterns: A Comparison of the Netherlands and the U.S." In R. Block, ed., *Victimization and Fear of Crime: World Perspectives,* op. cit.

Brown, Barbara. "Territoriality, Street Form, and Residential Burglary: Social and Environmental Analysis." Ph.D. dissertation, University of Utah, Salt Lake City, 1983.

Buggs, D. E., and C. Bridges. *Burglary Protection and Insurance Surveys*. London: Stone & Cox Ltd., 1982.

Clarke, R., A. Ekblom, M. Hough, and P. Mayhew. "Crime and the Elderly." *Howard Journal of Criminal Justice*, February 1985.

————, and T. Hope. *Coping with Burglary*. Boston: Kluwer-Nijhoff Publishing, 1984.

Clifford, Martin. *The Complete Guide to Security*. Indianapolis: Howard W. Sams & Co., 1982.

————. *Security*. New York: Drake & Co., 1974.

Cook, Roger, B. Smith, and A. Harrell. *Helping Crime Victims: Levels of Trauma and Effectiveness of Service*. Washington, D.C.: U.S. Department of Justice, National Institute of Law Enforcement and Criminal Justice, 1987.

The Cost of Negligence. Washington, D.C.: U.S. Department of Justice, National Institute of Law Enforcement and Criminal Justice, 1979.

Cowan, T. *Popular Mechanics Home Security Handbook*. New York: Cloverdale Press/ Hearst Books, 1982.

Cox, Wesley. *Crime Stoppers*. New York: Crown Publishers, 1983.

Currie, Elliott. *Confronting Crime*. New York: Pantheon, 1985.

Davis, Mick. *Prevent Burglary*. Englewood Cliffs, N.J.: Prentice-Hall, 1986.

DuBow, Fred, E. McCabe, and G. Kaplan. *Reactions to Crime: A Critical Review of the Literature*. Washington, D.C.: U.S. Department of Justice, National Institute of Law Enforcement and Criminal Justice, 1979.

Federal Bureau of Investigation. *Crime in the United States*. Washington, D.C.: U.S. Department of Justice, 1987 and 1988.

Friedman, Kenneth, Helen Bischoff, Robert Davis, and Andrea Person. *Victims and Helpers: Reactions to Crime*. Washington, D.C.: U.S. Department of Justice, National Institute of Law Enforcement and Criminal Justice, May 1982.

Greenback, Anthony. *Survival in the City*. New York: Harper & Row, 1974.

Greenberg, Stephanie, William Rohe, and Jay Williams. *Safe and Secure Neighborhoods: Physical Characteristics and Informal Territorial Control in High- and Low-Crime Neighborhoods.* Washington, D.C.: U.S. Department of Justice, National Institute of Law Enforcement and Criminal Justice, May 1982.

Guarino, Vincent Joseph. *Everyman's Guide to Better Home Security.* Boulder, Colo.: Paladin Books, 1981.

Hair, Robert A., and Samm Sinclair Baker. *How to Protect Yourself Today.* New York: Stein & Day, 1970.

Hall, Gerald. *How to Completely Secure Your Home.* Blue Ridge Summit, Pa.: Tab Books, 1978.

Harmon, A. J. *Remodeling for Security.* New York: McGraw-Hill, 1979.

Hellman, Daryl A., and Jack L. Naroff. *The Urban Public Sector and Urban Crime.* Washington, D.C.: U.S. Department of Justice, National Institute of Law Enforcement and Criminal Justice, 1980.

Herbert, Anthony B. *Complete Security Handbook.* New York: Macmillan, 1983.

Home Security. Alexandria, Va.: Time-Life Books, 1979.

Household Burglary. Washington, D.C.: U.S. Department of Justice, Bureau of Justice Statistics Bulletin, January 1985.

Households Touched by Crime in 1984. Washington, D.C.: U.S. Department of Justice, Bureau of Justice Statistics Bulletin, June 1985.

Hunter, George. *How to Defend Yourself, Your Family, and Your Home.* New York: David McKay, 1967.

Jacobs, Jane. *The Death and Life of Great American Cities.* New York: Viking, 1961.

Kelley, Clarence M., and Carl A. Roper. *Security for You and Your Home: A Complete Handbook.* Summit, Pa.: Carl A. Roper/Norback & Co., Inc., 1984.

Kirkpatrick, Doug. *The Burglar Alarm Book.* Van Nuys, Calif.: Baker Publishing, 1983.

Koppel, Herbert. *Lifetime Likelihood of Victimization*. Washington, D.C.: U.S. Department of Justice, Bureau of Justice Statistics, March 1987.

Lentzner, Harold. *Losses from Preventable Household Burglaries*. Washington, D.C.: U.S. Department of Justice, National Criminal Justice Information and Statistics Service, 1979.

McDermott, Robert. *Stop Thief*. New York: Macmillan, 1978.

MacLean, Jack. *Secrets of a Superthief*. New York: Berkley Books, 1983.

McNamara, Joseph D. *Safe and Sane*. New York: Putnam, 1984.

Mandel, Mel. *Being Safe*. New York: Saturday Review Press, 1972.

Mandelbaum, Albert J. *Fundamentals of Protective Systems*. Springfield, Ill.: Charles A. Thomas, 1973.

Mayhew, Peter. "Target-Hardening: How Much of an Answer?" In R. Clarke and T. Hope, eds., *Coping with Burglary*, op. cit.

Merry, Sally. *Life in a Neighborhood of Strangers*. Philadelphia: Temple University Press, 1981.

Moolman, Val. *Practical Ways to Prevent Burglary and Illegal Entry*. New York: Cornerstone Library, 1970.

Moriarty, Thomas. "Crime, Commitment, and the Responsive Bystander: Two Field Experiments." *Journal of Personality and Social Psychology* 31:2, 1975.

National Advisory Commission on Criminal Justice and Standards. *Community Crime Prevention*. Washington, D.C.: U.S. Department of Justice, National Institute of Law Enforcement and Criminal Justice, 1973.

National Automobile Theft Bureau. *1987 Passenger Vehicle Identification Manual*. Palos Hills, Ill.: National Automobile Theft Bureau, Inc., 1987.

————. *1986 Annual Report*. Palos Hills, Ill.: National Automobile Theft Bureau, Inc., 1987.

National Crime Survey: Criminal Victimization in the United States 1978–82. Washington, D.C.: U.S. Department of Justice, Bureau of Justice Statistics, 1983.

Newman, Oscar. *Architectural Design for Crime Prevention*. Washington, D.C.: U.S. Department of Justice, National Institute of Law Enforcement and Criminal Justice, March 1973.

———. *Defensible Space: Crime Prevention Through Urban Design*. New York: Collier Books, 1972.

———. *A Design Guide for Improving Residential Security*. Washington, D.C.: U.S. Department of Housing and Urban Development, December 1973.

New York City Police Department, Auto Crimes Division. *Insurance Fraud: The Perfect Crime—or Is It?* New York: NYCPD, 1987.

———. *Who Steals Cars?* New York: NYCPD, 1987.

New York City Police Department, City Community Affairs Division. *Crime Prevention Manual*. New York: NYCPD, 1972.

New York State Office of Crime Prevention. *Basic Crime Prevention Course Notebook*. Albany: New York State Division of Criminal Justice Services, 1987.

O'Block, Robert T. *Security and Crime Prevention*. Boston: Butterworth Publishers, 1981.

Panzarella, Robert, et al. *Residential Burglar Alarms as Deterrents to Intrusion and Aids to Apprehension*. John Jay College, New York: Research proposal submitted to the National Institute of Justice, February 1987.

Reppetto, Thomas A. *Residential Crime*. Cambridge, Mass.: Ballinger Publishing Co., 1974.

———. "Urban Design, Security, and Crime." Seminar, National Institute of Law Enforcement and Criminal Justice. Washington, D.C.: U.S. Department of Justice, April 1972.

Sampson, Robert J., and Thomas C. Castellano. *Juvenile Criminal Behavior and Its Relation to Neighborhood Characteristics*. Washington, D.C.: U.S. Department of Justice, National Institute of Justice, 1981.

Scarr, Harry A., Joan L. Pinsky, and Deborah S. Wyatt. *Patterns of Burglary*. 2nd ed. Washington, D.C.: U.S. Department of Justice, National Institute of Law Enforcement and Criminal Justice, June 1973.

Schwartz, Ted. *Protect Your Home and Your Family*. New York: Arco Publishing, 1984.

Short, James. "A Note on Relief Programs and Crime During the Depression of the 1930s." *American Sociological Review,* April 1952.

Sloane, Eugene A. *The Complete Book of Locks, Keys, Burglar and Smoke Alarms and Other Security Devices.* New York: New American Library, 1977.

Smith, Dennis. *Dennis Smith's Fire Safety Book.* New York: Bantam Books, 1983.

Standard for Safety: Household Burglar Alarm System Units. 4th ed. Northbrook, Ill.: Underwriters' Laboratories, December 1986.

Standard for Safety: Key Locks. 5th ed. Northbrook, Ill.: Underwriters' Laboratories, Inc., 1986.

Sviridoff, Michelle, and James W. Thompson. "Links Between Employment and Crime: A Qualitative Study of Rikers Island Releases." *Crime and Delinquency,* April 1983.

Traine, Robert. *Home Security and Protection.* London: Willow Books/Collins, 1984.

Weber, Thad L. *Alarm Systems and Theft Prevention.* Boston: Butterworth Publishers, 1984.

White, Thomas W., et al. *Police Burglary Prevention Programs.* Washington, D.C.: U.S. Department of Justice, National Institute of Law Enforcement and Criminal Justice, 1975.

Wilson, L. A., and A. L. Schneider. "Investigating the Efficiency and Equity of Public Initiatives in the Provision of Private Safety." Paper presented at the Western Political Science Association Annual Meeting, Los Angeles, Calif., 1978.

Yin, Robert K., Mary E. Vogel, Jan M. Chaiken, and Deborah R. Both. *Citizen Patrol Projects, National Evaluation Program. Phase 1 Summary Report.* Washington, D.C.: U.S. Department of Justice, National Institute of Law Enforcement and Criminal Justice, 1977.

Yin, Robert K., et al. *Patrolling the Neighborhood Beat: Residents and Residential Security.* Santa Monica, Calif.: The Rand Corporation, 1976.

Index